Managerial Issues of Enterprise Resource Planning Systems

David L. Olson
University of Nebraska

Boston Burr Ridge, IL Dubuque, IA Madison, WI New York San Francisco St. Louis
Bangkok Bogotá Caracas Kuala Lumpur Lisbon London Madrid Mexico City
Milan Montreal New Delhi Santiago Seoul Singapore Sydney Taipei Toronto

The McGraw-Hill Companies

MANAGERIAL ISSUES OF ENTERPRISE RESOURCE PLANNING SYSTEMS
International Edition 2004

10 09 08 07 06 05 04 03
20 09 08 07 06 05
CTF SLP

Library of Congress Cataloging-in-Publication Data

Olson, David Louis,
Managerial Issues of enterprise resource planning systems / David L. Olson.— 1st ed.
p. cm.
Includes index.
ISBN 007-286112-6
1. Information resources management. 2. Management information systems. I. Title.
T58.64.049 2004
658.4'038'011—dc21 2003054079

When ordering this title, use ISBN 007-123628-7

Printed in Singapore

www.mhhe.com

To my son, Daniel.

Preface

Enterprise resource planning (ERP) systems have played a major role in changing organizational computing for the better. ERP systems can be developed internally, but because of the difficulty of doing this, the majority of organizations adopt vendor products. Vendors offer their products in many modules, each of which can be used alone or in combination to meet the organization's design decisions. Vendors also provide customized systems for specific industries or organizational sectors. ERP systems can cost organizations millions of dollars, and some smaller firms have spent more than 10 percent of revenues to adopt an ERP.[1] Adopters expect significant economic returns through lower information system costs and through more responsive operating efficiencies. These systems are intended to last anywhere from 3 to 10 years, with some users hoping for longer product lives, given the scale of investment required. This is countered by vendors developing improvements and often dropping maintenance support for older systems to enhance adoption of the new versions.

Two recent studies examined the motivations for ERP adoption. Mabert et al. surveyed over 400 Midwestern U.S. manufacturing organizations about ERP adoption. Olhager and Selldin replicated that study with 190 manufacturing firms in Sweden.[2] Table 1 lists the results of these studies reporting the motivation for implementing an ERP.

Initially, fear of Y2K was a major concern. The Swedish survey was later than the United States one, and that might explain the lower rating for this item in the Swedish study. The U.S. response was actually neutral (only slightly higher than 3), but Y2K clearly was a factor in ERP adoption in the mid- to late-1990s. However, more important reasons were always present. In both studies, replacing legacy systems received a high positive response. The desire to simplify and standardize systems was the second highest reason in both studies.

Two other reasons received relatively high ratings in the United States (a bit lower in Sweden). These were to improve interactions with suppliers and customers, which is one way to gain strategic advantage. The supply-chain aspects of ERP have led vendors to modify their products to be more open, although work continues to be needed in this direction (and seems to be proceeding). Linking to global activities was slightly positive in the U.S. survey, and less important in the Swedish study.

Three potential reasons received low ratings in both studies. Pressure to keep up with competitors received neutral support in the U.S. study. Ease of upgrading systems is a technical reason that received neutral support both in the United States and in Sweden. Restructuring the organization was rated lower.

From these studies, we infer that ERP systems are an important means to upgrade the quality of information systems. They can provide organizations with coordinated systems

[1]V.M. Mabert, A. Soni, and M. A. Venkataramanan, "Enterprise Resource Planning Survey of U.S. Manufacturing Firms," *Production and Inventory Management Journal* 41, no. 20 (2000), pp. 52–58.

[2]Ibid., and J. Olhager and E. Selldin, "Enterprise Resource Planning Survey of Swedish Manufacturing Firms," *European Journal of Operational Research* 146 (2003), pp. 365–73.

TABLE 1 Reasons for Implementing ERP—Rating 1 (Not Important) to 5 (Very Important)

Reason	United States	Sweden
Replace legacy systems	4.06	4.11
Simplify and standardize systems	3.85	3.67
Improve interactions with suppliers & customers	3.55	3.16
Gain strategic advantage	3.46	3.18
Link to global activities	3.17	2.85
Solve the Y2K problem	3.08	2.48
Pressure to keep up with competitors	2.99	2.48
Ease of upgrading systems	2.91	2.96
Restructure organization	2.58	2.70

Source: Extracted from V.M. Mabert et al. "Enterprise Resource Planning Survey of U.S. Manufacturing Firms." *Production and Inventory Management Journal* 41, no. 20 (2000); and J. Olhager and E. Selldin, "Enterprise Resource Planning Survey of Swedish Manufacturing Firms." *European Journal of Operational Research* 146 (2003).

TABLE 2 ERP Issues by Chapter

Chapter	Issues
1	Implementation failures
2	Total system vs. modular implementation
	Customization
3	Cost budgeting in ERP
	Intangible and hidden factors
4	The value of reengineering
	Clean slate vs. technology enabled
	Vendor best practices vs. firm competitive advantage
5	ERP risk
	Installation options and comparative advantages
	External sources of ERP
6	ERP installation project management
7	ERP critical success factors
	Implementation options
	Expectation management
	ERP maintenance
	ERP system migration
8	Data warehouses and ERP
	Data mining potential in ERP
9	Supply-chain aspects of ERP
	Advanced planning systems
10	ERP openness
	Middleware
	Security

that have higher-quality data available in a more responsive way. Not all evidence indicates lower costs, but most evidence does indicate higher-quality information systems.

This book will guide the reader in understanding the issues affecting ERP systems and the implementation of ERP. Table 2 outlines some of these issues.

Real applications are reviewed in each of these chapters. These reviews focus on the essential points and provide a grounding in real practice. Students would benefit from visiting real firms in their locale that have adopted ERP systems.

Brief Contents

Contents

About the Author

David L. Olson *University of Nebraska*

David L. Olson is the James & H.K. Stuart Professor in MIS at the University of Nebraska. He received his Ph.D. in Business from the University of Nebraska in 1981 and has published research in more than 60 refereed journal articles, primarily on the topic of multiple objective decision making. He teaches in the management information systems, management science, and operations management areas. He has written the books *Decision Aids for Selection Problems* and *Introduction to Information Systems Project Management,* and co-authored the books *Decision Support Models and Expert Systems; Introduction to Management Science; Introduction to Simulation and Risk Analysis; Business Statistics: Quality Information for Decision Analysis; Statistics, Decision Analysis, and Decision Modeling;* and *Multiple Criteria Analysis in Strategic Siting Problems.* He has made over 100 presentations at international and national conferences on research topics and is a member of the Association for Information Systems, the Decision Sciences Institute, the Institute for Operations Research and Management Sciences, and the Multiple Criteria Decision Making Society. He has coordinated the Decision Sciences Institute Dissertation Competition, Innovative Education Competition, chaired the Doctoral Affairs Committee, served thrice as nationally elected vice president, and as National Program Chair. He was with Texas A&M University from 1981 through 2001, the last two years as Lowry Mays Professor of Business in the Department of Information and Operations Management. He received a Research Fellow Award from the College of Business and Graduate School of Business at Texas A&M University and held the Business Analysis Faculty Excellence Fellowship for two years. He is a Fellow of the Decision Sciences Institute.

Chapter 1

Enterprise Resource Planning Systems

Enterprise resource planning (ERP) systems have become very important in modern business operations. One study found more than 60 percent of Fortune 500 companies had adopted of ERP systems.[1] These systems have been credited with reducing inventories, shortening cycle times, lowering costs, and improving supply-chain management practices. ERP systems are designed to integrate all of an organization's information system computing. ERP has been credited with increasing the speed with which information flows through a company.[2]

ERP has also been credited with creating value through integrating activities across a firm, implementing best practices for each business process, standardizing processes within organizations, creating one-source data that results in less confusion and error, and providing on-line access to information.[3] All of these features facilitate better organizational planning, communication, and collaboration. Applied Robotics increased on-time deliveries 40 percent after implementing ERP, and Delta Electronics reduced production control labor requirements by 65 percent.[4]

ERP merits study for a number of reasons. From a *technical* perspective, the idea of integrating all aspects of an organization's computing is attractive because it fosters consistency across the system through use of single-source files and efficiency through making single data entry possible for all of the organization's applications. ERP has *financial* attraction, promising economic savings through integrating all applications into one big system. ERP also is attractive from an *organizational* perspective, as all

[1] G. Stewart, M. Milford, T. Jewels, T. Hunter, and B. Hunter, "Organizational readiness for ERP implementation," *Proceedings of the Americas Conference on Information Systems* (August 2000), pp. 966–971.

[2] T. H. Davenport, "Putting the Enterprise into the Enterprise System," *Harvard Business Review*, July–August 1998, pp. 121–31.

[3] D. E. O'Leary, *Enterprise Resource Planning Systems: Systems, Life Cycle, Electronic Commerce, and Risk* (Cambridge: Cambridge University Press, 2000). For business process reengineering, see M. Hammer and S. Stanton, "How Process Enterprises *Really* Work" *Harvard Business Review*, November–December 1999, pp. 108–18.

[4] M. Weil, "Managing to Win," *Manufacturing Systems* 17, no. 11 (November 1999), p. 14.

members of the organization learn to use the same system, thus enhancing intraorganizational communication.

While there are problems between the conception of an ERP system and the delivery, ERP is an attractive idea. ERP can provide lower costs of doing business, making it a competitive tool in many industries. Often business partners within supply chains require use of ERP. The concept of ERP has revolutionized the information system/information technology (IS/IT) field.

This chapter:

- Provides an initial description of ERP.
- Reviews development of ERP.
- Briefly looks at the current state of the market.
- Discusses advantages and disadvantages of ERP.
- Presents an example of a real ERP implementation failure as well as a subsequent success.
- Outlines where we are going with the rest of the book.

The Market for ERP

ERP has become a major software product line. An idea started by SAP in the early 1970s has evolved into a major information system software product line, which has revolutionized how large organizations approach business computing. Initial arguments were for integrated systems, yet vendors usually made sales in the form of modules, covering only limited functions of a business's computing needs. Because of the high price tags involved, companies apparently wanted to minimize their risks by trying only part of the ERP system. ERP vendor sales peaked in the late 1990s, driven in part by concerns about Y2K problems. This induced many large organizations to adopt ERP as a way to kill two birds with one stone—cleaning up and integrating their organizational computing services at the same time that they assured themselves they would be Y2K compliant. After that pre-Y2K rush, sales dropped. Vendors then shifted gears, seeking to fill in missing modules in large company systems and developing products more attractive to small to midsize firms. Additionally, vendors have made great strides in reducing some of the trauma of implementing ERP, making it possible to implement systems much faster (a matter of months rather than years) and offering more sophisticated functionality, such as customer relationship management and e-business system support. Furthermore, ERP is being marketed heavily in both government and educational sectors.

The prosperity of ERP vendors is a matter of dispute. The market for this product does not appear to have recovered its pre-Y2K boom levels, but there still appears to be a viable market. Vendor survival seems to depend on the ability to adapt to new market realities, which will continue to evolve.

There are currently more than 100 vendors of ERP products, although this field is dominated by the firms shown in Table 1.1. These firms are often referred to by the acronym BOPSE, using the initial letters of the five vendors.

SAP began ERP product development in Germany in the early 1970s. Former IBM employees designed their new product with the intent of implementing the **best practices**

TABLE 1.1
Major ERP Vendors

Source: T. H. Davenport, "Putting the Enterprise into the Enterprise System." *Harvard Business Review,* July–August 1998.

Vendor	Origin	Salient Features
BAAN	Holland	An early ERP vendor
Oracle	United States	A relative newcomer, but quickly gaining share
PeopleSoft	United States	Originally focused on human resources management
SAP	Germany	The pioneer and the largest firm
JDEdwards	United States	Internet emphasis

for a firm's information system processes. The idea of best practices is fundamental to an ERP system. SAP devotes significant resources to identify the best way to deal with common business functions and then incorporates those practices within its systems. However, these best practices are not best for each particular firm.[5] The business world is dynamic, and a rigid approach has drawbacks. Additionally, some firms develop a core competency, something that they do better than their competitors. The idea of a best practice implies that everyone ought to do things the same way. Yet, if a firm develops a core competency, it would be foolish to sacrifice that competitive advantage to utilize the ERP system to its fullest extent.

ERP systems were designed to integrate all information processing support for a business. Table 1.2 presents some business functions supported by ERP.

In the early 1970s, information systems were supported by mainframe architectures. SAP marketed R/2, a mainframe-supported software product in 1974. In the early 1990s, **client/server** architectures became popular, with an organization's computation supported by one or more servers linked to allow distribution of computing and storage. Client/server architectures are more flexible than mainframe systems, and thus are capable of better supporting dynamic ERP environments. In the mid-1990s, SAP developed a client/server version of its ERP product, which was named R/3. About this time, the field for ERP took off, with SAP holding the dominant portion of the market worldwide. Typically, an organization uses one server for application software, another for database software, and yet another server for user interface. Associated servers can also be used for additional support, such as dialog management and gateway services. Currently R/3 is the most popular ERP product on the market in terms of dollar volume. As noted, the market for ERP peaked in early 1999, when many firms were concerned with potential Y2K problems. Since ERP products are for the most part large-scale systems (typically involving multiple years for installation), the demand dropped off after mid-1999, when it was too late to implement a system in time for the feared calendar turnover. However, SAP and Oracle business continued to be brisk, primarily by expanding sales to existing clients and to midsize firms. The general business malaise for technology firms has been a notable factor in reducing sales growth in the latter portion of 2000 through the time of writing this book.

Chapter 2 discusses ERP modules. Other major business functions supported by ERP are customer relationship management (Chapter 8) and Web-based systems (Chapter 9).

[5] Davenport, "Putting the Enterprise into the Enterprise System."

TABLE 1.2
Business Functions Potentially Supported by ERP

Source: T. H. Davenport, "Putting the Enterprise into the Enterprise System." *Harvard Business Review*, July–August 1998.

Financial	Human Resources	Operations and Logistics	Sales and Marketing
Accounts receivable and payable	Time accounting	Inventory management	Order management
Asset accounting	Payroll	Materials Requirement Planning (MRP)	Pricing
Cash forecasting	Personnel planning	Plant maintenance	Sales management
Cost accounting	Travel expenses	Production planning	Sales planning
Executive information systems		Project management	
Financial consolidation		Purchasing	
General ledger		Quality management	
Profitability analysis		Shipping	
Standard costing		Vendor evaluation	

ERP Advantages and Disadvantages

There are many reasons to adopt ERP. It offers an integrated system shared by all users rather than a diverse set of computer applications, which rarely can communicate with each other and which each possess its own set of data and files. ERP provides a means to coordinate information system assets and information flows across the organization. The main benefit is the elimination of suborganizational silos that focus on their own problems rather than serving the interests of the overall organization. On the downside, ERP systems impose one procedure for the entire organization, which requires everyone to conform to the new system. But the benefits of integration are usually much greater than the costs of conformity.

Data can be entered once, at the most accurate source, so that all users share the same data (**data integration**). This can be very beneficial. As the shared data are used more and by more people, it becomes more complete and accurate. As errors are encountered, users demand correction. Procedures are needed to ensure that changes do not introduce new errors. This makes it harder to correct data, but again, this added inconvenience is usually well worth the gains of data integration.

ERP systems also can provide better ways of doing things. This idea is the essence of best practices, a key SAP system component. The downsides to best practices are that identifying the best way to proceed with specific business functions takes great effort, and such practices can involve significant change in how organizational members do their work. Further, as with any theory, what is considered best by one is often not considered best by all.

TABLE 1.3
ERP Pros and Cons

Factor	Pro	Con
System integration	Improved understanding across users	Less flexibility
Data integration	Greater accuracy	Harder to make corrections
Best practices	More efficient methods	Imposition of how people do their work Less freedom and creativity
Cost of computing	More efficient system planned	Changing needs Underbudgeted training expense Hidden costs of implementation

ERP systems are usually adopted with the expectation that they will yield lower computing costs in the long run. Ideally, adopting one common way of doing things is simpler and involves less effort to provide computing support to an organization. In practice, savings are often not realized, due to failure to anticipate all of the detailed nuances of user needs, as well as the inevitable changes in the business environment that call for different best practices and computer system relationships. As we will discuss in Chapter 7, training needs are typically underbudgeted in ERP projects. Furthermore, these training budgets don't usually include the hidden costs of lost productivity as employees cope with complex new systems. Table 1.3 recaps these pros and cons of ERP systems.

The key rationales for implementing ERP systems are:

- Technology—more powerful, integrated computer systems.
  - Greater flexibility.
  - Lower IT cost.
- Business practices—better ways of accomplishing tasks.
  - Better operational quality.
  - Greater productivity.
- Strategic—cost advantages gained through more efficient systems.
  - Improve decision making.
  - Support business growth.
  - Build external linkages.
- Competitive—Keep up with competitors adopting ERP. Greater cost efficiencies.
  - Better customer service.

We conclude this chapter with a case based on one of the most popularly discussed implementations of ERP. The SAP implementation has been claimed as a technical success. However, the overall impact was a spectacular failure, leading to bankruptcy of the adopting firm. The ultimate cause of this failure is subject to debate (in the court system).

Real Application: How Not to Implement ERP

Probably the most famous implementation of ERP was by FoxMeyer Drug, a holding company in the health care services industry specializing in wholesale distribution of drugs and beauty aids. Its customers were drugstores, chains, hospitals, and care facilities. FoxMeyer had 23 distribution centers across the United States. Due to an aging population and growth in health care in the United States, FoxMeyer anticipated high growth in the industry; but extreme price competition in the industry threatened FoxMeyer's margins. FoxMeyer adopted long-term strategies of efficiently managing inventory, seeking low operating expenses, building stronger sales and marketing efforts, and expanding services.[6]

Before adoption of SAP's ERP, FoxMeyer had three linked data processing centers. Its old system involved customers filling out electronic orders, which were sent to one of three data processing centers. Orders were filled manually and packaged within 24 hours. The company had recently completed a national distribution center with multiple carousels and automated picking, with the capability of tracking inventory to secondary locations.

The new distribution system was adopted to capitalize on growth. FoxMeyer anticipated large volumes to enable it to lower unit costs, and thus undercut competitors on price. The company hoped to save $40 million in annual operating costs. The new ERP would need to handle hundreds of thousands of transactions, and meet Drug Enforcement Administration (DEA) and Food and Drug Administration (FDA) regulations. SAP's R/3 system was selected, and Andersen Consulting was hired to integrate the $65 million system. At the same time, FoxMeyer adopted an $18 million project with another firm to install a warehouse automation system.

The major fundamental error FoxMeyer seems to have committed was to anticipate full savings from its ERP and warehouse systems based upon timely project completion within 18 months. To take full advantage of these anticipated savings, the company signed large new contracts, underbidding competitors based upon new expected lower costs. However, there were coordination problems across systems, as might reasonably have been anticipated. The new contracts that FoxMeyer signed also forced changes in system requirements. Unfortunately, these changes needed to be made after testing and development were under way. Because the ERP project was running late, FoxMeyer revised its schedule arbitrarily, telling project management to complete it 90 days earlier than project management thought reasonable.

At the same time, the warehouse system consistently failed, suffering from late orders, incorrect and lost shipments, and operating losses of more than $15 million. In August 1996, FoxMeyer filed for bankruptcy. Subsequently, the firm's assets were purchased by McKesson.[7]

While it is impossible to know exactly why the project went amiss, some issues seem relatively clear. SAP takes the position that its system was successfully installed and functioned appropriately. The apparent factor of concern was an unmerited confidence in the project keeping on schedule, and working as planned. Historically, IS/IT projects tend not to do that. It is only prudent to allow for some slippage in time and budget, and to not count on full project functionality until after testing and installation are complete.

[6] Most information on FoxMeyer Drug was gathered by Jason Donalson, Julie Seibold, Matthew Welch, and Sok Woo Yoon, graduate students at Texas A&M University, as part of the requirements of a semester project.

[7] T. Ehrhart, "Tech Lawsuits, Insurance Costs Escalate–as Does Cost of Doing Nothing," *National Underwriter* 10, no. 46 (November 12, 2001), pp. 17–20.

Case Questions

1. Risk analysis: FoxMeyer's project management failed to consider the possibility of project delays. Unfortunately, information systems projects are notorious for time overruns (Gartner Group often cites figures in the 70 percent range). The magnitude of FoxMeyer's ERP project, and its importance to operations, made delays very damaging. There are two broad approaches to developing an information system project—do it all at once (referred to as the "big-bang" approach in ERP literature) or develop the project in phases. Would FoxMeyer have benefited from a more conservative project development approach?
2. Change management: Another risk-related factor was reliance upon key customers. FoxMeyer suffered the loss of a key customer in the midst of its ERP development. It reacted by aggressively seeking replacement business by assuming the system was going to work as planned, and cost no more than planned. Using these optimistic costs, FoxMeyer bid low on new work. Costs did not turn out to be as low as expected. Should FoxMeyer have anticipated this? What would have been a better approach to solve its problem of lost business?
3. Human issues: FoxMeyer included a warehouse automation project in its strategic plans. Employees at the warehouse saw the writing on the wall and apparently did not cooperate to the fullest. One primary reason information systems projects are adopted is to reduce cost by getting more done with fewer people, which means fewer employees if there is not significant increase in volume of work. The employees accurately perceived the impact of the automated system on their futures. What could FoxMeyer have done to avoid this problem?

After FoxMeyer's bankruptcy filing, the major drug firm McKesson purchased FoxMeyer's assets and reported some success with ERP. But before that, McKesson had adopted SAP's R/3 for an initial implementation in the mid-1990s. This project was cancelled in 1996 after spending $15 million. It had included **business process reengineering** but the new processes didn't mesh well with R/3. In 1997, McKesson acquired FoxMeyer Corporation. Based upon its past experiences, McKesson carefully designed a new R/3 implementation project.[8]

The new project was scaled back by dropping a number of modules, and it was implemented one module at a time to ensure proper functionality. The project management team developed a cautious rollout schedule and rigorously held to that schedule. A separate group was formed to test the ERP system to avoid developer bias. This approach proved successful. The final phase of the $50 million system neared on-time completion within budget and without business disruptions.

The system imposed tremendous changes in end-user jobs. The implementation included careful analysis of these changes, with surveys, focus groups, demonstrations, and computer-based training adopted before formal training classes. Over 3,000 end users were expected to work on the system by completion of project implementation.

This example demonstrates that it is possible to bring an ERP implementation project in on time, within budget, and with full functionality. However, as demonstrated by

[8] C. Wilder and S. Davis, "False starts strong finishes," *Information Week* 711 (November 30, 1998), pp. 41–46; C. Stedman, "Flash! ERP works if you're careful," *Computerworld* 33, no. 11 (December 13, 1999), pp. 1, 14.

McKesson's experience, such success comes at the cost of a great deal of planning and project management effort.

The Rest of the Book

Chapter 2 will review the historical development of ERP from the aspect of manufacturing applications. The next two chapters will look at ERP from the perspective of the projects needed for its implementation. Chapter 3 will discuss techniques available for analysis of ERP adoption proposals. Methods will be demonstrated with examples, and factors in selecting from these techniques will be discussed. Chapter 4 will examine alternative configurations of ERP, to include consultant support and outsourcing and will look at the concept of reengineering and its relationship to ERP. Reengineering is directly related to the concept of best practices, which SAP includes as a key element of its system. Chapter 5 will discuss ERP implementation and its risks. Chapter 6 will present basic project management tools that can be used to support ERP implementation. Chapter 7 is concerned with ERP system maintenance and the need to train organizational members in the use of ERP to gain maximum benefit from the system. Chapter 8 presents supplemental tools that are often used to extend ERP into areas of customer relationship management and other data mining forms. Chapter 9 concerns Web and e-business aspects of ERP. Chapter 10 discusses some advanced features of ERP, including bolt-ons that expand ERP outside of its client organization into supply-chain and Web environments. Chapter 10 also addresses the related topic of ERP security.

This introductory look at ERP reveals a number of issues. First, ERP can be adopted in a variety of forms. Vendors would prefer to sell complete systems, but are happy to start organizations with modules of parts of their systems. Organizations could also develop their own ERP system, although this is usually much more expensive and slower. A number of options are available, calling for careful analysis of expected costs and benefits.

Another major element of an ERP system is the opportunity to reengineer how organizations accomplish the business they do. SAP uses the idea of "best practices" as a key component of its product. SAP has spent a great deal of research identifying how particular common activities should be done. These best practices are incorporated within SAP's products. Implementing such best practices, however, often involves dramatic changes in how people do their work. This leads to difficulty in the initial year or so of ERP implementation, as organizations get used to the new ways of doing things. While best practices are often adopted, a lot of people get lost along the way, and best practice for one organization has not always proven best for all organizations.

Implementing an ERP is a massive project. Information technology projects are time-consuming, costly activities, with high levels of risk. Adopting a vendor product completely is usually less time consuming than redesigning the system from scratch. Sound IS project management approaches will be needed to successfully implement ERP. A major element of this implementation process involves human subjects. If a new ERP system is expected to succeed, either current employees must buy in to the system, or new employees must be found. In either case, extensive training is needed.

The basic idea of ERP systems has proven beneficial, but the market continues to change, and vendors have found it necessary to keep up with new demands. Two of the more interesting new features offered within ERP systems are customer relationship management and e-business. Customer relationship management involves the use of large sets of data (obtainable from ERP systems, for instance) to better identify the value and needs of specific customers. E-business has been a very important new development (although the past few years have shown that any new opportunity needs to have sound business uses behind it). Incorporation of e-business within ERP has been a matter of interest to organizations and vendors. This need in part is driven by the growth of supply-chain operations, linking organization ERP systems. While a great deal of efficiency can be gained, a number of problems are created as well, especially in the area of security.

Summary

ERP is a software system that has had a tremendous impact on organizational computing. It offers technological, process efficient, financial, strategic, and organizational benefits over disparate and diverse computing systems. This chapter gave a brief review of the evolution of the ERP market, as well as a brief overview of the current state of this market. ERP has a number of advantages, primarily in centralized efficiency. But it also has disadvantages. ERP is usually very expensive, involving millions of dollars in vendor purchase price, as well as additional millions for consultant expertise and in-house development. Costs of ERP often do not fully reflect the negative impact of changing how an organization does business. This involves massive impact on personnel, who often have to relearn their jobs and need to spend many hours in training. Sound management requires careful consideration of benefits and costs of proposed ERP systems.

Humans learn best from failure. An ERP system can be very helpful to organizations. Any vendor will swamp you with success stories from its website. You are encouraged to look at these. However, keep in mind the motivations of the source. ERP vendors do not make money publicizing problems. It is good to review such failures as the FoxMeyer case from the perspective of gaining better understanding of problems to be overcome through planning.

Key Terms

Best practices Application of business processes in a manner deemed the best way.

Business process reengineering (BPR) Analysis of a business process (typical task the organization needs done) to accomplish it in a better way.

Client/Server Architecture Computer system where users (clients) are linked to one or more servers so computing and storage can be distributed.

Data integration Information system designed so that data are ideally entered only once and accurately, and is easily accessible by all organizational users.

Enterprise resource planning system (ERP) Integrated system engineered to apply best practices to organizational computing.

Questions

1. At the library and/or on the Web, review current sales claims by the five BOPSE vendors over the past year. Identify any trends. Are other vendors making progress to break into the top tier of this market?

2. What is the principle behind the idea of best practices?
3. What is the difference between a client/server system and alternative computer platforms?
4. What is the alternative to ERP?
5. If the idea behind ERP is centralization and uniformity, why is it often sold in modules?
6. What advantage is there to an organization in purchasing only a few modules of an ERP vendor product?
7. Why would an ERP system developed by an organization be expected to be more expensive and take longer to implement than a vendor system?
8. Discuss the pros and cons of computer system integration within an organization.
9. What is attractive about data integration? What does ERP have to do with data integration?
10. Visit ERP vendor websites, and compile a list of advantages they claim for ERP systems. Are all vendors relatively consistent?
11. Research the library and/or Web for updated information about FoxMeyer.

Chapter 2

ERP Modules and Historical Development

Enterprise resource planning systems arose from a variety of origins. SAP developed its product around supporting the function of manufacturing, integrating that with financial and accounting functions. Other vendors developed products from other sources. For instance, PeopleSoft began by developing a respected human resources software product, which it expanded to include a slate of other modules. Before entry into the ERP market directly, Oracle was the leading database software vendor.

This chapter:

- Reviews development of ERP.
- Presents the concept of ERP modules.
- Views relative use and modification of modules.
- Discusses issues of customization versus adoption of vendor software as is.

Development of ERP

In the early 1970s, business computing relied upon centralized mainframe computer systems. These systems proved their value by providing a systematic way to measure what businesses did financially. The reports these systems delivered could be used for analysis of budgets and plans, and the systems served as a place to archive business data. Computing provided a way to keep records much more accurately and on a massively larger scale than was possible through manual means.

Business computing systems were initially applied to those functions that were easiest to automate and that called for the greatest levels of consistency and accuracy. Payroll and accounting functions were an obvious initial application. Computers can be programmed to generate accurate paychecks, considering tax and overtime regulations of any degree of complexity. They also can implement accounting systems for tax, cost, and other purposes. Because these functional applications tend to have precise rules that cover almost every case, computers can be entrusted to automatically and rapidly take care of everything related to these functions.

ERP Modules

ERP systems in concept cover all computing for an organization. The idea is to centralize data and computation, so that data can be entered once in a clean form, and then be used by everyone in the organization (and even by supply-chain partners outside the organization) with confidence that the information is correct. However, in practice, ERP vendors sell their software in **modules**. Table 2.1 lists SAP modules and parallel sets of modules offered by other vendors.

One of the more popular computer systems supporting manufacturing before ERP was **materials requirement planning (MRP)**. SAP'S module MM covers the functions of MRP. MRP began as an inventory reordering tool in operations involving dependent demand (the demand for materials depends upon the demand for end items in which the materials are used). The capability of MRP systems evolved to support planning of all company resources, and currently can support business planning, production planning, purchasing, inventory control, shop-floor control, cost management, capacity planning, and logistics management. The use of MRP resulted in better inventory and raw materials control, reduced need for clerical support, and reduced lead times in obtaining materials. Improved communication and better integration of planning were also gained.

MRP II (manufacturing resource planning) is a method to plan all resources for a manufacturer. A variety of business functions are tied into MRP II systems, including order processing as in MRP, business planning, sales and operations planning, production planning, master production scheduling, capacity requirements planning, and capacity planning. MRP II systems are integrated with accounting and finance subsystems to produce reports including business plans, shipping budgets, inventory projections, and purchase plans. There is a tendency within the operations management field to consider ERP as a natural extension of MRP II. Manetti gave the American Production Inventory Control Society (APICS) definition for ERP as a method for effective planning and control of all resources needed to take, make, ship, and account for customer orders.[1] There is at least some truth to this view, but ERP systems fit more than manufacturing operations. ERP systems are found in practically all types of large organizations, including chemical facilities and universities. MRP II functions are covered by SAP's PP module as well as other modules.

Another interesting aspect of the ERP vendor market is industry-specific product lines. BAAN has similar modules to those in Table 2.1, but focuses its marketing on industry-specific product variations. This demonstrates the specialization that all ERP vendors have adopted since 2000. Table 2.2 shows some industry-specific product variations.

PeopleSoft also lists product lines of Customer Relationship Management, an add-on function offered by most vendors, and Portal Solutions, a Web access service also provided by most vendors.

An interesting development is Microsoft's entry into the ERP market. Its website includes a catalog for Microsoft Great Plains Business Solutions (and eight other products related to ERP), which seem very similar to ERP vendor functionality, offering

[1] J. Manetti, "How Technology Is Transforming Manufacturing," *Production and Inventory Management Journal* (first quarter, 2001), pp. 54–64.

TABLE 2.1 Modules Offered by Leading Vendors

Functional Description	SAP	Oracle	PeopleSoft	JDEdwards
Records sales orders and scheduled deliveries, customer information	**SD** (Sales and Distribution)	Marketing Sales Supply Chain	Supply chain management	Order management
Purchasing and raw materials inventory, work-in-process, finished goods	**MM** (Materials Management)	Procurement	Supplier Relationship Management	Inventory Management Procurement
Production planning and scheduling, actual production	**PP** (Production Planning)	Manufacturing		Manufacturing Management
Product inspections, material certifications, quality control	**QM** (Quality Management)		Enterprise Performance Management	Technical Foundation
Preventive maintenance, resource management	**PM** (Plant Maintenance)	Service	Enterprise Service Automation	
Recruiting, hiring, training, payroll, benefits	**HR** (Human Resources)	Human Resources	Human Capital Management	Workforce Management
General ledger account transaction, generates financial statements	**FI** (Financial Accounting)	Financials	Financial Management Solutions	Financial Management
Internal management, cost analysis by cost center	**CO** (Controlling)			Time and Expense Management
Fixed-asset purchase and depreciation	**AM** (Asset Management)	Asset Management		Enterprise Asset Management
R&D, construction, marketing projects	**PS** (Project System)	Projects		Project Management
		Contracts		Subcontract Management
				Real Estate Management
Automate system, task-flow analysis, prompt actions	**WF** (Workflow)			
Best practices	**IS** (Industry Solutions)			

Source: Vendor websites and J. A. Brady, E. F. Monk, and B. J. Wagner, *Concepts in Enterprise Resource Planning* (Boston: Course Technology, 2001).

TABLE 2.2 Industry-Specific Variants

Vendor	BAAN	BAAN	PeopleSoft	PeopleSoft
Product	Discrete Manufacturing	Process Manufacturing	Industry Solutions	Nonprofit
Industries served	Aerospace and defense	Chemicals	Communications	Federal government
	Automobile	Food and beverage	Financial services	Higher education
	Industrial machinery and equipment	Pharmaceuticals	High technology	Public sector
	Electronics	Cable and wire	Professional services	Human resources and payroll
	Telecommunications	Pulp and paper	Utilities	Manufacturing
	Construction	Metals	Consumer products	Project accounting
	Logistics		Health care	
			Industrial products	
			Staffing	
			Wholesale distribution	

Sources: www.baan.com, www.peoplesoft.com.

solutions for accounting and finance, customer relationship management, e-business, human resources and payroll, manufacturing, project accounting, and supply-chain management.

Relative Module Use

The degree of module use was reported by Mabert et al., and replicated by Olhager and Selldin.[2] Mabert et al. surveyed 479 ERP users from the American Inventory and Inventory Control Society in the Midwest. Olhager and Selldin patterned their study after Mabert et al., using 190 Swedish manufacturing firms. Table 2.3 and Figure 2.1 present information extracted from that study.

The most popular module in the United States was financial and accounting, which is the most obvious application needed by an organization. The Swedish study indicated that materials management, production planning, order entry, and purchasing modules were very popular. Other modules, listed in Table 2.3 with adoption rates or less than 50 percent, are either not considered as critical or involve less specificity in best practices. These are similar for both studies, although human resources modules were more popular in Sweden.

There have been noted differences in the ease with which modules are implemented. All financial modules tend to be relatively easy to implement. Those modules relating to manufacturing and human resources also have been implemented with noted success. But modules supporting less structured activities, such as sales and marketing, have encountered notable implementation difficulty.

[2] V. M. Mabert, A. Soni, and M. A. Venkataramanan, "Enterprise Resource Planning Survey of Manufacturing Firms," *Production and Inventory Management Journal* 41, no. 20 (2000), pp. 52–58 and J. Olhager and E. Selldin, "Enterprise Resource Planning Survey of Swedish Manufacturing Firms," *European Journal of Operational Research* 146 (2003), pp. 365–73.

TABLE 2.3
Relative ERP Module Use

Sources: V. M. Mabert, A. Soni, and M. A. Venkataramanan, "Enterprise Resource Planning Survey of Manufacturing Firms," *Production and Inventory Management Journal* 41, no. 20 (2000), and J. Olhager and E. Selldin, "Enterprise Resource Planning Survey of Swedish Manufacturing Firms," *European Journal of Operational Research* 146 (2003).

Module	Midwestern ERP Users	Swedish ERP Users
Financial and Accounting	91.5%	87.3%
Materials management	89.2	91.8
Production planning	88.5	90.5
Order entry	87.7	92.4
Purchasing	86.9	93.0
Financial control	81.5	82.3
Distribution/logistics	75.4	84.8
Asset management	57.7	63.3
Quality management	44.6	47.5
Personnel/human resources	44.6	57.6
Maintenance	40.8	44.3
R&D management	30.8	34.2

FIGURE 2.1
Display of Relative ERP Module Use

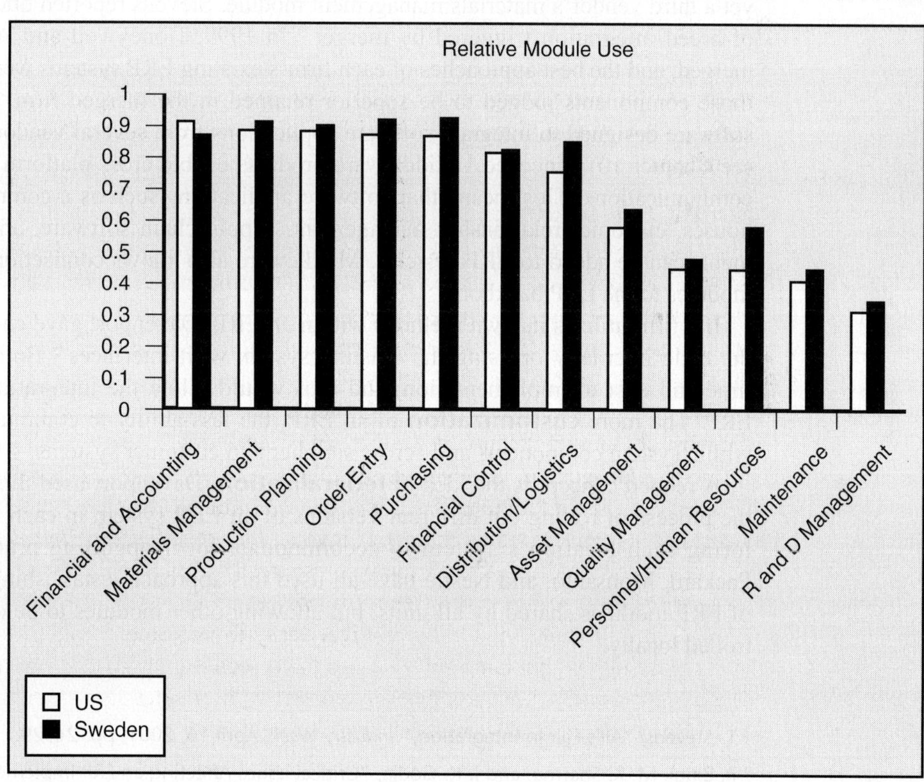

One reason to implement ERP in modules is to obtain specific functionality. Another (and probably the compelling) reason is cost. Full ERP systems cost a reported $5 million for very small versions to more than $100 million for very large implementations. The fewer modules implemented, the lower the cost. Additionally, it sometimes makes sense to implement the system in bits (phased implementation) rather than try to bring the entire massive system on-line at one time (big-bang implementation). Thus, rolling out an ERP by module sometimes makes sense.

Often firms will apply the concept of **best-of-breed,** mixing modules from different vendors. The Mabert et al. study found that a single ERP package was utilized as the vendor designed by only 40 percent of the more than 400 survey respondents. The most common strategic approach in the United States, used by 50 percent of respondents, was to supplement a single ERP package. The idea of best-of-breed was applied in only 4 percent of cases. As might be expected by the enormity of the undertaking, less than 1 percent of the surveyed implementations were entirely constructed in-house.

The idea of best-of-breed approaches is to utilize what is perceived as a specific vendor relative advantage in particular areas of application. One vendor's human resource module might be used in conjunction with another vendor's financial and accounting system, and yet a third vendor's materials management module. Stevens reported one instance of best-of-breed integration triggered by merger.[3] In 1999, Honeywell and AlliedSignal were merged, and the best approaches of each firm's existing ERP systems were examined, with those components judged to be superior retained in the merged firm. Often third-party software designed to integrate software applications from several vendors (**middleware;** see Chapter 10) is needed.[4] Middleware products enable cross-platform operating system communications. This means that software applications such as e-commerce, data warehouses, customer relationship management, supply-chain software, and other enhancements can be added to ERP systems. Middleware also allows connection of best-of-breed modules to the ERP backbone.

If a firm utilizes its own methods within an ERP, Davenport gave choices of rewriting the code internally or using the existing system with interfaces.[5] Both approaches add time and cost to implementation, and thus would dilute the integration benefits of the ERP. The more **customization** of an ERP, the less ability to communicate seamlessly within system components and across supplier and customer systems.

A related concept is the idea of **federalization**. Davenport used this term to describe the process of rolling out different versions of an ERP system in each regional unit, tailoring each location's system to accommodate local operating practices.[6] Hewlett-Packard, Monsanto, and Nestlé have all used this approach, establishing a common core of ERP modules shared by all units, but allowing other modules to be operated and controlled locally.

[3] T. Stevens, "All's Fair in Integration," *Industry Week*, April 16, 2001, pp. 24–29.

[4] P. Bingi, M. K. Sharma, and J. K. Godla, "Critical Issues Affecting an ERP Implementation," *Information Systems Management*, Summer 1999, pp. 7–14.

[5] T. H. Davenport, "Putting the Enterprise into the Enterprise System," *Harvard Business Review*, July–August 1998, pp. 121–131.

[6] Ibid.

Customization Issues

Organizations adopting ERP systems face the dilemma of deciding what degree of customization to adopt. The best fit with organizational needs would involve intensive reengineering and development of ERP software by internal staff. But this method is extremely slow and expensive. It is much faster and less troublesome to adopt a vendor's software directly. However, in practice, almost every organization adopting an ERP system must modify vendor software to some degree. The following applications report modifications of ERP systems adopted by two organizations (referred to here as Firm A and Firm B).[7] These experiences demonstrate typical modifications required when vendor ERP software is implemented.

Firm A's experiences emphasize the extra effort involved in almost any ERP implementation . If the system is obtained from a vendor, as it was here, modifications will be requested. The organization has choices—it can modify the vendor software, as in items 1, 2, 5, and 6 below; it can create new tools to cope with problems, as in items 3 and 4 above, or it can deny requests, as Firm A did. In some cases, the vendor would argue that if the system's procedures were adopted, the users would do their work better in the long run. Information technology personnel are focused on getting the system up and running quickly and within budget, which are the performance indicators by which they are usually evaluated. They also are interested in making the system relatively painless to operate. Users would usually prefer more modifications, and information technology staff would usually prefer fewer modifications. The first year of operation of an ERP tends to be quite traumatic, with users learning to do their work differently, and information technology staff struggling to run the system, often leading to conflict. Usually this extra work was unanticipated, sometimes leading to much longer implementation times, as in item 1. Often decisions must be made with respect to getting the system functioning now at the risk of future problems (items 2 and 5) or developing solutions now at the cost of extra work (items 3 and 4). Future impact was also a major consideration in the decision not to change labels and terminology.

There is inherently a divergence of interest between users and information technology staff members. Users are interested in getting the information they need. Making the system more responsive to users would lead to fewer changes in how they do their work, but would also require more modifications of the vendor system. Early in the implementation of the ERP system, a number of requests for changes in labels and terminology were received. *These requests were denied*, seeking to retain systematic terminology across all users. Another reason for denying requests was the implication on future maintenance that such customizations would have generated.

Again, the modification of vendor ERP software involved many compromises. In items 1 and 3, this burden was entirely placed on internal IT resources, taxing the budget. Items 2, 4, 5, 6, and 7 emphasize the impact of modifications on future operations.

[7] B. Light, "The Maintenance Implications of the Customization of ERP Software," *Journal of Software Maintenance and Evolution: Research and Practice* 13, no. 5 (2001), pp. 415–29.

Real Application: ERP Customization

Firm A was an international firm producing and distributing copper cable. The organization had evolved primarily through acquisition, and thus had a variety of computer systems. In the late 1990s, there were 10 manufacturing systems, 13 sales systems, 15 purchasing systems, 5 planning systems, 18 finance systems, and 18 personnel systems. This resulted in a variety of data views that often conflicted and in systems using incompatible platforms. The options that every ERP adopter has are represented by the extremes of:

- An all-internal system—revising how the software works to fit the organization
- An all-vendor system—revising how the organization works to fit the software
- Practical compromise—varying degrees available between the two extremes.

The Firm A ERP implementation was intended to be as close to the vendor design as possible. However, instances cited here show where customization was required.

1. In the MRP system, cable lengths needed by the corporation did not fit the vendor setup. A customization was specified by Firm A. The ERP vendor built a customization into the ERP system, which provided Firm A with a working solution. However, this customization *delayed system delivery by five months*, emphasizing the impact of modifications to vendor ERP systems.
2. Copper prices vary daily. Firm A coped with this risk through inventory stocks of copper, valued at the purchaser price. Therefore, details of purchase time, price, and contractual information had to be retained. This functionality was incorporated into the ERP software by the vendor. However, this *led to requirements for recustomization in future software upgrades.*
3. The ERP system reporting screens for shop-floor control were complex and cluttered. Test trials found a data entry error rate of 17 percent. Implementation of a software applications programming *interface tool* (automation of a process) solved this problem.
4. Every sales order required dispatch notes. The original ERP setup involved about 16 user operations to generate the required notes. Another *software applications programming interface* developed one screen that the user could mark to accomplish all needed work. The average time to accomplish the business process was thus reduced from 20 minutes to 5 minutes.
5. A number of documents associated with each sales order were standardized to include addition of a company logo. These changes were not affected by upgrades. However, *subsequent acquisitions led to the need to revise documents*, a typical adaptive maintenance activity.
6. The inventory reports generated by the ERP system did not provide all needed management information. The development team had to devote considerable *effort to create new reports.* In the meantime, users created their own reports through SQL queries. Firm A's IT staff sought to curb such activity and generate needed reports within the system.

Firm B provided a second example of a real ERP implementation, confirming the results experienced by Firm A. Firm B was a British retailer with 20 outlets. This organization's legacy systems were very fragmented. ERP was adopted to integrate systems, avoid data entry duplication, and replace a number of manual systems. Maintenance issues in this case included the following:

1. Pricing was based in part on travel distance to deliver the product. Thus, there were millions of prices in the system. Customization to support this was extensive. Maintenance issues involved were that this *customization was not supported by the service agreement*, and that only one IT person at Firm B fully understood the customization.
2. Because costs were a function of delivery distance, addresses had to be accurate and easy to find. The ERP software allowed free format. Firm B required a predefined list of addresses from post office address files. Some delivery sites were to streets that did not yet physically exist. Regular updates were not easy to apply. The scope of addresses in the system was expected to cause *future problems in any ERP software upgrades.*
3. Firm B utilized a number of shipping firms, which traditionally used self-billing, a *function not supported by the ERP software.* A customization was implemented producing shipper statements each month with details, as well as the amount Firm B intended to pay each shipper. Queries were collected and adjustments made the following month. This extensive customization was found to be very expensive.
4. Dispatch procedures embedded in the ERP system led to entry of the same data a number of times. Keystroke emulation software was used to automate this data entry. Future *upgrades would likely require heavy redevelopment.*
5. Corporate document sets were modified and standardized, and the company logo was added. Future upgrades were expected, realizing that such *upgrades would require additional changes* in the document set.
6. Many ERP software screens were modified, removing unused fields. Many Sales module screens were changed, while only four Purchasing module screens required change. These *changes had to be carefully documented* to reduce problems in future upgrades (which would wipe out changes).
7. A large number of control reports were developed, designed to highlight exceptions. Business users developed 908 control reports. The resources needed to *revise in the future as required* presented maintenance implications.

Both cases demonstrate the importance of considering future ERP system maintenance. Future modifications to ERP systems will arise from organizational changes (mergers and acquisitions, significant organizational growth or contraction, radically changing markets, etc.) or from vendor changes (ERP vendors systematically improve their software, and upgrades rarely will accommodate using organization modifications).

Key performance indicators are essential in ERP systems. Both Firm A and Firm B examples involved identification of key performance indicators. For Firm A, these were:

- Production cycle time.
- Daily cost of production receipts.

- Monthly production volume analysis.
- Daily cost of sales dispatches.
- Goods in the warehouse longer than a specified maximum number of days.

This information was captured by ERP reports, but led to increased maintenance activity. For Firm B, most key performance indicator reports were obtained from the organization's data warehouse rather than from the ERP. However, some key performance indicator reports were obtained directly from the ERP. IT staff had to devote resources to create and revise these reports.

Summary

The core idea of ERP is complete integration of an organization's computing system. Almost none of ERP implementations involve installing a vendor's entire suit of modules.[8] It is very common for organizations to select modules, which makes great sense because not every organization needs every module vendors develop. In fact, vendors seem to recognize this through their recent emphasis on products tailored to a specific industry.

There are also other very important reasons for implementing ERP products different from the vendor's design. A very important one is that full system implementation is very expensive. By selecting particular modules, organizations can cut initial implementation costs significantly. While vendors might argue that in the long run this might be less effective than full implementation now, in practice information systems projects rarely go as planned, nor do they tend to stay within originally planned budgets. Thus, organizations reduce their risks by trying particular modules first, often seeing how the new system is digested by the organization before going ahead with additional modules.

There also is a difference in the difficulty of implementing different modules. Financial and accounting modules are typically installed first, as they involve the most structured application. This makes it easier to implement, and easier for the organization to digest. Other modules such as materials management and planning also tend to work well. Conversely, support to less structured environments, such as sales and marketing, tends to be more problematic.

Related to the idea of implementing ERP in modules are the concepts of best-of-breed, middleware, customization, and federalization. Best-of-breed implementation is idealistic, seeking the best module across vendors and combining whatever mix is viewed as best for the particular organization. This approach is not widely adopted, probably because it involves obvious coordination risks. It also tends to be more expensive. Middleware is an important type of software making it possible to add on specialty software products. Customization is an approach to implement a vendor's ERP system tailored to organizational needs. Customization is done internally, as opposed to middleware, which is usually accomplished from third-party vendor software. Federalization allows different parts of the organization to utilize different modules, or possibly different levels of customization.

[8]Mabert et al., "Enterprise resource planning survey of manufacturing firms."

Key Terms

Best-of-breed Concept of mixing ERP modules from different vendors.

Customization Modification of vendor software to meet specific organizational requirements.

Federalization Tailoring ERP systems differently for each regional unit of an organization.

Key performance indicators Measures of organizational performance in areas deemed critical to success.

Manufacturing resource planning (MRP II) Computer system created to add planning support to MRP.

Material requirements planning (MRP) Computer system created to organize the materials purchasing of an assembly operation.

Middleware Third-party software created to integrate software applications from multiple sources.

Module Vendor software capable of independent operation that provides ERP support for a specific function.

Questions

1. What is the relationship between MRP and ERP?
2. What is the most commonly used ERP module, and why?
3. Have manufacturing-related modules been the basis of all ERPs?
4. Quality is an important emphasis in manufacturing. What has been the relative use of quality modules in ERP?
5. What is the relative importance of manufacturing-related modules in ERP?
6. What is the best-of-breed concept?
7. Describe the concept of federalization.
8. Research the library and/or Web and identify current modules offered by the BOPSE firms.
9. Research the library and/or Web and identify Microsoft's ERP system success.

Chapter 3

ERP System Options and Selection Methods

Enterprise resource planning systems are very large IS/IT projects. The cost range is enormous, depending upon the size of the firm implementing the system, as well as on how many modules are used. An additional factor is the cost of training users. It is difficult to develop much of any system for less than $5 million. Some of the largest systems have cost in excess of $100 million. Training organizational users to utilize ERP systems in their jobs has cost as much as an additional 20 percent of an ERP system's cost. Some ERPs are installed with much less training, but this usually proves to be a major mistake.

All IS/IT projects begin with a project proposal, generated by users or management. Because of an ERP system's large size and pervasive impact on an organization, the first step should be a thorough analysis of the proposal as an investment. Once ERP projects are adopted, their cost and progress should be carefully monitored.

This chapter will discuss the options in obtaining an ERP system. It will also address ERP project selection and will show how commonly used selection methods work. Analytic methods support this selection process in two ways. First, they provide decision makers with analysis of expected outcomes from adopting specific projects. Second, they provide a basis for communication, so that the reasoning behind a selection decision can be explained to others.

This chapter:

- Discusses optional ERP system configurations.
- Considers factors in ERP adoption decisions.
- Details IS/IT project selection techniques.
- Reports the duration of ERP implementations.
- Outlines ERP system component costs.
- Discusses the relationship of ERP cost to organization size.
- Presents value analysis as a basis for adoption decisions.
- Presents multiple objective analysis as a basis for adoption decisions.
- Details Dell's ERP analysis.

Optional Means of Developing an ERP

There are a number of ways to build an ERP, briefly outlined in Table 3.1.

The simplest way is to adopt a vendors product completely. This is what vendors prefer. This option has some strong advantages, especially with respect to relative time and cost. The opposite extreme is to develop an ERP totally with in-house assets. This approach offers the greatest opportunity to gain competitive advantage. However, the in-house approach is a very difficult information systems project, probably the most difficult imaginable. The ideal way to do this is to combine it with extensive business process reengineering (see Chapter 4), identifying the best way to do everything, and then building the computer system to accomplish this. This is a very slow and expensive way to obtain an ERP, but it is the most flexible and responsive to organizational needs.

As with many other aspects of life, compromises are available within these extremes. As discussed in Chapter 2, most firms adopt only a few ERP modules of vendor software, which has the relative advantage of minimizing organizational risk and expenditure in the short run, and reducing the trauma of incorporating the ERP into organizational operations. The disadvantage is that the full functionality of the vendor system is not obtained, and users still must conform to the procedures that the vendor programmed into the system.

Many companies adopt another hybrid approach, customizing a vendor software product. This gains flexibility over simply adopting the vendor system, but risks loss of the efficiencies built into the system through best practices. A form of this hybrid approach is

TABLE 3.1 Advantages and Disadvantages of Alternative ERP Development Methods

Method	Advantages	Disadvantages
Develop in-house	Best fit with organizational needs	Most difficult to develop Most expensive Slowest
In-house system with vendor supplements	Gain commercial advantages combined with organizational fit	Difficult to develop Expensive Slow
Best-of-breed	Theoretically gain best of all systems	Difficult to link modules Slow Potentially inefficient
Customized vendor system	Retain flexibility while keeping vendor expertise	Slower Usually more expensive
Selected vendor modules	Less risk Relatively fast Least expensive	If expand, long run time and cost higher
Full vendor system	Fast Less expensive Efficient	Inflexible
Application service provider	Least risk Least cost Fastest Least subject to vendor change	At the mercy of ASP provider No control Subject to price increases

best-of-breed (discussed in Chapter 2). In the best-of-breed approach, modules considered to be competitively strong are selected from multiple vendors. Custom interfaces can be developed using in-house information system development assets.

The final approach is to rent an ERP through an application service provider (ASP). This topic will be discussed more in Chapter 5. The benefit of an ASP is that the using organization doesn't have to worry about system development or about being at the mercy of vendors when they change their software. However, the risk is simply transferred, because the user is now subject to the mercy of the ASP. The decision is similar to that of deciding whether to buy or rent housing. In the long run, you are usually better off buying a house. However, the cash flow impact and risk avoidance of renting is much better than buying.

Each organization needs to analyze the costs and benefits of various forms of ERP. This should involve consideration of a number of factors, not just cash. Estimates of future revenue impacts need to be made under conditions of high uncertainty. Another possible option is to not adopt an ERP, which is demonstrated with the real case at the end of the chapter.

Measurement of Project Impact

Information systems projects typically involve benefits that are difficult to measure in terms of concrete monetary benefits. This vastly complicates matters, because **cost-benefit analysis**, the ideal tool for evaluating project proposals, will not always accurately reflect project benefits. Hinton and Kaye cited cost and benefit intangibility, **hidden outcomes** involved in information technology investment, and the changing nature of information technology systems as important issues.[1]

Intangible Factors

Both costs and benefits tend to have intangible features. Many of the benefits of any IS/IT project are expected in the future and are very difficult to measure. These include expected increases in market share, improved customer service, and better corporate image. Other types of **intangible factors** include the impact of soft benefits, such as employee satisfaction (or dissatisfaction), supply-chain integration, and the ability to support e-business operations. These intangible benefits often lead to real competitive advantage, although the precise economic impact is often difficult to accurately estimate.

Hidden Outcomes

Other aspects of ERP projects often involve complex results. ERP may change organizational power. Specific groups may have held power in the older system, and a new ERP system can hamper teamwork. ERP systems include components of the organization's communications network. Experienced employees may have established power bases because they were efficient at accessing key information. An ERP system can be viewed as a threat, by making more information readily available to those who need it. On the other hand, an ERP system is complex, and those who are involved in its implementation may

[1] M. Hinton and R. Kaye, "Investing in Information Technology: A Lottery?" *Management Accounting* 74, no. 10 (November 1996), p. 52.

temporarily gain a power base because they know how to access information from the ERP while others are still learning its intricate workings.

There also is the behavioral factor of working with more automated systems. Computers can make work more productive and more attractive. But they also can change work roles to emphasize skills in which specific employees have no training, making them feel less productive.

Failure to identify the impact of projects often is not noticed until implementation. At that stage, the problems are more difficult to deal with. It is important to consider the systems aspects of projects, and try to predict how the project will change how people do their jobs. Thorough user involvement early in the process can make project impact more obvious, as well as easier to reconcile and convince users of the project's benefits.

The Changing Nature of Information Technology

There are many excellent applications of computer technology to aid businesses. But because technology is highly dynamic and some ERP projects take years to implement, a new system may be outdated by the time it's installed. McLeod and Smith suggest a maximum of nine months between management approval and project component construction in information systems projects.[2] This rule of thumb is not intended for ERP systems, which are so massive that they have longer-range impact. However, many recent vendor products are designed to be implemented in six months or less, given that there is no system customization. If long-term projects to implement ERP are adopted, understanding their impact on organizational operations is even more important.

Information Technology Selection

Hinton and Kaye surveyed 50 members of a professional organization whose members were responsible for appraising key organizational investments. [3] Methods used for information technology projects were appraised and compared to projects in other areas (operations, marketing, and training). Treatment of a project as a capital investment involves cost-benefit analysis to establish profitability. Treatment as a revenue-related project does not require cost-benefit analysis, as the project is expected to foster key organizational goals, and the benefits are recognized as being difficult to measure accurately. Table 3.2 gives the results of their survey. Information technology tended to be treated as a capital investment. This means that executives expect IT projects to have measurable profit benefits.

Decision makers treat information technology investment more like operations projects with measurable profitability requirements rather than the revenue-based appraisals appropriate for training and marketing. Operations investments focus on efficiency-related measures. Conversely, marketing investments are usually viewed in terms of their expected impact on improving competitive position, or increasing market share. The capital approach is appropriate for hardware proposals, but difficulties are encountered when

[2] G. McLeod and D. Smith, *Managing Information Technology Projects* (Cambridge, MA: Course Technology, 1996).

[3] Hinton and Kaye, "Investing in Information Technology."

TABLE 3.2 IS/IT Project Treatment — Capital Investment or Revenue Enhancement

Investment Type	Treated as Capital Investment	Treated as Mixed	Treated as Revenue Enhancement
Training	0%	1%	99%
Marketing	4	9	87
Information technology	39	41	20
Operations	58	31	11

Source: M. Hinton and R. Kaye, "Investing in Information Technology: A Lottery?" *Management Accounting* 74, no. 10 (November 1996).

justifying software. Intangible benefits such as competitive advantage or improved practices tend to be disregarded because they are hard to quantify. The most commonly cited justification is reduction in expenses, usually in payroll. The second most common justification involves the subjective aspect of accomplishing some strategic objective. Intangible benefits include example such as enhanced patient care and satisfaction for a health care organization, better speed of responding to customers, and the need to satisfy governmental regulations.

Information systems projects involve risks from a number of sources. Most of these risks have to do with estimating the time for a specific organization to accomplish required work. The amount of time, on average, will depend on a number of factors, including:

1. Project manager ability.
2. Experience with this type of application.
3. Experience with the programming environment.
4. Experience with the language or system used.
5. Familiarity with modern programming practices.
6. Availability of critical equipment, software, and programming language.
7. Completeness of project team (are all team members on board).
8. Personnel turnover.
9. Project team size.
10. Relative control of project manager over project team.[4]

Of these factors, probably the most important is the ability of the project manager. Experience can take a variety of forms. Familiarity with modern programming practices concerns exposure to current best practices. These items are a checklist of characteristics that should be at minimum acceptable levels. If satisfactory ratings are not assigned for all items, this organization's ability to complete this particular project may be in doubt.

Financial techniques often used to assess viability are payback, discounted cash flow, and cost-benefit analysis. Focus on bottom-line justification misleads companies

[4] J. Simms, "Evaluating IT: Where Cost-Benefit Can Fail," *Australian Accountant*, May 1997, pp. 29–31.

evaluating information technology investment.[5] Net present value masks some of the true value of information technology proposals. On the other hand, some projects that have low impact on corporate performance often appear attractive in cost-benefit analyses. For instance, a project may provide an organization with a key competitive advantage, although expected benefits from this improvement may not be acceptably measurable to accounting personnel. Cost-benefit analysis emphasizes those features most easily measured. The value of information technology projects is in making organizations more competitive, increasing customer satisfaction, and operating more effectively. These sometimes intangible strategic benefits are often disregarded because they are not measurable.[6]

Cost-benefit analysis should consider costs over the entire life cycle of the project. Life cycle costs are roughly four times development costs for most information systems projects.[7] But these long-range costs are much less predictable, and therefore often not included in cost-benefit analyses.

Many companies tie up valuable developmental resources on low-cost, unevaluated projects. A comprehensive information technology management program needs to evaluate the costs and benefits, strategic impacts, risk, and life-cycle costs of all of its projects. There seems to be an evolutionary progression in information technology management, with firms starting with conventional cost-benefit evaluation. When this stage is mastered, they tend to implement risk analysis along with cost-benefit analysis. Finally, they add consideration of strategic, intangible benefits. This final approach is said to provide up to 50 percent higher returns on investment.[8]

Many companies simply disregard important intangible factors because these factors in assessing the worth of information technology project proposals involve high levels of uncertainty and even speculation. But there are many important intangible factors involved. **Value analysis** or **multiple criteria analysis** offer means of considering such factors.

Information Technology Project Approval

Bacon surveyed 80 American, British, Australian, and New Zealand companies about their practice in approving information system technology projects.[9] The study consisted of a list of 15 criteria, divided into financial, management, and development groupings. **Financial criteria** included net present value, internal rate of return, and **payback** methods as discussed above, as well as a profitability index and a budgetary constraint method. The accounting rate of return method, like payback, does not consider the time value of money. Its attractiveness is due in all likelihood to its simplicity. Another reason accounting rate of return is used is that managerial bonuses are often based on accounting

[5] Ibid.

[6] Hinton and Kaye, "Investing in Information Technology."

[7] Simms "Evaluating IT."

[8] Ibid.

[9] C.J. Bacon, "The Use of Decision Criteria in Selecting Information Systems/Technology Investments," *MIS Quarterly* 16, no. 3 (1992), pp. 335–353.

TABLE 3.3 IS/IT Project Evaluation Technique Use

Criteria	% of Companies Using	% of Projects to Which Applied	Ranking by Total Project Value
Financial:			
Budgetary Constraint	68%	64%	8
Payback	61	51	5
IRR	54	54	2
NPV	48	58	4
Accounting rate of return	16	47	10
Profitability index	8	47	14
Management:			
Explicit business objectives	88	57	1
Support decision making	88	29	7
Legal/government requirement	71	13	13
Implicit business objectives	69	44	3
Response to competition	61	28	6
Probability of achieving benefits	46	63	9
Development:			
Technical/system requirements	79	25	12
Introduce/learn new technology	60	13	15
Probability of project completion	31	62	11

Source: C.J. Bacon, "The use of Decision Criteria in Selecting Information Systems/Technology Investments." *MIS Quarterly* 16, no. 3 (1992).

rates of return.[10] Bacon's survey also included a profitability index, which is a variant of net present value analysis (as are rates of return). The budgetary constraint method would adopt projects in order of rate of return, until some budget limit was exceeded. This method can be optimized by using mathematical programming.

Five **management criteria** were listed in the Bacon survey: support of business objectives (explicit and implicit), response to competition, seeking better support to management decision making, consideration of probability, and satisfaction of legal requirements. Project proposals that support business objectives may not always be quantifiable, and accurate measurement of the impact on net present value is usually impractical. Support of management decision making reflects the importance of information technology as an objective in itself. Probability can sometimes be included with other criteria (in the form of expected value), but risk represents a fundamental consideration in itself.

There were three **development criteria.** These were technical system requirements (projects needed for effective operation of the organization), to introduce or learn new technology, and probability of project completion. We saw in Chapter 1 that probability of project completion on schedule is highly problematic.

The results of Bacon's survey of 203 companies are displayed in Table 3.3. The column for ranking by total project value compiled the responses of the ranking of a criterion in

[10] S.C. Weaver, D. Peter, R. Cason, and J. Daleiden, "Panel Discussions on Corporate Investment: Capital Budgeting," *Financial Management* 18, no. 1 (1989), pp. 10–17.

terms of overall value of projects to which it applies. This was intended to reflect each method's value in important cases. Among financial criteria, the budgetary constraint method was reported to be used most often. Payback was the second most widely reported. Firms with more projects used **net present value (NPV)** and **internal rate return (IRR)** more often, providing one possible explanation for their higher ranking in the percent of projects in which the method was applied and their higher ranking by total project value. Bacon found that 25 percent of these large organizations did not report any use of discounted cash flow methods. Among those firms that did use it, it was used primarily for evaluating large projects. IRR was used more often than NPV, despite the theoretical superiority of NPV. Bacon concluded that managers may be able to grasp the significance of IRR, and that NPV involves many assumptions about discount rates that are not accurate. IRR and NPV were ranked highest, however, in the value of the projects analyzed. This indicates that their use tends to be reserved for larger projects. Accounting rate of return and profitability index were used by a small proportion of the companies.

Of the management criteria, explicit business objectives was ranked first on all three measures. Many companies reported the criterion of support decision making. The survey also indicates that information technology projects are often adopted to keep up with competition or to satisfy legal requirements. The need to keep up with competition is often expressed by the statement: "We cannot afford not to invest." The risk-related criterion of the probability of achieving benefits was reported by less than half of the companies surveyed. But of those who reported its use, Bacon stated that it was applied to 63 percent of the projects analyzed.

The most commonly reported development criterion was technical/system requirements. Organizations may invest in upgraded information technology because their existing systems might be outdated or of insufficient capacity. Technical managers may deem it necessary to have state-of-the-art systems, an opinion possibly not shared by business managers. Companies with such technical managers may have invested more in information technology than was merited by business needs. Justification based on introducing new technology can be subject to the same criticism. Often the probability of project completion is used as the basis for project adoption. While only 31 percent of the companies reported using probability of completion as a justification criterion, those who did were reported to apply it to over 60 percent of their projects. The rest of this chapter will demonstrate most of the basic methods reported. The first method demonstrated is screening, a common form of the checklist method that can be and often is combined with other criteria.

ERP Proposal Evaluation

Mabert et al. surveyed a large number of Midwestern U.S. manufacturing firms that had implemented ERP systems. Olhager and Selldin replicated the study in Sweden.[11] These

[11] V. M. Mabert, A. Soni, and M. A. Venkataramanan, "Enterprise Resource Planning Survey of U.S. Manufacturing Firms," *Production and Inventory Management Journal* 41, no. 20 (2000), pp. 52–58, and J. Olhager and E. Selldin, "Enterprise Resource Planning Survey of Swedish Manufacturing Firms," *European Journal of Operational Research* 146 (2003), pp. 365–373.

TABLE 3.4 ERP Proposal Evaluation Technique Use

Financial Method	Reported Use in United States	Reported Use in Sweden
ROI	53%	30%
Payback	35	67
Expected NPV	15	12
Other	11	20

Sources: V.M. Mabert, A. Soni, and M.A. Venkataramanan, "Enterprise Resource Planning Survey of U.S. Manufacturing Firms." *Production and Inventory Management Journal* 41, no. 20 (2000), and J. Olhager and E. Selldin, "Enterprise Resource Planning Survey of Swedish Manufacturing Firms," *European Journal of Operational Research* 146 (2003).

TABLE 3.5 Expected ERP Project Installation Time Requirements

Installation Time	United States	Sweden
12 months or less	34%	38%
13 to 24 months	45	49
25 to 36 months	11	8
37 to 48 months	6	4
Over 48 months	2	1

Sources: V.M. Mabert, A. Soni, and M.A. Venkataramanan, "Enterprise Resource Planning Survey of U.S. Manufacturing Firms." *Production and Inventory Management Journal* 41, no. 20 (2000), and J. Olhager and E. Selldin, "Enterprise Resource Planning Survey of Swedish Manufacturing Firms," *European Journal of Operational Research* 146 (2003).

surveys yielded the proportions of analysis use applied to ERP adoption decisions as shown in Table 3.4. Note that payback use reported in the United States was much lower than that reported for general IS/IT projects by Bacon (although the Swedish percentage was even higher than Bacon's number). It seems counterintuitive that not all firms implementing ERP applied formal **return on investment (ROI)** analysis, although the argument still holds that detailed analysis of imprecise estimated figures is often a waste of time. In this study, some firms used multiple evaluation methods. Most of these firms anticipated that the adopted system would serve their organizations over seven years.

Table 3.5 reveals the expected ERP installation time. The reported times are very similar. Obviously, the scope of the ERP project would be a major factor in this time expectation. Projects implemented in less than one year would have to be relatively small (implementation of one or only a few modules, for instance).

Table 3.6 reports expected ERP system costs. Again, the two studies provided similar numbers (assuming a scale error of 10 in the Swedish study for installation cost system). For smaller firms, with revenues less than $50 million per year, anticipated ERP installation costs were solidly in the less than $5 million range, with an associated implementation cost of about 14 percent of revenues. Firms with annual revenues above $250 million had larger ERP implementation budgets, but their implementation cost as a percent of revenue was only 3 percent or less.

While almost half of the surveyed firms reported expected implementation expense to be less than $5 million, we consider that figure to still be representative of the minimum

TABLE 3.6 ERP Estimated Installation Project Cost

Installation Cost	United States	Sweden
Less than $5 million	42%	40%
$5 million to $25 million	33	35
$26 million to $50 million	10	18
$51 million to $100 million	7	7
Over $100 million	7	(in prior category)

Sources: V.M. Mabert, A. Soni, and M.A. Venkataramanan, "Enterprise Resource Planning Survey of U.S. Manufacturing Firms." *Production and Inventory Management Journal* 41, no. 20 (2000), and J. Olhager and E. Selldin, "Enterprise Resource Planning Survey of Swedish Manufacturing Firms," *European Journal of Operational Research* 146 (2003).

TABLE 3.7 ERP Installation Project Cost Proportions

Installation Cost Proportion Project	Installation Cost Proportion in United States	Cost proportion in Sweden
Software	30%	24%
Consulting	24	30
Hardware	18	19
Implementation team	14	12
Training	11	14
Other	3	1

Sources: V.M. Mabert, A. Soni, and M.A. Venkataramanan, "Enterprise Resource Planning Survey of U.S. Manufacturing Firms." *Production and Inventory Management Journal* 41, no. 20 (2000), and J. Olhager and E. Selldin, "Enterprise Resource Planning Survey of Swedish Manufacturing Firms," *European Journal of Operational Research* 146 (2003).

TABLE 3.8 Expected ROI from ERP Projects

Expected ROI	United States	Sweden
Less than 5%	14%	17%
5% to 15%	18	38
16% to 25%	36	30
26% to 50%	18	11
Over 50%	13	4

Sources: V.M. Mabert, A. Soni, and M.A. Venkataramanan, "Enterprise Resource Planning Survey of U.S. Manufacturing Firms." *Production and Inventory Management Journal* 41, no. 20 (2000), and J. Olhager and E. Selldin, "Enterprise Resource Planning Survey of Swedish Manufacturing Firms," *European Journal of Operational Research* 146 (2003).

scope required because IS/IT projects often significantly exceed their time and cost estimates. However, recent trends on the part of vendors to reduce implementation time probably have reduced ERP installation cost.

Mabert et al. also investigated the proportion of total costs by ERP component, with results given in Table 3.7. In the United States, vendors take the biggest chunk of the average implementation. Consultants also take a big portion. These proportions are reversed in Sweden The internal implementation team accounts for an additional 14 percent (12 percent in Sweden). These proportions are roughly reversed for training.

The expectations of return on their investment varied widely as given in Table 3.8. From these numbers, it appears that Swedish manufacturers expect a bit less return than did those in the United States (much of which might be explained by timing of the surveys). Because the motivations for adopting ERP in some cases was either competitive or viewed as forced for other reasons, some firms expect low payoff from their ERP systems. However, roughly as many adopters expect clearly significant returns on their investment.

Project Evaluation Techniques

This section will demonstrate some of the most widely used methods mentioned above and show how other methods can be used to consider other factors describing expected project performance.

Cost-benefit analysis seeks to identify accurate measures of benefits and costs in monetary terms, and uses the ratio benefits/costs (the term benefit-cost ratio seems more appropriate, and is sometimes used, but most people refer to cost-benefit analysis). Because ERP projects involve long time frames (for benefits if not for costs as well), considering the net present value of benefits and costs is important.

Cost-Benefit Example

Consider a proposed ERP implementation involving a study in year 1 conducted by a small team of company personnel, aided by a hired consultant. This is a fairly small implementation, and at this stage of the analysis, expected costs typically are underestimated. It has numbers that are relatively small compared to average ERP implementation projects, but represent ballpark costs for a small firm implementing one or a few modules. This analysis in year 1 includes a business process reengineering study and the formation of a training team. This cost analysis assumes purchase of a $3 million software system from a reputable vendor. The internal team is expected to double in payroll cost during year 2, and consulting expertise will double as well. The second year will also see investment in extra hardware to support the proposed system. Finally, in year 3, the internal implementation team, assisted by consultants, will finish implementation. An extra budget of $500,000 is allowed for additional hardware. The training team will grow after the first year. The firm wants to treat all expenses in the first three years as investment.

There will be costs for a team to operate the system. This budget is expected to be $2 million in year 4, growing at a rate of 10 percent per year thereafter. There will be a continued need for training personnel during years 4 and 5, but at lower rates than during system development and implementation.

The firm's cost of capital is 20 percent, because it has a strong average return on its money. There is some disagreement among the firms board of directors concerning the expected growth rate of benefits. The dominant group on the board expects benefits from the ERP to be $4 million per year in year 4 and to last for 7 years, growing at 30 percent per year. A vocal minority thinks this expectation is far too high, and benefits will probably grow only 10 percent per year. This data is summarized in Table 3.9. These numbers reflect the expectations of the majority of the board. A minority expects the benefits to be lower after year 4, by growing at 10 percent per year instead of the 30 percent per year shown here.

TABLE 3.9 Cost-Benefit Analysis Input Data — Example Proposal

Year	Internal Team	Consultants	Software	Hardware	Training	Benefit
1	$500,000	$500,000			$200,000	
2	1,000,000	1,000,000	$3,000,000	$2,000,000	500,000	
3	1,500,000	1,000,000		500,000	2,000,000	
4	2,000,000				1,000,000	$4,000,000
5	2,200,000				300,000	5,200,000
6	2,420,000					6,760,000
7	2,662,000					8,788,000
8	2,928,200					11,424,400
9	3,221,020					14,851,720
10	3,543,122					19,307,236

TABLE 3.10 Net Present Value Calculation

Year	Investment	Operation	Benefits (30%)	NPV30	Benefits (10%)	NPV10
1	$1,200,000			$-1,000,000		$-1,000,000
2	7,500,000			-5,208,333		-5,208,333
3	5,000,000			-2,893,519		-2,893,519
4		$3,000,000	$4,000,000	482,253	$4,000,000	482,253
5		2,500,000	5,200,000	1,085,069	4,400,000	763,567
6		2,420,000	6,760,000	1,453,457	4,840,000	810,453
7		2,662,000	8,788,000	1,709,654	5,324,000	742,915
8		2,928,200	11,424,400	1,975,945	5,856,400	681,006
9		3,221,020	14,851,720	2,254,108	6,442,040	624,255
10		3,543,122	19,307,236	2,545,992	7,086,244	572,234
NPV				2,404,627		-4,425,168

Net Present Value Calculation

We will first demonstrate calculation of net present value of the project proposal, using both expected rates of benefit growth, in Table 3.10. Using the 30 percent benefit growth rate assumed by the majority of the board, and a cost of capital of 20 percent per year, the net present value for the majority board opinion shows that adopting the ERP project (and investing $13.7 million) is equivalent in worth to a gain of $2.4 million. This takes some faith, as most of the outflow of cash is at the beginning of the time frame, while expected benefits are late. Furthermore, in 10 years, technology will undoubtedly have changed significantly, making the value of the current system dubious. That is a good reason to cut off the analysis at 10 years. The problem is that the expected benefits peak at that distant time horizon.

The more conservative group on the board would view the proposal as equivalent to throwing away $4.4 million today. This would be the basis for a strong argument against the proposal. There is a possible mitigation in that competitive pressures or other reasons may compel adoption of more modern computer systems.

TABLE 3.11 Payback Calculation Assuming 30% Benefit Growth

Year	Investment	Operation	Benefits (30%)	Net	Cumulative
1	$1,200,000			$-1,200,000	-1,200000
2	7,500,000			-7,500,000	-8,700,000
3	5,000,000			-5,000,000	-13,700,000
4		$3,000,000	$4,000,000	1,000,000	-12,700,000
5		2,500,000	5,200,000	2,700,000	-10,000,000
6		2,420,000	6,760,000	4,340,000	-5,660,000
7		2,662,000	8,788,000	6,126,000	466,000
8		2,928,200	11,424,400	8,496,200	
9		3,221,020	14,851,720	11,630,700	
10		3,543,122	19,307,236	15,764,114	

Return on Investment

The internal rate of return (IRR) on investment of a proposal is simply the discount rate (20 percent per year was used in Table 3.9) that would yield a zero net present value. This can be identified easily on a spreadsheet by placing the discount rate used in net present value calculations in a particular cell and entering data until the net present value is closest to zero. In the example, assuming a 30 percent rate of benefit growth per year would yield an internal rate of return of 25.2 percent per year. For the conservative group on the board, the corresponding IRR would have been 5.0 percent.

Payback

One of the most common reasons for company failure in the United States is lack of cash flow. Webb has examined the trade-off between cash flow and net present value in economic analysis.[12] In this case, if the firm has cash-flow difficulties, the investment would be less attractive than if it had adequate cash reserves.

Another measure of value is to identify the time for an investment to be repaid. A time-related factor is the need for cash flow. One alternative may be superior to another on the net present value of the total life cycle of the project. However, cost-benefit analysis does not consider the impact of negative cash flow.

Payback is usually a simplified form of analysis. Its calculation is very simple in cases where investment is heavy up front, and benefits are later in the time horizon. That is usually the case with ERP proposals, although care must be taken that possible negative cash flows in later periods don't mess up the calculations. The operation is to identify cumulative net cash flow, and identify how long it will be before it turns positive, as in Table 3.11.

Here the payback period is almost seven years. The calculation using the more conservative rate of growth in benefits is given in Table 3.12, showing payback delayed until late in year nine.

[12] D. C. Webb, "The Trade-off between Cash Flow and Net Present Value," *Scandinavian Journal of Economics* 95, no. 1 (1993), pp. 65–75.

TABLE 3.12 Payback Calculation Assuming 10% Benefit Growth

Year	Investment	Operation	Benefits (10%)	Net	Cumulative
1	$1,200,000			$-1,200,000	$-1,200,000
2	7,500,000			-7,500,000	-8,700,000
3	5,000,000			-5,000,000	-13,700,000
4		$3,000,000	$4,000,000	1,000,000	-12,700,000
5		2,500,000	4,400,000	1,900,000	-10,800,000
6		2,420,000	4,840,000	2,420,000	-8,380,000
7		2,662,000	5,324,000	2,662,000	-5,718,000
8		2,928,200	5,856,400	2,928,200	-2,789,800
9		3,221,020	6,442,040	3,221,020	431,220
10		3,543,122	7,086,244	3,543,122	

Payback analysis converts the analysis from currency into time. In this case, the firm would have to wait seven to nine years (based upon some rather heroic assumptions) to get its investment back. Negative cash flow would be expected to reach almost $14 million.

We present two methods that provide ways to quantify the analysis of ERP investment problems in ways that consider more than simply estimates of cash flow.

Value Analysis

A number of complications can affect the calculation of cost-benefit ratios. One of the most obvious limitations of the method is that benefits, and even costs, can involve high levels of uncertainty. The element of chance can be included in cost-benefit calculations by using expected values.

Peter Keen proposed value analysis as an alternative to cost-benefit analysis in the evaluation of proposed information system projects. These projects, clearly attractive to business firms, suffer in that their benefits are often heavily intangible. For instance, decision support systems are meant to provide decision makers with more complete information for decision making. But what is the exact dollar value of improved decision making? We all expect the success of firms to be closely tied to effective decision making, but there is no rational, accurate measure of making better decisions.[13]

Value analysis was presented as a way to separate the benefits measured in intangible terms from costs, which are expected to be more accurately measurable. Those tangible benefits as well as costs can be dealt with in net present terms, which would provide a price tag for proposed projects. The value of the benefits would be descriptive, with the intent of showing the decision makers accurate descriptions of what they were getting, along with the net present price. The decision would then be converted to a shopping decision. Many of us buy automobiles, despite the fact that the net present cost of owning an automobile is negative. Automobiles provide many intangible benefits, such as mak-

[13] P. G. W. Keen, "Value Analysis: Justifying Decision Support Systems," *MIS Quarterly* 5, no. 1 (1981), pp. 1–16.

TABLE 3.13 Alternative System Implementation Options for Example ERP

Alternative	Investment	Benefits (NPV)
A Full vendor implementation, all modules	$15 million	$21 million
B Vendor, only FA and MM modules	11 million	17 million
C Vendor, only FA module	8 million	12 million
D In-house development	25 million	27 million
E Current situation	0	0

TABLE 3.14 Qualitative Features of ERP Options in Example

Alternative	BPR	Standardize	Internet	Advantage	Keep Up	Disruption
A	Complete	Complete	Best	Equal	Best	5 years
B	Partial	Partial	Best	Less than A	Less than A	4 years
C	Minimal	Partial	Best	Less than B	Less than B	1 year
D	Complete	Complete	Problematic	Best	Mediocre	7 years
E	Nothing	Nothing	Worst	Worst	Worst	0

ing the driver look very sporty, letting the driver speed over the countryside, and letting the driver transport those he would like to impress. The dollar value of these intangible benefits is a matter of willingness to pay, which can be identified in monetary terms by observing the purchasing behavior of individuals. This measurement requires some effort and is different for each individual.

Assume a firm is considering four different ways to implement some or all of an ERP system (also including an alternative of doing nothing). The options, with estimated investments and benefits, are given in Table 3.13.

Value analysis would consist of presenting the decision maker with the intangible comparisons in performance, and asking the decision maker thought the improvements provided by the new machine were worth their price tag. This requires an analysis of expected benefits from each system. Reasons this particular management team is interested in an ERP project are:

- To update current business processes (through business process reengineering).
- To standardize procedures within the organization.
- To make interaction with suppliers and customers over Web technology possible.
- To gain strategic advantage.
- To keep up with competitors.
- To minimize system disruption.
- To maximize positive net financial impact.

The expected performance of each alternative on the six qualitative factors is given in Table 3.14.

In this approach, the expected benefits are understood to be highly variable and are treated as a rough estimate. Costs are assumed to be a bit more reliable. Thus, the options, in descending order of price, are:

A—Full implementation of vendor product: expected cost $15 million.
Complete business process reengineering (BPR) analysis and standardization.
Top-of-the-line Internet access for suppliers and customers.
State-of-the-art ERP system, which competitors also have access to.
Serious disruption of operations through installation in five years.
Expected benefit NPV: $21 million, for net gain of $6 million.

B—Partial implementation of vendor product: expected cost $11 million.
Partial BPR analysis and standardization.
Top-of-the-line Internet access for suppliers and customers.
State-of-the-art ERP system, which competitors also have access to.
Serious disruption of operations through installation in four years.
Expected benefit NPV: $17 million, for net gain of $6 million.

C—Minimal implementation of vendor product: expected cost $8 million.
Minimal BPR analysis, partial standardization.
Top-of-the-line Internet access for suppliers and customers.
State-of-the-art ERP system, which competitors also have access to.
Serious disruption of operations through installation in one year.
Expected benefit NPV: $12 million, for net gain of $4 million.

D—In-house implementation: expected cost $25 million.
Complete BPR analysis and standardization.
Suspect Internet access for suppliers and customers.
Custom-designed ERP system, with features competitors don't have.
Serious disruption of operations through installation in seven years.
Expected benefit NPV: $27 million, for net gain of $2 million.

E—Do nothing: expected cost $0.
No BPR analysis and standardization.
Primitive Internet access for suppliers and customers.
No ERP system, in market where competitors do.
No disruption of operations.
Expected benefit NPV: $0, for net gain of $0 million

Management can now view each option as a market basket of benefits, each with its own price tag. In this case, the key difference is building the system in-house, adopting a variant of the vendor system, or doing nothing. Building the system in-house clearly has many risks and involves the most out-of-pocket investment. Management might well discard that option unless the company is very confident in its ability to develop complex software projects. Among the vendor options, alternative A has the best features on reengineering, standardization, and Internet connectivity. But it would involve five years of disruption and call for a $15 million investment. Option B would save $4 million in investment with the same Internet access at only four years of disruption, but sacrifice a bit on BPR factors, standardization, relative competitive advantage, and keeping up with competitors. Management might feel that the gains in disruption are worth the sacrifices in BPR, standardization, competitive advantage, and competitiveness. For only an an $8 million investment, option C would involve sacrifice of even more BPR, strategic advantage, and competitiveness, but would save three additional years of disruption. However, it may be paramount to obtain higher degrees of methods improvement through business process reengineering and standardization of business functions across the organization. By focusing on the important features involved, management may be able to conclude that option A or B is preferable to the other options available.

Taking value analysis one more step, to quantify these intangible benefits in terms of value (not in terms of dollars), leads us to multiple criteria analysis.

Multiple Objectives

Profit has long been viewed as the determining objective of a business. However, as society becomes more complex, and as the competitive environment develops, businesses are finding that they need to consider multiple objectives. While short-run profit remains important, long-run factors such as market maintenance, product quality, and development of productive capacity often conflict with measurable short-run profit.

Conflicts

Conflicts are inherent in most interesting decisions. In business, *profit* is a valuable concentration point for many decision makers because it has the apparent advantage of providing a measure of worth. Minimizing *risk* becomes a second dimension for decision making. Cash flow needs become important in some circumstances. Businesses need *developed markets* to survive. The impact of advertising expenditure is often very difficult to forecast. Yet decision makers must consider advertising impact. *Capital replenishment* is another decision factor that requires consideration of trade-offs. The greatest short-run profit will normally be obtained by delaying reinvestment in capital equipment. Many U.S. companies have been known to cut back capital investment to appear reasonably profitable to investors. *Labor* policies can also affect long-range profit. In the short run, profit will generally be improved by holding the line on wage rates and risking a high labor turnover. However, such a policy incurs less obvious costs. First, there is training expense involved with a high turnover environment. The experience of the members of an organization can be one of its most valuable assets. Second, it is difficult for employees to maintain a positive attitude when their experience is that short-run profit is always placed ahead of employee welfare. And innovative ideas are probably best found from those people who are involved with the grass roots of an organization—the workforce.

This variety of objectives presents decision makers with the need to balance conflicting objectives in ERP option selection. The simple multiattribute rating technique (SMART) is an easy to use method to aid selection decisions with multiple objectives.

TABLE 3.15 Criteria Considered for IT and ERP Supplier Selection

Information Systems Selection Criteria (n=2,401)	ERP Supplier Selection Criteria (n=2,623)
1. Fit with business procedures	1. Product functionality
2. Flexibility	2. Product quality
3. Cost	3. Implementation speed
4. User friendliness	4. Interface with other systems
5. Scalability	5. Price
6. Support	6. Market leadership
	7. Corporate image
	8. International orientation

Source: Y. Van Everdingen, J. Van Hellegersberg, and E. Waarts, "ERP Adoption by European Midsize Companies," *Communications of ACM* 43, no. 4 (2000).

Multiple Criteria Analysis

Multiple criteria analysis considers benefits on a variety of scales without directly converting them to some common scale such as dollars. The method (there are many variants of multiple criteria analysis) is not at all perfect. But it does provide a way to demonstrate to decision makers the relative positive and negative features of alternatives, and it gives a way to quantify the preferences of decision makers.[14]

Van Everdingen et al. conducted a survey of European firms in mid-1998 with the intent of measuring ERP penetration by market.[15] The survey included questions about the criteria considered for information systems selection, as well as criteria for supplier selection. The criteria reportedly used are given in Table 3.15, in order of ranking.

Fit with business procedures was selected among the three most important criteria by about one-half of the respondents and was listed as the single most important criterion by over one-third. While ERP vendors have devoted a great deal of effort to making their packages match existing business processes, the importance of this criterion is based upon the high cost and bother of configuring and implementing ERP systems. Selection of a vendor involved less variance among criteria. Product functionality and quality were the criteria most often reported to be important.

Perhaps the easiest application of multiple criteria analysis is the simple multiattribute rating theory (SMART), which identifies the relative importance of criteria in terms of weights, and measures the relative performance of each alternative on each criterion in terms of scores.[16] We will first explain scores.

Scores

Scores in SMART can be used to convert performances (subjective or objective) to a zero—one scale, where zero represents the worst acceptable performance level in the

[14] See D. L. Olson, *Decision Aids for Selection Problems* (New York: Springer, 1996) for description of methods.

[15] Y. van Everdingen, J. van Hellegersberg, and E. Waarts, "ERP Adoption by European Midsize Companies," *Communications of the ACM* 43, no. 4 (2000), pp. 27–31.

[16] W. Edwards, "How to Use Multiattribute Utility Measurement for Social Decisionmaking," *IEEE Transactions on Systems, Man, and Cybernetics* SMC-7, no. 5 (1977), pp. 326–340.

TABLE 3.16 Scores by Criteria for Each Option in Example

Option	BPR	Standard	Internet	Advantage	Competition	Disruption	Financial
A	1.0	1.0	1.0	0.7	1.0	0.1	0.8
B	0.9	0.7	1.0	0.5	0.8	0.3	0.9
C	0.6	0.7	1.0	0.2	0.6	0.9	1.0
D	1.0	1.0	0.6	1.0	0.3	0.0	0.2
E	0.0	0.0	0.0	0.0	0.0	1.0	0.0

TABLE 3.17 Worst and Best Measures by Criteria

Criteria	Worst Measure	Best Measure
Update systems (BPR)	Nothing	Complete
Standardize business processes	Nothing	Complete
Internet connectivity to suppliers and customers	None	Modern
Gain strategic advantage	Do nothing	Develop unique system
Keep up with competition	Do nothing	State-of-the-art vendor
Minimize disruption	7-year installation	Current system
Financial implications	Risk $25 million, gain $2 million	Risk $8 million, gain $4 million

mind of the decision maker, and one represents the ideal, or possibly the best performance desired. Note that these ratings are subjective, a function of individual preference. Scores for the criteria given in the value analysis example could be as in Table 3.16.

Weights

The next phase of the analysis ties these ratings into an overall value function by obtaining the relative weight of each criterion. To give the decision maker a reference about what exactly is being compared, the relative range between best and worst on each scale for each criterion should be explained.[17] There are many methods to determine these weights. In SMART, the process begins with rank-ordering the four criteria. A possible ranking for a specific decision maker might be as given in Table 3.17.

To obtain relative criterion weights, the first step is to rank-order criteria by importance. Two estimates of weights can be obtained. The first assigns the most important criterion 100 points and assesses the relative importance of each of the other criteria on that basis. This process (including rank-ordering and assigning relative values based upon moving from worst measure to best measure based on most important criterion) is demonstrated in Table 3.18.

The total of the assigned values is 283. One estimate of relative weights is obtained by dividing each assigned value by 283. Before we do that, we obtain a second estimate from the perspective of the least important criterion, which is assigned a value of 10 as in Table 3.19.

[17] B.F. Hobbs and G.T.F. Horn, "Building Public Confidence in Energy Planning: A Multimethod MCDM Approach to Demand-Side Planning at BC Gas," *Energy Policy* 25, no. 3 (1997), pp. 356–75.

TABLE 3.18 **Weight Estimation from Perspective of Most Important Criterion**

Criteria	Worst Measure	Best Measure	Assigned Value
1—Gain strategic advantage	Do nothing	Develop unique system	100
2—Keep up with competition	Do nothing	Use state-of-the-art	70
3—Internet connectivity	None	Modern	50
4—Update systems (BPR)	Nothing	Complete	30
5—Minimize disruption	7-year installation	Current system	20
6—Financial implications	Risk $25 million, gain $2 million	Risk $8 million, gain $4 million	10
7—Standardize business processes	Nothing	Complete	3

TABLE 3.19 **Weight Estimation from Perspective of Least Important Criterion**

Criteria	Worst Measure	Best Measure	Assigned Value
7—Standardize business processes	Nothing	Complete	10
6—Financial implications	Risk $25 million, gain $2 million	Risk $8 million, gain $4 million	25
5—Minimize disruption	7-year installation	Current system	30
4—Update systems (BPR)	Nothing	Complete	50
3—Internet connectivity	None	Modern	60
2—Keep up with competition	Do nothing	Use state-of-the-art	70
1—Gain strategic advantage	Do nothing	Develop unique system	100

TABLE 3.20 **Criterion Weight Development**

Criteria	Based on Best		Based on Worst		Compromise
1—Gain strategic advantage	100/283	0.35	100/345	0.29	**0.33**
2—Keep up with competition	70/283	0.25	70/345	0.20	**0.23**
3—Internet connectivity	50/283	0.18	60/345	0.17	**0.17**
4—Update systems (BPR)	30/283	0.11	50/345	0.14	**0.12**
5—Minimize disruption	20/283	0.07	30/345	0.09	**0.08**
6—Financial implications	10/283	0.04	25/345	0.07	**0.05**
7—Standardize business processes	3/283	0.01	10/345	0.03	**0.02**

These add up to 345. The two weight estimates are now as shown in Table 3.20. The last criterion can be used to make sure that the sum of compromise weights adds up to 1.00.

Value Score

The next step of the SMART method is to obtain value scores for each alternative by multiplying each score on each criterion for an alternative by that criterion's weight, and adding these products by alternative. Table 3.21 shows this calculation.

This value score (shown in the totals row) provides a relative score that can be used to select (take the alternative with the highest value score) or to rank-order (by value score). In this case, the SMART analysis indicates a preference for Option A, the full version of

Real Application: Dell Chooses to Cancel

The expected sequence of an ERP project life includes careful consideration of the initial proposal, followed by a carefully controlled project to implement this plan. The following case, however, demonstrates that it is also necessary to keep evaluating such projects. While hindsight will always be able to say that changes should have been anticipated, real life tells us that it is impossible to anticipate everything. The example reviews how one of the more successful firms in the United States found it rational to shift gears after undertaking one ERP plan. It also demonstrates the concept of best-of-breed, which the dynamic requirements of the organization found to be more suitable than adopting widely accepted best practices.

In 1994, Dell Computer began an implementation of SAP's R/3 enterprise software suite. Dell spent more than one year selecting from SAP's 3,000 configuration tables.[18] However, after two years and $200 million of effort, it revised this plan at the end of 1996.[19] Public accounts indicate that Dell's business model shifted during that period from global focus to a segmented, regional focus. Dell is a make-to-order operation, which Dell found to require more flexibility than typical ERP installations could support. Rather than relying on one integrated, centralized system, Dell shifted to a more flexible system supportive of its make-to-order operation. Company executives did not believe that the full SAP system could keep up with Dell's growth, but instead selected a more flexible architecture to allow for quick addition or deletion of applications from a variety of vendors.[20]

The revised project adopted a best-of-breed strategy. I2 Technologies Inc. software was selected to manage raw materials flow. Oracle software was selected for order management. Glovia software was included for manufacturing control, to include inventory control, warehouse management, and materials management. Glovia's system interfaced with Dell's own shop-floor system and the I2 supply-chain planning software, retaining one of Dell's core competencies. The SAP module was selected for human resources management.

In a similar case, Songini reported that Kellogg Co. encountered severe problems in installing high-end systems, and it scuttled the project.[21]

[18] T. H. Davenport, "Putting the Enterprise into the Enterprise System," *Harvard Business Review*, July–August 1998, pp. 121–131.

[19] S. Holt, "Dell Takes on a Multivendor Approach to ERP Applications," *InfoWorld 20*, no. 19 (May 11, 1998), p. 8; T. Stein, "Dell Takes 'Best-of-Breed' Approach in ERP Strategy," *Informationweek*, no. 681 (May 11, 1998), p. 34; and J. P. Mello, Jr., "Small Now Big," *CFO* 17, no. 8 (2001), p. 10.

[20] D. Slater, "An ERP Package for You, and You, and Even You," *CIO Magazine*, February 15, 1999, www.cio.com.

[21] M. L. Songini, "Teddy Bear Maker Prepares for Second Attempt at ERP Rollout," *Computerworld* 11 (February 2002), www.computerworld.com.

TABLE 3.21 Value Score Calculation

Criteria	Weight	Option A	Option B	Option C	Option D	Option E
Strategic advantage	0.33	× 0.7 = 0.231	× 0.5 = 0.165	× 0.2 = 0.066	× 1.0 = 0.330	× 0.0 = 0.000
Competition	0.23	× 1.0 = 0.230	× 0.8 = 0.184	× 0.6 = 0.138	× 0.3 = 0.069	× 0.0 = 0.000
Internet	0.17	× 1.0 = 0.170	× 1.0 = 0.170	× 1.0 = 0.170	× 0.6 = 0.102	× 0.0 = 0.000
Update (BPR)	0.12	× 1.0 = 0.120	× 0.9 = 0.108	× 0.6 = 0.072	× 1.0 = 0.120	× 0.0 = 0.000
Minimize disrupt	0.08	× 0.1 = 0.008	× 0.3 = 0.024	× 0.9 = 0.072	× 0.0 = 0.000	× 1.0 = 0.080
Financial	0.05	× 0.8 = 0.040	× 0.9 = 0.045	× 1.0 = 0.050	× 0.2 = 0.010	× 0.0 = 0.000
Standardize	0.02	× 1.0 = 0.020	× 0.7 = 0.014	× 0.7 = 0.014	× 1.0 = 0.020	× 0.0 = 0.000
Totals	1.00	0.819	0.710	0.582	0.651	0.080

the vendor ERP system. This is followed relatively closely by Option B, which is to reduce functionality to finance and accounting and materials management modules. Building the system in-house has a low rating, while doing nothing is practically off the chart in a negative way.

Other Multiple Criteria Methods

There are many other approaches implementing roughly the same idea. The best known is multiattribute utility theory, which uses more sophisticated (but not necessarily more accurate) methods to obtain both scores and weights.[22] The analytic hierarchy process is another well-known approach.[23]

This chapter concludes with an example of a firm making an ERP project decision. Initial analysis (in the early 1990s) must have shown positive expectations from a centralized ERP system. Analysis three years later led to a different conclusion, probably considering the relative risk of ERP adoption to be too great. The point is that ERP project adoption analysis should not stop once the initial decision is made.

Summary

We have reviewed some of the primary methods used to evaluate ERP proposals. Screening provides a way to simplify the decision problem by focusing on those projects that are acceptable on all measures. Profiles provide information that displays trade-offs on different measures of importance. Cost-benefit analysis (with net present value used if the time dimension is present) is the ideal approach from the theoretical perspective, but has limitations. It is very difficult to measure benefits, and it is also difficult to measure some aspects of costs accurately. One view of dealing with this problem is to measure more accurately. Economists have developed ways to estimate the value of a life and the value of scenic beauty. However, these measures are difficult to sell to everybody.

A more common view is that it is wasted effort to spend inordinate time seeking a highly unstable and inaccurate dollar estimate for many intangible factors. Value analysis

[22] R. L. Keeney and H. Raiffa, *Decisions with Multiple Objectives: Preferences and Value Trade-offs* (New York: John Wiley & Sons, 1976).

[23] T. L. Saaty, "A Scaling Method for Priorities in Hierarchical Structures," *Journal of Mathematical Psychology* 15 (1977), pp. 234–81.

is one such alternative method. Value analysis isolates intangible benefits from those benefits and costs that are more accurately measurable in monetary terms and relies upon decision maker judgment to come to a more informed decision. The SMART method, one of a family of multiple criteria decision analysis techniques, provides a way to quantify these intangible factors to allow decision makers to trade off values.

Cost-benefit provides an ideal way to proceed if there are no intangible factors (or at least no important intangible factors). However, usually such factors are present. Intermediate approaches, such as payback analysis and value analysis, exist to deal with some cases. More complex cases are better supported by multiple criteria analysis.

Key Terms

Cost-benefit analysis Generically, the set of financial analyses that consider return on investment. Specifically, the ratio of gains to expenses for a project.

Development criteria Estimates of system impact on technical system operations.

Financial criteria Measures based on quantified estimates of cash flows.

Hidden outcomes Unexpected results of implementing a complex system.

Intangible factors Factors involved in estimating costs and benefits that include subjective elements that are difficult to quantify.

Internal rate of return (IRR) Discount rate that returns a net present value of 0 for a given stream of cash flow.

Management criteria Estimates of impact of a system on nonfinancial business measures.

Multiple criteria analysis Quantification of subjective elements in terms of preference value functions of various kinds.

Net present value (NPV) Current worth of a stream of cash flow given a stated discount rate.

Payback Estimated amount of time required to recover an investment.

Return on investment (ROI) Average gains obtained from investing in a project.

Value analysis View of information system projects considering costs as in cost-benefit analysis, but gains in subjective terms.

Questions

1. Describe some of the intangible costs and benefits typically found in ERP proposals.
2. Describe the relative advantages in the extremes of an ERP system developed in-house versus a full vendor ERP system.
3. Describe hidden outcomes of adopting ERP systems.
4. Why are ERP systems usually treated as capital expenditures rather than required business expenses?
5. Discuss financial criteria typically used to analyze information system technology proposals.
6. Discuss management criteria sometimes used for analyzing information system technology proposals.
7. Discuss development criteria sometimes used for analyzing information system technology proposals.

8. Discuss the relative costs involved in ERP installation projects.
9. Given the following data for an ERP proposal, estimate payback, net present value, and cost-benefit ratio. Use a discount rate of 10 percent per year.

Time	Outflow	Inflow
Begin year 1	$5,000,0000	0
End year 1	10,000,000	$1,000,000
End year 2	5,000,000	9,000,000
End year 3	3,000,000	10,000,000
End year 4	3,300,000	11,000,000
End year 5	3,700,000	12,000,000

10. Estimate net present value for the data in question 9 using a discount rate of 25 percent per year.
11. Use a spreadsheet to calculate internal rate of return for the data in question 10.
12. Discuss the difference between value analysis and cost-benefit analysis.
13. Why are other objectives besides profit important in business?
14. Apply SMART analysis to the following data. Develop your own weights of relative importance for NPV, market share, and technical learning, as well as scores for each of these measures with respect to each project.

Option	NPV	Market Share	Technical Learning
Vendor	$80 million	Little impact	Minor gain
Vendor-custom	90 million	Significant	Minor gain
In-house	110 million	Very significant	Major gain
ASP	150 million	Average	Minor gain

Develop weights of attribute importances using your own judgment. Then use your own judgment to score each option on each of the three criteria. Finally, apply SMART analysis to rank the three options.

15. In question 14, apply managerially imposed weights of: NPV, 0.7, market share, 0.2, technical learning, 0.1. Use the same scores for NPV, market share, and technical learning for the four projects that you developed in question 14.

Chapter 4

Business Process Reengineering and Best Practices

Once an organization decides what form of ERP system it wants to adopt, it will next need to specify how the ERP system will be designed. In conventional IS/IT projects, requirements analysis involves much effort to identify what users need. ERP projects vary highly in the amount of effort needed to identify system requirements. In vendor ERP projects, the functionality is given, based on vendor research into best practices. (SAP in particular has devoted significant effort to identification of best practices.) In ERP implementations developed with in-house assets, an integrated system serving all of the organization's information system needs must be developed through extensive **business process reengineering** (BPR).[1] BPR is an effort to identify the best way to do each business task supported by the system.

This chapter:

- Describes business processes.
- Demonstrates business process reengineering and why it is needed.
- Reviews best practices and related concepts.
- Compares clean slate and technology-enabled business process reengineering.
- Presents a discussion of how BPR was used in a real case.

Business Processes

A **process** is a logical set of related activities taking inputs, adding value through doing things, and creating an output.[2] In business, there are many different ways to get work done. Information systems play a key role in providing a means to collect data, store it efficiently,

[1] An article on BPR by its most vocal academic proponent is M. Hammer and S. Stanton, "How Process Enterprises Really Work," *Harvard Business Review*, November–December 1999, pp. 108–18.

[2] H. J. Harrington, E. K. C. Essing, and H. van Nimwegen, *Business Process Improvement Workbook: Documentation, Analysis, Design, and Management of Business Process Improvement*. (New York: McGraw-Hill, 1997), p. 1.

generate reports to let management know what the organization is doing, and archive data for future reference as needed. Tables 4.1 and 4.2 provide a generic view of two kinds of processes—operational and infrastructure. Operational processes help accomplish typical business functions, including product development, order management, and customer support. Infrastructure processes are more administrative, such as establishing and implementing strategy, and managing many aspects of the organization, including human resources, physical assets, and information systems. Each of these processes involves sets of tasks needed to accomplish work. For example, in the operational process of order management, it is necessary to forecast the volume of demand expected for the products produced by an organization. Forecasting can be accomplished in many ways:

- Using last month's demand as a prediction for this month.
- Using the monthly demand from a year ago as the prediction for this month.
- Applying a spreadsheet algorithm such as exponential smoothing over available monthly data.
- Incorporating seasonality indices into such a spreadsheet algorithm.
- Taking known orders and adjusting forecasts based on past demand records.
- Relying upon managerial judgment.
- Using a Ouija board (throwing darts; rolling dice; guessing).

Business process reengineering involves identifying the best way to design the flow and processing of information to obtain forecasts that yield the organization the greatest profit. That requires avoiding the most damaging kinds of forecast error and giving the organization the greatest flexibility to respond to risk.

Business Process Reengineering

BPR analyzes the way an organization accomplishes each business task with the intent of identifying the best way of doing things. BPR is closely tied to ERP, because for ERP to benefit the organization, at least some of the ways in which that organization does business must change.

Hammer and Stanton note that reengineering has sometimes been a euphemism for mindless downsizing but they provide an example of how reengineering should work.[3] In the early 1990s, Texas Instruments faced long cycle times and declining sales. BPR was applied to calculator development, which was to be accomplished by cross-disciplinary teams from engineering, marketing, and other departments. These teams were to be in control of every aspect of product development, from design through marketing. The first pilot teams failed, sabotaged by the existing organization, which felt threatened. Functional departments were unwilling to give up good people, space, or responsibility. Power continued to lie in the old functional departments. Texas Instruments responded by changing the way it was organized. Development teams became the primary organizational units. Functional departments focused on redefined missions supporting the product teams. Budget was accomplished by process instead of by department. Office space

[3] Hammer and Stanton, "How Process Enterprises Really Work."

TABLE 4.1
Typical Operational Business Processes

Function	Process
Develop new products/services	Plan and manage the development process
	Research and analyze need
	Define customer requirements
	Develop and design new product/service concepts
	Refine existing product/service concepts
	Conduct prototype and market tests
	Plan, release, and roll out new products/services
	Plan, release, and roll out changes to existing products/services
Market and sell products/services	Develop and execute market plans
	Conduct market and consumer research
	Develop competitor intelligence
	Manage product/service pricing
	Identify and qualify target customers
	Develop/maintain customer relationships
	Define customer's buying requirements
	Develop and propose a solution to the customer
	Estimate solution cost and price
	Influence customer buying process
	Negotiate and close the sale
Order management	Forecast order volumes
	Enter and process orders
	Manage customer credit exposure
	Plan production/service delivery
	Bill and collect revenue
Manufacture products and/or provide services	Manage overall production/service requirements and capacity
	Plan production/service delivery
	Design and engineer customer solution
	Produce products and/or provide service
	Manage change orders
	Plan and manage subcontract services
	Control production/service schedule
Manage logistics	Define logistics strategy
	Establish and maintain supplier relationships
	Measure and certify supplier performance
	Procure materials/services
	Manage inventory storage and movement
	Manage packing and packaging
	Manage outbound logistics
Provide customer support	Provide customer training
	Provide customer interface to the organization
	Receive and respond to customer inquiries
	Receive and respond to internal inquiries
	Dispatch and provide field service/support
	Manage return/warranty activities

TABLE 4.2 Typical Infrastructure Business Processes

Function	Process
Plan and manage performance	Formulate business strategy and vision
	Establish and prioritize goals and objectives
	Develop financial/operational performance
	Measure and monitor financial/operational performance
	Manage business performance
	Plan and manage quality and service levels
	Design and improve business processes
	Design and improve organizational structures and job roles
	Manage change
	Establish policies and procedures
Manage finances and accounting	Manage accounts receivable
	Manage accounts payable
	Manage payroll
	Manage the general ledger
	Plan and manage taxes
	Plan and manage cash
	Plan and manage budgets
	Plan and manage capital expenditures
	Plan and manage risk to corporate assets
	Plan and manage loans and equity
	Report financial performance
	Perform financial analysis and cost accounting
	Maintain financial records
	Ensure financial control
Manage human resources	Define human resource needs and skill requirements
	Manage the acquisition and termination of human resources
	Educate, train, and develop employees
	Ensure employee communication
	Establish reward and recognition systems
	Manage compensation and benefits
	Provide employee services
Manage information resources	Define and plan for information resource needs
	Develop and enhance data architecture
	Develop and enhance communications infrastructure
	Develop and enhance software applications
	Manage information systems operations
	Provide information user support
	Archive and dispose of information
Manage physical assets	Acquire production/service equipment and technology
	Maintain production/service equipment and technology
	Acquire facilities
	Manage and maintain facilities
	Manage other fixed assets
Manage support services	Manage public/external relations
	Perform the legal function
	Manage administrative services
	Plan and manage environmental programs

was reallocated. After the new system became established, time to new product launch was cut by as much as half, and profitability was enhanced, with return on investment multiplied fourfold.

A business process is what the organization does to get its work done. For instance, if you go into a drugstore to purchase prescription medicine, the process is for the drugstore to sell merchandise to a customer and collect money. There are a number of actions in this process. Before computer automation, this manual business process went like this:

Customer gives pharmacist prescription.
Pharmacist recognizes face, checks doctor's signature.
If both OK, pharmacist checks controlled substance list.
If OK, pharmacist fills prescription.
Pharmacist gives bill to customer.
Customer pays by cash or check (if pharmacist finds that acceptable).

A number of elements in this process involve risk. First, there is a need to control some substances that drugstores deal in. While in the above process, the expertise of the pharmacist might catch most problems, computer support would be more reliable, especially if the pharmacist faces a large population of customers and cannot possibly know all of them. Second, many drugs involve the risk of reactions. It is the pharmacist's business to understand some of these risks, but as the number of drugs on the market has grown dramatically, computer automation can help track these risks and to add a step in the process where the pharmacist reads the warnings to the customer and obtains some assurance of customer understanding. There also is a more complex set of payment possibilities, much of which can be supported by Internet connection to insurance providers and to credit providers. Therefore, a new automated business process might be:

Customer gives clerk prescription.
Clerk checks doctor's authorization via an electronic authorization system.
If authorization OK, clerk gives prescription to pharmacist.
Pharmacist checks computer file for controlled substances.
System connects to insurance carrier and confirms how much insurance will cover.
If both OK, pharmacist fills prescription.
System automatically computes bill to customer and prints out receipt.
System prints out dosage instructions and warnings for clerk to read to customer.
Clerk collects payment from customer.
  If cash, records in cash register.
  If check, checks file for bad check writers, and if OK, records in cash register.
  If credit or debit card, connects to credit source for approval, and if OK, obtains signature; records in cash register.

This is only one of many ways to perform this business process. Business process reengineering would analyze how a particular operation is performed and seek better ways to do it, either through more automation or by adding people to do specific tasks to relieve bottlenecks in the process. For instance, if a particular pharmacy averages 100 customers per hour, extra personnel performing specific specialty activities can be included to relieve the pharmacists from collecting payment or other administrative tasks not calling for their higher-paid expertise. Additionally, other professional specialists might be introduced into the system to take care of drug inventories and security activities.

Business process reengineering predates the popular phase of ERP. Most reengineering efforts in the 1980s, which sought more efficient ways to do business, degenerated into wholesale layoffs.[4] The bad ways of doing business sometimes remained, but with fewer people to do them. Reengineering's primary impact has been massive reductions in workforce and other short-term cost savings, with less impact on diffusing computer-based automation. ERP software has been credited with rescuing the idea of BPR, forcing companies to redefine and redesign work flows to fit the new software.

Deregulation and competition are drivers for the creation of new business models (BPR) in many fields, such as telecommunications. ERP systems provide a higher level of flexibility in meeting growing customer demands, while demanding higher levels of automation and integration in almost all business processes.[5]

The change implicit in BPR has many risks. Even advocates of BPR cite failure rates of 50 to 70 percent.[6] Sutcliffe reviewed reasons for the difficulty of implementing BPR:[7]

- Employee resistance to change.
- Inadequate attention to employee concerns.
- Inadequate and inappropriate staffing.
- Inadequate developer and user tools.
- Mismatch of strategies used and goals.
- Lack of oversight.
- Failure in leadership commitment.

Blanket adoption of an ERP product could discard processes in which the organization has developed a competitive advantage.[8] Instead of changing those processes, the ERP system should be modified. Other activities might be better done following the ERP system's best practices. Even here, a transition period can be expected when employees have to radically change what they do. Productivity will decline while users adapt to the new system. In the long run, the new system is usually better. Those who refuse to adapt to it usually have to learn new skills with their next employer.

The following example demonstrates business process reengineering in an ERP system applied to an academic institution.[9] Babson College implemented a three-year project to

[4] M. Hammer, "Reengineering Redux," *CIO* 13, no. 10 (March 1, 2000), pp. 143–56.

[5] S. Levine, "The ABCs of ERP," *America's Network* 103, no. 13 (September 1, 1999), pp. 54–58.

[6] G. Hall, J. Rosenthal, and J. Wade, "How to Make Reengineering Work," *Harvard Business Review*, November–December (1993), pp. 119–31.

[7] N. Sutcliffe, "Leadership Behavior and Business Process Reengineering (BPR) Outcomes: An Empirical Analysis of 30 BPR Projects," *Information & Management* 36, no. 5 (1999), pp. 273–86.

[8] J. D. Schultz, "Hunt for Best Practices," *Traffic World,* September 25, 2000, pp. 41–42.

[9] R. M. Kesner, "Building an Internet Commerce Capability: A Case Study," *Information Strategy,* Winter 1998, pp. 27–36.

transform its business processes. The primary objective was to improve the quality of service delivery to students for admission, records, registration, advising, financial aid, career services, and field-based learning. The college also sought to reduce administrative costs so as to redirect these funds to teaching and academic support. Change management teams were formed to reengineer each of the operational areas supported by the system. Critical performance measures were established for each application. The focus was on easy-to-use and effective information systems that students could access themselves. The existing system was a mainframe system with dial-up network and text-based applications. The new system was a multitiered client/server infrastructure with 6,000 nodes, over 50 servers, and 1,500 workstations. Data warehousing was used. The system reduced operating costs about 20 percent after the system was implemented, half of the planned 40 percent, because some vendor systems were late. One problem faced by the information technology team was how to organize system access for customers or service providers. Initially, it was decided that a graphical electronic-mail system front end would be used, with applications written as executables within mail system file folders. But end users rejected this design because the mail system was not robust or fast enough for the transaction volume experienced. The Internet proved to be a solution. The Internet provided widespread access, and while the platform was not as reliable as it needed to be, it was expected to improve with time.

In another example of how best practices in BPR can be implemented, Nestlé obtained a very large mySAP.com system from SAP for over $200 million in 2000.[10] This system affected the way in which all 230,000 Nestlé employees in 80 countries did their work. Each Nestlé employee has a customized browser-based start page relating to his or her job function to guide the employee to the selected best practice.

Yet another example is Sunoco Products Co., which implemented e-procurement software allowing the company to reduce purchasing costs for operating resources.[11] The software aided the company in monitoring and enforcing business process changes as part of the ERP implementation. Sunoco was able to reduce its supplier base by 5 percent to 10 percent. It had a goal of a 10 percent reduction in spending on operating resources, which if attained would more than pay back the investment.

On the negative side, lack of up-front business process changes has been blamed for installation problems at Farmland Industries Inc.[12] Without BPR, finance and order-entry operations were unable to get the savings anticipated. This forced the company having to redo BPR and revise system implementation.

Within the manufacturing arena, a concept related to BPR is **lean manufacturing.** We will look more at lean manufacturing in Chapter 9. Lean manufacturing is an effort to cut waste by avoiding activities that don't add value. Throughout a supply chain, manufacturing can often involve continuous flows of material without bottlenecks, producing only what the customer has ordered. This reflects a system of demand pull rather than supply push. In the personal computer market, for instance, Dell has a demand-pull system. Some of its competitors had a supply-push system, where product was made in the

[10] S. Konicki, "Nestlé Taps SAP for e-Business," *Informationweek* 792 (June 26, 2000), p. 185.

[11] M. Shaw, "ERP and e-Procurement Software Assist Strategic Purchasing Focus at Sunoco," *Pulp & Paper* 74, no. 2, (February 2000) pp. 45–51.

[12] C. Stedman, "ERP Flops Point to Users' Plans," *Computerworld* 33, no. 46 (November 15, 1999), pp. 273–86.

most efficient way from the perspective of manufacturing. Finished goods are inventoried in a supply-push system. It appears that Dell's demand-pull approach is outperforming the supply-push approach.

Best Practices in ERP

One primary feature of the SAP ERP product has been **best practices.** A best practice is a method that has been judged to be superior to other methods. This implies the most efficient way to perform a task. Business process reengineering is designed to identify a best practice. Once a best practice that would seem applicable to most organizations is identified, it can be incorporated into an ERP system. SAP devotes considerable research to identifying the best way of doing conventional ERP tasks. Between 800 and 1,000 best practices are included in SAP's R/3 software.[13] Consultants often develop further specialized expertise that firms can purchase.

A related concept is **benchmarking.** Benchmarking compares an organization's methods with peer groups, with the purpose of identifying the best practices that lead to superior performance. Best practices are usually identified through the benchmarking phase of a business process reengineering activity. Best practices often change the organizational climate and attempt to bring about dramatic improvements in performance.

Vendors attempt to be comprehensive and to be all things to all people. Yet Scott and Kaindle state that at least 20 percent of the functionality needed by ERP users is missing from vendor packages.[14] There are also many reports of missed deadlines, excessive costs, and employee frustrations in ERP implementation. A more participative design approach could help in implementing ERP. If a client implements the entire suite of SAP modules, as well as the tools for system implementation, SAP can ensure timely implementation within budget. However, this approach disregards the human factors of the client business culture.

While business process reengineering was designed to consider human values and business purposes, Taylor states that these factors are clearly neglected in ERP application, and he outlines a process emphasizing human factors in ERP implementation.[15] The human factor costs of training and obtaining cooperative participation are key to the successful implementation of ERP.

Reengineering Options

O'Leary gives two basic ways to implement reengineering: clean slate versus technology-enabled BPR.[16] While these are not the only choices (they are the extremes of a spectrum

[13] J. E. Scott and L. Kaindle, "Enhancing Functionality in an Enterprise Software Package," *Information & Management* 37, no. 2 (2000), pp. 111–22, and C. Dean, "ERP Best Practices Checklist," www.deansystem.com, (2002).

[14] Scott and Kaindle (2000), "Enhancing Functionality."

[15] J. C.Taylor, "Participative design: Linking BPR and SAP with an STS approach," *Journal of Organizational Change Management* 11, no. 3 (1998), pp. 233–45.

[16] D. E. O'Leary, *Enterprise Resource Planning Systems: Systems, Life Cycle, Electronic Commerce, and Risk* (Cambridge: Cambridge University Press, 2000).

of reengineering implementation possibilities), they are good concepts to explain the choices available in accomplishing reengineering.

Clean Slate Reengineering

In **clean slate reengineering,** everything is designed from scratch. In essence, clean slate engineering involves reengineering, followed by selection of that software best supporting the new system design. Processes are reengineered based on identified needs and requirements of the organization. As its name implies, clean slate reengineering has no predefined constraints. This theoretically enables design of the optimal system for the organization. This approach is more expensive than technology-enabled reengineering, but clean slate reengineering is more responsive to organizational needs.

Clean slate reengineering is slower and harder to apply than the technology-enabled approach to implementation. However, clean slate reengineering offers a way to retain competitive advantages that the organization has developed. Ideally, this approach can develop the optimal system for the organization. Clean slate reengineering can also involve significant changes in the way the organization does business. However, the adjustment in how organization members do their business often retains the features that were found to work well in the past. Thus, while training is required, the impact is probably less than in the technology-enabled approach.

Technology-Enabled Reengineering

In **technology-enabled reengineering,** first the system is selected and then reengineering is conducted. O'Leary refers to this approach as constrained reengineering. The reengineering process is thus constrained by the selected system. This approach is faster and cheaper than clean slate reengineering, because the software does not have to be changed (it is the basis of the design). Cap Gemini refers to technology-enabled reengineering as **concurrent transformation.**

The technology-enabled approach designs the organizational system around the abilities of the vendor software. SAP's best practices, for instance, are designed to do things right in the first place. If SAP's research came up with better methods for everything a company does, this would be the best option. Technology enabled reengineering is the easiest to implement, is usually much faster to implement, and thus costs less to implement. On the negative side, it also usually involves the most change in organizational practice, and thus the most complications for training. In practice, therefore, while the ERP installation project looks great from time, budget, and functionality perspectives, the actual benefits to the organization are often disappointing.

O'Leary calls the technology-enabled approach the most dominant in practice. He cited a survey of SAP R/3 implementers that found only 16 percent had planned reengineering before they obtained SAP. Of this set of implementers, 33 percent felt that no BPR was needed before implementation, although only 10 percent felt that way after implementation. The most common approach was to undertake BPR simultaneously with implementation of R/3. After the fact, 35 percent thought that reengineering should have come first (the clean slate approach). Table 4.3 compares advantages and disadvantages of both extremes.

TABLE 4.3 Comparison of Clean Slate and Technology-Enabled Reengineering

Clean Slate Advantages	Technology-Enabled Advantages
Not constrained by tool limitations	Focus on ERP best practices
Not limited by completeness of best practice database	Tools help structure and focus reengineering
Company may have unique features where vendor best practices aren't appropriate	Process bounded and thus easier
Not subject to vendor software changes	Know that design is feasible
May be only way to embed processes such as Web and bar coding into new technology	Experience of others ensures design will work
Maintain competitive advantage	Greater likelihood of cost, time achievement
	Software available (already developed)
Clean Slate Disadvantages	**Technology-Enabled Disadvantages**
No preexisting structure to design	Reengineering limited by tool
Greater likelihood of infeasibility	System evolution possibly limited by technology
May involve more consultants	System evolution may be limited by technology
May be more costly, slower	No relative advantage (others can purchase same system)
May not work with selected ERP	All best practices may not be available

Source: D. E. O'Leary, *Enterprise Resource Planning Systems: Systems, Life Cycle, Electronic Commerce, and Risk* (Cambridge: Cambridge University Press, 2000).

O'Leary's advice is that clean slate reengineering should be used by large firms with ample reserve funds. Such firms would have the needed resources and would be more likely to use processes as a basis of strategic advantage. Technology-enabled reengineering should be used by firms that are constrained by budgets or with urgent time requirements. The more standard processes used by an organization, the more attractive technology-enabled reengineering is. Whichever approach is used, business process reengineering is considered a necessity for firms adopting ERP.

The technology-enabled strategy dominated the survey cited by O'Leary. Firms were surveyed before and after their ERP implementation. Before their experience, only 16 percent of those firms surveyed thought BPR should be applied before installation of the SAP system. This statistic jumped to 35 percent after the experience. Before implementation, 33 percent of those surveyed thought that BPR was unnecessary. After their experience, only 10 percent felt the same. Thus, even if the technology-enabled strategy is adopted, it seems clear that BPR is needed.

There are other implementation issues in ERP installation. Many organizations focus on one vendor's products. As discussed in Chapter 2, the best-of-breed approach involves mixing modules from multiple vendor sources.

Many organizations have difficulty switching from old legacy systems to ERP. These legacy systems included distribution, financial, and customer service systems developed in-house over the years. A case in point is Russ Berrie and Co., which makes teddy bears. It selected J. D. Edwards & Co.'s OneWorld ERP for customer relationship management and financial applications. The ERP installation project was

Real Application: McDonnell Douglas's Integrated Manufacturing Control System [17]

In the early 1990s, the St. Louis McDonnell Aircraft & Missile Systems factory (a Boeing subsidiary) was one of the world's largest manufacturing plants. But its IS/IT systems were not very up-to-date. They consisted of an antiquated material control system, with inadequate resource planning and no MRP. The St. Louis factory was one of the few aircraft producers without MRPII. It had just tried to update a mainframe system, and while the pilot test was successful, it was not scalable, in that it was unable to cope with the full volume of plant information. In 1994 a task force was formed to recommend methods to reduce costs in light of declining defense budgets and to refocus the information system to return on net assets.

The task force recommended implementation of a Western Data Systems ERP (which McDonnell Douglas named IMACS, the first use of commercial, off-the-shelf, client/server ERP in military aircraft).[18] The system was built around Hewlett-Packard hardware and an Oracle relational database. The task force felt that a large, expensive, vendor-supplied ERP was not needed. The functional goals of the IMACS system were to reduce inventory levels by several hundreds of millions of dollars, reduce support costs by hundreds of people, make it easier to move work between Boeing sites and suppliers, institutionalize improvements, and improve return on investment.

The first activity undertaken after adoption of the project was business process reengineering. BPR was conducted from 1994 through 1996. Customers were involved in this BPR study. The starting point of BPR was with business processes rather than systems. Thus, a clean slate approach was adopted. Efforts were made to modify selected software as little as possible. The BPR process yielded best practices.

Extensive employee training was applied. Eight courses were developed and delivered on CD-ROMs for 18 positions. This training media was estimated to save McDonnell Douglas more than $250,000 over alternative means of delivering training.

The IMACS integrated 38 systems. The ERP project team consisted of 150 Boeing employees, supplemented by vendor team members from Western Data Systems, Hewlett-Packard, and Oracle. The system was tested in 1995 and modified in 1997. In 1999, all products were converted to the system. The IMACS measured inventory, cycle time, cost, delivery performance, and product quality. Work in process was much easier to identify. Lead times were reduced, and there were fewer materials shortages. Product costs were lowered through the use of the IMACS as well.

[17] The information for this section was generated by Ratnesh Dubey, Sharon King, Laurie Lewandowski, Lucia Rodriguez, and Geoffrey Woodbury, graduate students at Texas A&M University, as part of the requirements of a class on information systems project management.

[18] T. Womeldorf, "Aerospace Defense Turns to Enterprise Apps," *Manufacturing Systems* 16, no. 8 (August 1998), pp. 56–66.

scheduled in phases over 18 months.[19] The system was adopted in an effort to more than quadruple sales revenue by accessing Customer Relationship Management (CRM) and Internet links.

Other organizations are supported by multiple ERP systems, sometimes a different system for each region. This would tend to be more attractive for larger firms. An example is Mobil, which is so large and spread out in global operations that it has operated with SAP, BAAN, and Oracle. Mobil was reported to be applying SAP's R/3 in the United States.[20] Mobil's Asia Pacific operations had smaller volume and different needs than the U.S. division and selected J. D. Edwards' software. Best practices have been applied throughout Mobil's operations, yielding standardized processes. Before use of this model, an ERP product took 18 months and cost $2.5 million to install. Using the standardized approach, a later installation at another affiliate took only six months and cost only $600,000. Mobil's approach discouraged local customization. In yet another regional ERP installation, it required six months to remove local customizations to the IT system before beginning installation of the new ERP system.

Summary

Business process reengineering is often a major component of an ERP installation. This implies massive changes in the way in which organizations conduct business. BPR has great potential payoff, but also implies a great deal of change in people's work lives, which requires a lot of attention to demonstrate benefits, as well as a great deal of retraining.

Requirements analysis is important in identifying what a proposed system is to do. In ERP projects, requirements analysis takes the form of business process reengineering to identify the best way (best practice) for each business process supported by the system. There are two extremes in the many ways in which business process reengineering can be accomplished. Clean slate reengineering starts from scratch. Technology-enabled reengineering begins with the software selected. This is faster and less expensive, as many of the processes are selected from the system. In practice, neither extreme is necessarily best.

BPR has enabled companies to operate faster and more efficiently, and to use information technology more productively. Employees often obtain more authority and a better understanding of the role their work plays for the organization as a whole. Customers get higher-quality products and more responsive service. Shareholders obtain larger dividends and higher stock value because BPR reduces cost and increases revenues. Executives no longer see their organizations as separate entities, but instead see them as related elements in larger systems linked through information flows across the business, reaching customers and suppliers.

[19] M. L. Songini, "Teddy Bear Maker Prepares for Second Attempt at ERP Rollout," *Computerworld*, February 11, 2002, www.computerworld.com.

[20] B. Zerega, "Mobil Model Simplifies ERP Overseas," *InfoWorld* 20, no. 25 (June 22, 1998), p. 76.

Key Terms

Benchmarking Comparison of organizational procedures with those of peer organizations.

Best practices The set of best ways to accomplish business processes.

Business process reengineering (BPR) Analysis of the set of tasks making up a business process with the intent of identifying the best way of accomplishing it.

Clean slate reengineering BPR conducted from scratch.

Concurrent transformation Synonym for technology-enabled reengineering.

Lean manufacturing BPR applied to cut waste in supply chains by eliminating non-value-adding activities.

Process Logical set of related activities taking inputs, adding value through doing things, and creating an output.

Technology-enabled reengineering BPR conducted after system is adopted, so that BPR is constrained by system features.

Questions

1. Describe business processes.
2. Define business process reengineering.
3. Search the library and/or Internet for business process reengineering practice.
4. Identify risks involved in adopting BPR.
5. Identify a specific business process, and analyze it with the intent of improvement through the use of information technology.
6. Describe the concept of best practices.
7. Search the library and/or Internet for best practices in ERP.
8. Describe benchmarking and its relationship to ERP.
9. Search the library and/or Internet for benchmarking practice in ERP.
10. Compare clean slate reengineering with technology-enabled reengineering.
11. Search the library and/or Internet for use of business process reengineering, especially associated with ERP.

Chapter 5

ERP System Installation Options

Implementation of any information systems (IS) project is risky. ERP system implementations are especially risky because of their size and because of the impact they have on the organization. ERP systems have some unique features. First, if a vendor system is adopted, there is much less system design than in conventional IS projects. Second, in most forms of ERP implementation there is usually a great deal of assistance: from the vendor, from consultants, and from a fairly extensive internal project management team. Third, there are opportunities to outsource all or parts of the ERP operation, or to use application service providers.

This chapter:

- Describes ERP as an information systems project.
- Discusses typical time, budget, and functionality performance of information systems projects.
- Outlines risk in IS/IT projects.
- Covers the systems failure method applied to IS projects.
- Describes architectures for ERP.
- Lists methods used to analyze and design information systems.
- Discusses the impact of outsourcing and application service providers on ERP project design.

ERP systems primarily are adopted to gain high-quality computing service for the organization. Vendors have spent a great deal of research in identifying better ways to provide organizational computing support. Research has indicated a very high payoff from high-quality information systems. ERP systems are designed to be efficient, integrating computing within organizations. They also are intended to provide high quality through improved business processes and also through linking to add-on software products.

ERP as an Information Systems Project

Information systems (IS) projects involve relatively higher levels of uncertainty than most other types of projects. ERP implementations tend to be on the large end of the IS project spectrum. As discussed in Chapter 3, there are many options for implementation of an ERP system.

1. Full ERP package from a single vendor source.
2. Single ERP vendor source with internally developed modifications.
3. Best-of-breed, or modules from different vendor sources.
4. Modules from vendor sources with internal modifications.
5. In-house development.
6. In-house development supplemented by some vendor products.
7. Application service provider (ASP).

The easiest method, barring item 7, is to adopt a system provided by a single vendor, without modifications (item 1). But this isn't necessarily the least expensive option, nor will it necessarily provide the greatest benefits to the firm. The reason to use the best-of-breed approach (item 3), using modules from different vendors, is that the functionality obtained from specific modules may be greater in one area for one vendor, but better in another module area (with respect to the needs of the specific adopting organization) from another vendor. ERP systems can be developed in-house (item 5), but is not recommended. This method requires a great deal of IS/IT project management effort. Blends of each of these forms of ERP implementation have been applied as well (items 2, 4, and 6). Finally, ERP could be outsourced (item 7), through application service providers. This can result in the lowest cost method of installation. As discussed later in this chapter, that may involve trading convenience at the expense of control.

Mabert et al. surveyed the strategic approach adopted in their sample of 479 manufacturing firms that had implemented ERP systems. ASP implementation was not surveyed. Of the other methods listed above, Table 5.1 gives their percentage of use.

The dominant **ERP implementation** strategy in this sector (manufacturing) was to rely upon a single developer, with half the firms supplementing the system for internal

TABLE 5.1
Relative Use of ERP Implementation Strategies

Strategy	Percentage using
Single ERP package with internally developed modifications	50%
Single ERP package	40
Vendor packages with internally developed modifications	5
Best-of-breed	4
In-house plus specialized packages	1
Totally in-house	<1

Source: V. A. Mabert, A. Soni, and M. A. Venkataramanan, "Enterprise Resource Planning Survey of U.S. Manufacturing Firms," *Production and Inventory Management Journal* 41, no. 2 (2000), pp. 52–58.

needs. The concept of best-of-breed was not widely applied. Few firms developed their own ERP system. Reliance upon vendor plans makes it much easier to control installation by following implementation procedures developed and tested by the vendors. This avoids many of the pitfalls of IS/IT projects, which are discussed in the next section.

IS/IT Project Management Results

Project management is one of the most important fields in information systems. It is difficult to bring an information systems project to completion on time, within budget, and meeting specifications. A partner of KPMG Peat Marwick said that, based on a survey of 250 companies, some 30 percent of information systems projects exceeded the original budget and time frame by at least a factor of two, or did not conform to specifications.[1] A report issued by The Standish Group in 1994 (based on a survey of 365 companies with over 8,000 development projects) found that only 16 percent came in on time and within budget. For large companies, the success rate was only 9 percent. It was also reported that only 42 percent of planned features and functions end up in the final version of the software.[2] A 1995 report of The Standish Group stated that over half the software development projects initiated by large companies would cost 189 percent more than originally estimated. American Express Financial Advisors experienced project budget overruns as high as 500 percent.[3] The Standish Group issued yet another report in 1997, reporting that in 1996 73 percent of U.S. software projects had been canceled, were over budget, or were late, but that this was much better than the corresponding 84 percent in 1995.[4] Meta Group, Inc., in 1997 reported that poor project planning and management had led to U.S. companies scrapping almost one-third of their new software projects at a loss of $80 billion annually. One out of every two projects ran more than 180 percent over budget for another $59 billion in losses.[5] Despite this information systems projects offer great value for companies.

While ERP systems involve a little more structure, problems still are encountered in implementing ERP. A typical problem is underestimation of the time to get an ERP system working.[6] However, a number of efforts have worked to make this type of installation less problematic. Vendors have a vested interest in making ERP installation less risky and more predictable.

While implementation of the basic ERP software systems is becoming less problematic, the situation is complicated a bit by the opportunity to enhance ERP. Enhancement tools include customer relationship management, supply-chain management, and knowledge

[1] E. Booker, "No Silver Bullets for IS Projects," *Computerworld,* July 11, 1994, www.computerworld.com.

[2] R. Cafasso, "Few IS Projects Come in on Time, on Budget," *Computerworld,* December 12, 1994, www.computerworld.com.

[3] J. King, "'Tough Love' Reigns in IS Projects," *Computerworld,* June 19, 1995, www.computerworld.com.

[4] J. King, "IS Reins in Runaway Projects," *Computerworld,* February 24, 1997, www.computerworld.com.

[5] J. King, "Project Management Ills Cost Businesses Plenty," *Computerworld,* September 22, 1997, www.computerworld.com.

[6] J. Romeo, "ERP:On the Rise Again," *Network Computing,* September 17, 2001, p. 46.

management. The Gartner Group has estimated up to 30 percent of in major enterprise applications involve the integration of such systems with ERP.[7] The increased use of application service providers is another complicating factor. However, while there will always be new challenges, many productivity tools are available to make it easier to install ERP and related systems. The use of extensible markup language (XML) to streamline data access and portals for making ERP data more accessible make installation and operation much less difficult. XML streamlines data access between applications. Many firms find it useful to include portals for end-user data access and other enterprise application integration tools.

Risk Identification and Analysis

Information systems involve high levels of risk, because it is very difficult to predict what problems are going to occur in system development. In 1982 a major insurance company began development of an $8 million computer system from a major software provider. This system was intended to serve all the computing needs of the insurance company and was due to be completed in 1987. However, a number of problems were encountered, resulting in delaying completion until 1993, with a new estimated cost of $100 million.[8] In the late 1980s, Bank of America undertook an anticipated two-year project with a budget of $25 million for on-line updating and automated generation of monthly statements. After five years and $80 million, the system was rejected by its intended users because it created accounting problems, was slow, and involved unreliable access to data. During project development, the bank had laid off a number of employees (evidently anticipating cost savings). After this project was installed, the number of institutional accounts dropped from 800 to 700, and assets under management shrank from $38 billion to $34 billion.[9]

All risks in information system project management cannot be avoided, but early identification of risk can reduce the damage considerably. Kliem and Ludin detail four activities managers can undertake to understand what is happening and where.[10] Risk identification focuses on identifying and ranking project elements, project goals, and risks. Risk identification requires a great deal of pre-project planning and research. Risk analysis converts data gathered in the risk identification step into understanding of project risks. Analysis can be supported by quantitative techniques, such as simulation, or qualitative approaches based on judgment. Risk control is the activity of measuring and implementing controls to lessen or avoid the impact of risk elements. This can be reactive, after problems arise, or proactive, expending resources to deal with problems before they occur. Risk reporting communicates identified risks to others for discussion and evaluation.

Risk management is not a step-by-step procedure, done once and then forgotten. The risk management cycle is a continuous process, occurring throughout a project. As the project proceeds, risks are more accurately understood.

[7] Ibid.

[8] H. Barki, S. Rivard, and J. Talbot, "Toward an Assessment of Software Development Risk," *Journal of Management Information Systems* 10, no. 2 (1993), pp. 203–225.

[9] N. Ahituv, M. Zviran, and C. Glezer, "Top Management Toolbox for Managing Corporate IT," *Communications of the ACM* 42, no. 4 (April 1999), pp. 93–99.

[10] R. L. Kliem and I. S. Ludin, *Reducing Project Risk* (Aldershot:Gower, 1998).

The primary way to identify risk is to discuss potential problems with those who are most likely to be involved. Chapman suggested three distinct methods of risk identification: individual work by a risk analyst, interviewing the project team, and discussion with a broader class of those impacted, especially users.[11]

Successful risk analysis depends on the personal experience of the analyst, as well as access to the project plan and historical data. Interviews with members of the project team can provide the analyst with the official view of the project, but risks are not always readily apparent from this source. More detailed discussion with those familiar with the overall environment within which the project is implemented is more likely to uncover risks. Chapman compared brainstorming, the nominal group technique, and the Delphi method.

Chapman recommended a formal risk management process at all stages of a project life cycle (project risk assessment method, PRAM).[12] PRAM steps include identifying the risk, assessing the impact of risk if negative consequences are realized, and deciding how to mitigate the negative consequences should they be realized.

One of the most attractive risk reduction methods is the systems failure approach. This approach tries to identify all cases where others tried similar projects (such as installing an ERP). Then as much information is gathered as possible about problems encountered by those others. Analysis of these cases can yield valuable insight into problems and pitfalls to avoid. A great deal can be learned by these failures.

The Systems Failure Method for Information Systems Projects

Fortune and Peters presented the **systems failure method,** a systems view intending to identify risk in proposed projects by examining failure that occurred in similar efforts in the past.[13] This approach has been applied in a wide variety of situations, including IS/IT project management. Ormerod demonstrated the application of soft-system modeling to business process reengineering of information systems strategies for a supermarket chain (1995), for two South African mines (1996; 1998), and for a UK power company (1999).[14] It is very suitable for organizations considering ERP installation. The idea behind this approach is that by reviewing past failures, future failures can be avoided.

[11] C. Chapman, "The Effectiveness of Working Group Risk Identification and Assessment Techniques," *International Journal of Project Management* 16, no. 6 (1998), pp. 333–343.

[12] R. Wyatt, "How to Assess Risk," *Systems Management* 23, no. 10 (1995), pp. 80–83; C. Chapman, "Project Risk Analysis and Management – PRAM the Generic Process," *International Journal of Project Management* 15, no. 5, (1997), pp. 273–281; C. Chapman and S. Ward, *Project Risk Management Processes, Techniques and Insights.* (Chichester: John Wiley & Sons, 1997).

[13] J. Fortune and G. Peters, *Learning from Failure:The Systems Approach* (New York: Wiley, 1995).

[14] R. Ormerod, "Putting Soft OR Methods to Work: Information Systems Strategy Development at Sainsbury's," *Journal of the Operational Research Society* 46 (1995), pp. 277–293; R. Ormerod, "Putting Soft OR Methods to Work: Information Systems Strategy Development at Richards Bay," *Journal of the Operational Research Society* 47 (1996), pp. 1083–1097; R. Ormerod, "Putting soft OR Methods to Work: Information Systems Strategy Development at Palabora," *Omega* 26, no. 1 (1998), pp. 75–98; R. Ormerod, "Putting Soft OR Methods to Work: Information Systems Strategy Development at PowerGen," *European Journal of the Operational Research* 118, no. 1 (1998), pp. 75–98.

In the context of information systems, disasters are systems that do not satisfactorily support users. As organizations rely more on computers, Fortune and Peters noted that there is a corresponding increase in significant business interruptions. Fortune and Peters differentiated between negative and positive disasters. **Negative disasters** come from decisions resulting in a change of policy, where a project is substantially modified, reversed, or abandoned after commitment of substantial resources.

Positive disasters involve some uncertainty. These are systems that are implemented despite heavy criticism and are believed by many informed people to have been a mistake. While the project output works, it does not work to the satisfaction of key users.

We have looked at some things that go wrong with ERP projects. Davenport mentioned classic examples such as FoxMeyer Drug (which blamed its bankruptcy on ERP; see the real case in Chapter 1), Mobil Europe, Dow Chemical (see the real case in Chapter 7), and Dell Computer (see the real case in Chapter 3). Other classic cases include Hershey's (see the real case in Chapter 9), Applied Materials, and Whirlpool. We also have looked at some ERP installations that appear to be doing well. Instituting ERP does take a lot of planning and effort.

This chapter presents an approach that is designed to improve the success rate of complex projects such as ERP implementations. The systems failure method seeks to avoid failure by studying things that went wrong with similar projects undertaken by others. It is a use of the systems view, viewing projects as collections of coordinated and interrelated activities, bringing diverse skills together to accomplish a set of goals.

The Systems Failure Method

The systems failure method is intended to improve the prospects of success by examining similar undertakings that have failed with the intent of avoiding those things that caused failure. The method consists of studying the process as a system, to enable modeling the system so that cause-and-effect relationships can be understood. Planned systems are compared with similar systems that have either succeeded or failed.

The approach begins with gathering as many similar cases as possible. Then each case is analyzed with the intent of studying the system aspects similar to the subject. The history of each case is developed and examined to determine why the system failed. The systems failure approach consists of the following processes:

- Preanalysis: define purpose, determine perspectives, gather source material.
- Identification of failures and select systems.
- Modeling: clarify the nature of the system.
- Comparison: gain understanding.
- Analysis.
- Synthesis.

Preanalysis involves conceptualizing the system being studied, including different viewpoints and perspectives. Information is gathered and analyzed to identify the system components, their interaction to accomplish system goals, and the hierarchical structure of system control.

Significant failures of similar systems are identified. Failure is the focus of the study. This requires modeling the system in some detail. Many of the more advanced systems involving human interaction consist of ill-structured, messy situations. Soft-systems methodology was proposed by Checkland as a way to study these systems.[15] Instead of identifying the optimal solution for a system, the purpose of soft systems is to involve users in a learning process. First, understanding of the system is required. The background and history of the problem are useful in gaining understanding. Then, the system is described, and this model of the system can be used to predict the outcome of alternative decisions.

Modeling allows the analyst to theorize about possible results of certain actions. By studying similar systems, better understanding can be gained. System components, as well as relationships, need to be described. Structural relationships describing system behavior are included.

Soft-system methodology consists of seven stages:[16]

1. Define the problem situation.
2. Structure the problem situation.
3. Identify human activity systems.
4. Conceptualize models of human activity systems.
5. Compare models with perceptions in the problem situation.
6. Identify feasible desirable changes.
7. Take action.

Stage 1 involves identifying the actors with interests in the situation. Stage 2 requires an analysis of the political aspects of the situation. Systems thinking leads to identification of the system relationships in stage 3. In stage 4, the analyst develops a model of the system capable of predicting the expected consequences of actions. Stage 5 uses the models to gain insight. Stage 6 involves developing and evaluating more refined alternatives, including benefit-cost analysis. Finally, the approach leads to action.

Comparison involves identifying what you think would happen with the system being studied, given the model based on similar systems. This requires developing a model laying out the system operation, including the decision-making subsystem. For instance, a medical information system would need to capture the flow of information and decision making in a medical process. A patient arrives with a malady. Information about this patient's medical history is needed. Patient's records are kept at each medical facility. Those in this medical facility system can be recalled by accessing the database records relating to this patient. The patient is questioned about medical history, and other sources that might have records are identified and additional records requested. The physician then examines the patient and diagnoses the causes of the current malady, in light of the historical data available relating to the patient, as well as the physician's knowledge about similar cases. Another database, organized by symptoms, can be accessed by the physician to obtain greater understanding of probable causes. The physician then prescribes a treatment plan, which is closely monitored for results. The overall process requires support in the way of data by patient and data by symptom. That portion of the information system focuses on

[15] P. B. Checkland, *Systems Thinking, Systems Practice* (Chichester: Wiley, 1981).

[16] Khisty,"Soft-systems methodology as learning and management tool,"*Journal of Urban Planning and Development* (September 1995), pp. 91–108.

the patient. Another portion of the information system monitors billing information, including charges and payment arrangements. The focus of comparison is on decision making and control. Relationships between the system and the wider system are needed, as well as understanding of the effects caused by the external environment.

Analysis uses the model output to draw inferences about the relationship of actions within the system and expected outcomes. In a medical information system, the administration may use the system to monitor productivity aspects by physicians in attempts to control costs. Physicians can use the system professionally by developing databases by disease and symptom that can be used to determine better treatment plans. Synthesis is obtained when the analyst feels that learning about the system has been gained.

According to Fortune and Peters, failure of systems is commonly a result of:

- Deficiencies in organizational structure and lack of performance control.
- Lack of a clear statement of purpose.
- Subsystem deficiencies.
- Lack of effective communication between subsystems.
- Inadequate design.
- Insufficient consideration of environment and insufficient resources.
- Imbalance of resources, and inadequate testing.[17]

Fortune and Peters were interested in the failure of all types of systems, not just information systems. Lack of a clear statement of purpose appears on their list of causes of failure, further confirming its importance in projects.

System Control

Control is action to reach or maintain a desired state. Classical feedback control monitors the output of the system. When a difference is identified between desired performance levels, such as the size of a ball bearing being produced or the characteristics of a microchip, then action is taken by throwing out the inferior product and adjusting machinery so that future production will be within specifications. A common example of feedback control is a thermostat. More modern forms of feedback control include a model predicting the final form of the output based upon a measurement early in the production process. These systems adjust according to the measures obtained. An example might be a chip in a refrigerator that monitors conditions within the enclosed environment and contacts the manufacturer's representative to send a repairperson before damage is done. This implies feedforward control, because the outcome of the system is predicted before production actually occurs.

System Communication

Many systems failures are due to problems with communications links between system components. These can be missing links, inadequate links, or links that are not used. There is a vicious circle in organizational communication. Information overload describes situations where so much information is provided that no understanding is obtained. A correc-

[17] J. Fortune and G.Peters, *Learning from Failure: The Systems Approach.* (Chichester: John Wiley & Sons, 1995).

tion for this condition is to filter communications to those bits that have important information content. However, this leads to distortion and omission of some information, some of which may turn out to be important. The reaction to this is more messages, which leads inevitably to information overload.

Each of us has to cope with the potential for information overload. Newspapers contain more information each day than any one individual cares to know. Therefore, newspapers classify articles by content. Some people spend their time reading the front page, others the comics, and yet others concentrate on the sports page. If one can filter out the advertising, the newspaper can be used to gain a good picture of the highlights of what is going on in the world. But modern technology provides even more concentrated news. There are television channels that purvey nothing but news, others that show nothing but cartoons, and others that have sports around the clock. With expanded cable coverage, one can specialize even more. There are headline news channels and classic sports networks. The age of information overload has certainly arrived.

Human Aspects of Systems

Part of understanding the system is to identify the structure of responsibility—who is responsible for what. Another part of the system is the set of organizational codes of behavior—what is appropriate conduct. Some information is communicable, and some things are not. For instance, in the nuclear energy field, some information is classified by the government. In any organization, some information may be considered sacrosanct, not to be broadcast. Understanding a system includes understanding what portions of the system are fixed and unchangeable, and what elements are merely there for temporary purposes. For control purposes, understanding the procedure followed to solve problems can be one of the most important system components.

Demonstration of the Systems Failure Method

Fortune and Peters used a medical information systems project to demonstrate the systems failure method. Medical records are the primary means that health professionals have to communicate with each other and facilitate continuity of care. However, medical records are often incomplete and inaccurate. Automation would speed care and improve efficiency. Automatic review of medical records would lower error and help control costs. Systematic analysis of medical records offers the ability to better select policies in the future.

Fortune and Peters presented experience with the electronic patient record, a three-year strategic research and development program for a computer system in the United Kingdom in 1993. The **prototyping** approach was applied to develop the system. Systems analysis was used to identify tangible and intangible benefits and costs, as well as to understand cultural issues.

The systems failure approach began with a review of published accounts of attempts to introduce clinical information systems in hospitals. These accounts were selected on the basis of providing sufficient detail to allow analysis of the systems involved. Each selected account was complex, with wide-ranging consequences. Eight cases were found, six in the United States, one in Canada, and one in the United Kingdom.

One of the eight cases was a 700-bed teaching hospital at an eastern U.S. university. In 1981, consultants had recommended expended use of information technology, which had successfully been applied to financial and accounting applications. The proposed medical information system was expected to provide more then $26 million in savings over five years, with a payback period of less than two years. It was designed to deliver administrative support to areas such as admissions by 1987 and to be extended to provide dietary and radiology support and to assist laboratories and the pharmacy by 1991.

The system encountered delays, increasing the cost to over three times the original estimate. Three communication links in the system were not sufficient to system needs. System development strained the relationships between medical staff and the administration. It was found that implementing a decision subsystem was not possible immediately. The new system challenged basic institutional assumptions and disturbed traditional patterns of conduct. The project builder had no authority, and medical professionals declined to use the system, which would require them to modify their established routines. Not only did the system fail in the sense that it ran over budget, but it also failed because it was not used as designed.

A second case was a project to develop an outpatient medical record system for a hospital that would have involved 1,400 terminals for direct entry of information by clinicians. The system was brought on line in 1989, using parallel operation with the preexisting (manual) system to ensure continuity of service. However, four years later both systems were still operating in parallel. The new system's printing requirements exceeded the designed output capability, and it was hard to find space for the printers. Also, data security and privacy were far more important than the project team had originally understood.

Based on study of these eight accounts, a formal system model was constructed. Common themes were identified as follows:

- Links with other systems were commonly deficient.
- There was a low ability to influence the environment.
- Decision making tended to be isolated.
- System expectations were not widely understood.
- Required resources were often lacking.

Major failures occurred when key system participants were not involved. Communication was also considered a major critical success factor. Complex user interfaces and lack of standard interfaces for communication also led to failure. Rules of information use were not clearly defined. On the human side, system failure occurred because there was a great deal of prejudice between the professional and administrative groups. With respect to the project, there was uncertainty about roles, responsibility, and power that led to anomie. Clinicians and the project staff were unable to form a team for consensus decision making for project implementation. Intended users resented the system, as they viewed it as something imposed by management.

The results of the systems failure analysis included a formal systems model for the proposed project at the system level for patient care, at the subsystem level for messages, and at the sub-subsystem level for computers. This led to better understanding of the organizational climate. Among the many things that the systems failure analysis provided was consideration of how records would be used, the level of detail required, usage patterns over time, and the need to support different individual styles.

The approach recognized of the need for a flexible design that practitioners could use for information about specific patients and researchers could use for information about particular diseases. Standardization of records led to greater consistency. Patient confidentiality was a major concern, placing extra security requirements on the system. The systems failure analysis led to a design in which the client had greater confidence.

System Architecture and ERP

A **system architecture** displays the layout of computer systems used to support an organization. Traditionally, ERP systems were focused internally, which eliminated many problems relative to security and compatibility with external systems. By using closed systems on dedicated servers (mainframe or client/server architecture), access to organizational data could be strictly controlled.

ERP systems that provide access to customers and suppliers (supply chains, for instance) need open system architectures.[18] Such applications facilitate the use of ERP systems in e-commerce environments. ERP data in such systems can be distributed over many systems, and the exchange of data across such systems can be problematic. This creates a need for common standards. It also creates the need for systematic and rational design of ERP systems.

Hasselbring suggests a vertical structure of three architectural layers for an organizational information system.[19] The business architecture layer defines organizational hierarchy and work flows for business processes and rules. This layer is conceptual, expressed in terms meaningful to application users. The application architecture layer defines implementation of business concepts in terms of enterprise applications. This layer provides the glue between the application domain described by the business architecture and the technical solutions described in the technology architecture. The technology architecture layer defines the information and communication infrastructure, where IT does the work required by the business users.

When ERP systems are tied to external systems, they must be integrated across organizations. This is usually done through messaging services. The SAP R/3 approach aims at enterprise integration via a single database, without boundaries between ERPs. But messaging services are still required to integrate autonomous ERP systems. There are products specializing in application adapters, data transformations, and messaging services across ERP systems based on different vendor products.

ERP implementations usually involve installation of vendor software. Custom-designed ERP systems are sometimes built, which would be a major information systems project. Although installation of a vendor system is much simpler, it is still a significant information systems project. A number of techniques have been developed to accomplish information systems projects. The standard approach is the waterfall model, a straightforward sequence of activities. For projects with higher levels of risk, alternative methods

[18] W. Hasselbring, "Information System Integration," *Communications of the ACM* 43, no. 6 (June 2000), pp. 33–38; and P. Fingar, "Component-Based Frameworks for e-Commerce," *Communications of the ACM* 43, no. 10 (October 2000), pp. 61–66.

[19] Hasselbring, "Information System Integration."

have been developed. Following are brief overviews of the **waterfall model,** which represents a sequence of activities within which a standard ERP installation might proceed, and the **spiral model,** intended to provide support when high levels of risk are involved.

The Waterfall Model

The waterfall model is the basic standard for software development of all types, including ERP. The waterfall model recognizes feedback loops between stages of software development to minimize rework, as well as incorporating prototyping as a means to more thoroughly understand new applications. The waterfall model (named because each step follows its predecessor in sequence) consists of the following stages, each of which can involve reversion to the prior stage if attempts at validation uncover problems. The waterfall model has the advantages of encouraging planning before design and it decomposes system development into subgoals with milestones corresponding to completion of intermediate products. This allows project managers to more accurately track project progress, and provides project structure, as shown in Table 5.2.

The list shown is for a **software life-cycle** product. Variations in the stage labels are used for different types of projects, such as acquisition of software, implementation of a vendor system, or other kinds of projects. In ERP projects, feasibility analysis is a major concern due to the scope of investment involved and the impact on future operations. Software plans and requirements are determined in large part by the implementation option selected. Product design is tied to business process reengineering efforts. Detailed design is expedited by vendor and consultant support, and their methodologies eliminate the need for most coding. (If the system is built in-house, a heavy coding burden would be required.) Integration is also expedited by vendor products. While design, coding, and integration efforts would be less following pure vendor implementation options, the implementation effort would be high, as extensive training is required to get each member of the organization to adopt the best practices imposed by the system. Conversely, in-house systems would often be built around existing business practices, and thus implementation would likely have less impact for in-house systems. The impact on operations and maintenance is expected to have high payoff for systems adopting improved business practices.

Each stage involves a test, either validation or verification. Validation is the process of evaluating software to ensure compliance with specification requirements. (Is this the right product?) Verification is the process of determining whether or not the software component functions correctly. (Is the product built right?)

TABLE 5.2 Waterfall Model of Software Life-Cycle Stages

Stage	Feedback Determinant
System feasibility	Validation
Software plans and requirements	Validation
Product design	Verification
Detailed design	Verification
Code	Unit test
Integration	Product verification
Implementation	System test
Operations and maintenance	Revalidation

Source: B. Boehm, *Software Risk Management* (Atlanta: Computer Society Press, IEEE Computer Society, 1988), p. 27.

In the original waterfall model, problems accumulated over stages and were not noticed until project completion, resulting in very expensive code. User needs were often not met, resulting in rejection of products after they were built. Therefore, feedback loops were added, along with prototyping, to catch problems early. The waterfall model does not allow rapid response to the pervasiveness of change in information system projects. The orderly sequence of activities in the waterfall model does not accommodate new developments.

In-house implementation of ERP, and even implementations involving vendor systems with some customization, can be expected to be problematic for the waterfall model. For complete in-house ERP development, higher levels of risk are present, and the spiral model might be appropriate. Rapid prototyping, object-oriented processes, or rapid application development might also apply. However, that form of ERP implementation is expected to be rare. Far more common is use of vendor software directly, in which case the implementation process is much more straightforward. The waterfall model still can apply, with the risk involved far less.

Prototyping is the process of developing a small working model of a program component or system with the intent of seeing what it can do. It is a learning device, especially appropriate when users are not absolutely sure what they want in a system.

Prototyping

When dealing with systems that involve features that are both difficult to predict and difficult to price, the systems development approach has proven ineffective. The hard, clear dollar benefits rarely are sufficient to justify adopting the system.

An evolutionary approach is useful for evaluating systems applied in unstructured environments because users often do not know what benefits or what features the system will provide until they see it in operation.[20] A prototyping approach involves building a small-scale mock-up system, and allowing the user to try it. The user could then ask for modifications based upon a better idea of what the system could do. Prototyping is a much less thoroughly planned approach, but is often appropriate for applications with low investment and low structure. This can result in much lower development cost and time, especially when there are many uncertainties about what the system should consist of.

Prototyping is useful in the installation of parts of ERP systems. It is especially appropriate for generating modifications to systems when there is not complete assurance that the proposed change will avoid unexpected complications. In ERP systems, risk is present in some implementation options. The spiral model has been suggested as a methodology to deal with information system project risk. The spiral model methodology includes prototyping.

The Spiral Model

The spiral model uses iterative prototypes.[21] This approach was developed for software projects involving high levels of risk. This might be an appropriate method for ERP implementations involving significant in-house work. Implementation of ERP vendor

[20] P. G. W. Keen, "Adaptive Design for Decision Support Systems," *Database* 12, nos. 1–2 (1980), pp. 15–25.

[21] B. Boehm, *Software Risk Management* (Atlanta: Computer Society Press, IEEE Computer Society, 1988), p. 27.

TABLE 5.3 The Spiral Model of Software Development

Cycle 1	Cycle 2	Cycle 3	Cycle 4
Risk analysis	Risk analysis	Risk analysis	Risk analysis
Prototype models	Prototype models	Prototype models	Operational prototype
Operation concept	Software requirements	Software product design	Detailed design
			CODE
Requirements plan	Requirements validation	Design validation and verification	Unit test
Life-cycle plan	Development plan	Integration and test plan	Integration and test
			Acceptance test
			Implementation

Source: B. Boehm, *Software Risk Managemeant* (Atlanta:Computer Society Press, IEEE Computer Society, 1988).

software involves major iterations, with each iteration often involving revision, reimplementation, and upgrades.[22] In the spiral model, risk analysis is performed for each portion of the system. Starting with a concept of system operation, a requirements plan is developed. Software requirements are generated and validated, followed by a development plan. Risk analysis is repeated, and a new prototype incorporating the new development plan is generated, followed by software product design, which is validated, verified, integrated, and tested. After another risk analysis, an improved prototype is developed with a more detailed design. Given this more complete information, coding proceeds, along with testing, integration, acceptance testing, and implementation. The spiral model is shown in Table 5.3.

Each cycle of the spiral begins with the identification of objectives, development of alternative means of implementing the particular stage of the product, and consideration of constraints. Each cycle involves risk analysis, an identification of what might go wrong, and a plan to deal with problems if they occur. Then prototypes are developed to demonstrate what the system can do at this stage. Models, in the form of simulation to determine risk and benchmarks to test system modules, are applied. This is followed in each cycle by design considerations.

Many risks exist in ERP projects. Management of these risks is critical to successful delivery of needed information system support. The spiral model emphasizes risk analysis to yield more consistent system performance.

The complexity of an ERP system installation depends primarily on the type of ERP system adopted. Full implementation of vendor software will involve the least risk because the implementation technique that has been developed and thoroughly tested through experience by the vendor can be adopted. At the other extreme, building an ERP internally from scratch would be a mammoth undertaking full of risk, calling for a spiral approach. In between, the more modification to the vendor software that is involved, the greater the consideration of risk elements.

22 G. G. Gable, T. Chan, and W.-G. Tan, "Large Packaged Application Software Maintenance: A Research Framework," *Journal of Software Maintenance and Evolution: Research and Practice* 13 (2001), pp. 351–371.

Other Options for Systems Development

ERP development includes modules, much the same idea as objects. Software development productivity tools include the use of **object-oriented enterprise frameworks (OOEFs)**.[23] OOEFs are designed to reduce the complexity and cost of enterprise systems. They are meant to establish a formal set of criteria to be used in building or selecting an enterprise framework. Distributed object computing is a recognized way to build enterprise information architectures that can operate in advanced client/server, intranet, and Internet environments.[24] By using objects to build information systems, complexity is reduced because programmers do not need to know how an object works internally. They only need to know what the object is and the services it provides.

There are negatives to object-oriented technology. There is a steep learning curve. Business objects can become unwieldy when combined with large-scale commercial applications (which is what a vendor-provided ERP is). More plug-and-play application services, and reuse of components, are attractive. Java portability (write once, run anywhere) is useful, and the extensible markup language (XML) is very useful in shared Internet file systems. Another productivity tool is the unified modeling language (UML), designed to model components and guide construction, assembly, and reuse.

External ERP Operation and Support

Recently, **outsourcing,** or hiring out large portions of information processing, has become popular. Outsourcing involves contracts with external vendors to operate your system on your premises. One purpose of outsourcing is downsizing. Unocal, like many other oil companies, pared its staff by 40 percent over a two-year period, with 130 layoffs in the information systems group.[25] Many functions can be outsourced, including data center management, telecommunications, disaster recovery, and legacy systems maintenance. This avoids the need to use scarce resources and can gain efficiencies by hiring vendors with expertise. Outsourcing can also be used for company Internet operations. Eastman Kodak, which began outsourcing in 1989, held on to its Internet activities because the environment was too dynamic, and its own plans were too uncertain. Internet functions that could be outsourced include connectivity, Web server hosting, firewall security, website development, and content development. These activities are complex, subject to change, and not particularly relevant to organizational core competencies.[26] Outsourcing makes sense when fast start-up is important, internal skills are lacking, and the vendor can provide strong features. Outsourcing for Internet operations is not as worthwhile if they are of strategic importance to the business or requirements are ill-defined. Rarely is outsourcing used for everything involved within a project. For one thing, there

[23] M. E. Fayad, D. S. Hamu, and D. Brugali, "Enterprise Frameworks, Characteristics, Criteria, and Challenges," *Communications of the ACM* 43, no. 10 (October 2000), pp. 39–46.

[24] P. Fingar, "Computers Based Frameworks For e-commerce."

[25] S. Moore, "Unocal's Outsourcing Decision Stirs up Networking Operations," *Computerworld,* November 14, 1994, www.computerworld.com.

[26] G. H. Anthes, "Net Outsourcing a Risky Proposition," *Computerworld,* April 7, 1997, www.computerworld.com.

will be need for internal training to implement the system and to integrate it with the existing system.

The most popular way to outsource ERP and related systems is the use of **application service providers** (ASPs). An ASP is a company that leases software applications and distributes them via the Internet or private communications lines. This is like returning to the time-sharing approach in the early days of management information systems (MIS). Boyd reported that most firms are not willing to outsource complex ERP or other complex applications because of the need for high levels of integration by these systems.[27] However, ASPs can offer lower costs and increased flexibility.[28] They often provide a way to obtain more reliable and less expensive service than from systems built in-house. This includes obtaining partial ERP services via an ASP rather than developing a full-scale ERP system.

Use of an ASP saves money in software development and upgrades. Kavanagh estimates that costs of system implementation and maintenance would be the same for traditional approaches as for an ASP.[29] Training costs would also be expected to be about the same. However, the cost of hardware and personnel would be eliminated, as would software upgrade costs. These cost savings would be expected to be far greater than the cost of the ASP. Kavanagh concludes that total operating cost for the ASP option over a five-year period would be about 30 percent less than for a conventional ERP model.

ERP is only one service offered through ASPs. Acquisition of customer relationship management services through an ASP often makes sense.

The ASP route to obtaining ERP services includes several risks:[30]

1. Security issues.
2. Service failures.
3. Confidentiality failure.
4. Performance issues.

Leaving your applications in the hands of others involves the primary risk that your ASP may discontinue product features that you were relying upon. It also might inadvertently leak information sensitive to your organization. Use of an ASP relinquishes a degree of control. On the positive side, ASPs can develop core competencies in training and support that can be very costly for customer organizations to develop on their own. ASPs also can agree to meet performance standards that are necessary to allow interaction with other systems for e-commerce or supply-chain management purposes. Kavanagh found that ERP vendors have been committed to at least some sort of ASP effort.[31]

A number of alternative approaches are available to obtain ASP support for ERP. The original vendor can deliver ERP through an ASP, or third-party resellers can be utilized.

[27] J. Boyd, "Technical Limitations Hold Back ASPs—Quality of Service, Security, App Interoperability, Responsiveness Still Question Marks," *Internetweek* 832 (October 9, 2000), pp. 12, 16.

[28] M. Apicella, "Alternatives to the Traditional ASP Model," *Infoworld,* June 26, 2000, p. 65, www.infoworld.com.

[29] S. Kavanagh, "Application Service Providers (ASPs): Can ASPs Bring ERP to the Masses?" *Government Finance Review* 17, no. 4 (August 2001), pp. 10–14.

[30] Apicella "Alternatives to the Traditional ASP Model."

[31] Kavanagh "Application Service Providers."

Smaller ERP companies selling to a variety of markets may find a third-party, value-added reseller best able to meet their needs. Those ERP-using organizations specializing in only a few markets may be better off hosting the application themselves because there is little the third party could add.

Organizing for Implementation

Implementing an ERP is a major organizational project, Regardless of the method adopted by an organization, there will be some project structure to create, and an individual will be appointed project manager. The effort can be carried by vendors, consultants, or in-house personnel to varying degrees. If a single vendor source is the method adopted, the vendor will provide people to coordinate the effort. Most organizations also feel the need to hire consultants. A major ERP implementation project concern is how to control the participation (and thus the cost) of such consultants.

The amount of effort depends a great deal on the form of implementation adopted. Table 5.4 compares this relative effort by entity.

Implementing an ERP is going to strain in-house information systems groups. Consultants are expensive, but there are times when their expertise is needed.

Project sponsors can have a major impact on the success of any information system project. Project sponsors could be those who control purse strings or those who persuade decision makers to adopt ERP systems. A project champion is an influential individual within an organization who makes sure a project has sufficient resources and attention to succeed. Project champions can come from the top of the organization, and in the case of ERP, the motivation to adopt an ERP system very often comes from chief executive officers. Project champions can be other higher-level people in an organization as well. The key feature is to provide enthusiastic interest in the project to overcome inevitable problems from undertaking such a large and pervasive system.

ERP implementation teams always include people from within the organization. What they do varies with the method of ERP implementation adopted. All systems involve extensive training. The level of coordination activity will vary as indicated in Table 5.4. If a vendor product is involved, vendor support personnel will be actively involved. Consultants are always available at the call of the organization. The degree of consultant activity

TABLE 5.4
Relative Implementation Effort

Method	In-House	Vendor	Consultant
Single vendor source	Significant	Heavy	Heavy
Single vendor with modifications	Significant +	Heavy	Heavy +
Best-of-breed	Significant +	Moderate	Heavy +
Multiple vendor modules with modifications	Significant ++	Moderate	Heavy +
In-house	Excruciating	None	Might be useful
In-house with modules	Painful	Moderate	Might be useful
Application service providers	Light	None	To select

TABLE 5.5 Relative Advantages and Disadvantages of Implementation Methods

Method	Relative Advantages	Relative Disadvantages
Single vendor source	Fastest of controlled methods Least amount of complications Proven business processes	Subject to vendor changes Potential loss of any internally developed competitive advantages
Single vendor with modifications	More responsive to organizational methods	Modifications involve high schedule risk
Best-of-breed	Allows selection of preferred approaches for each function	A highly risky method with many coordination problems
Multiple vendor modules with modifications	The most flexible approach	The riskiest of all methods
In-house	Custom design can match organizational needs Least change on the part of users	A massive undertaking—high budget and time risk Requires development of many expensive areas of expertise
In-house with modules	Supplement existing system with vendor features, minimizing user change	Moderately high budget and time risk
Application service providers	Least budget, time risk May provide access to latest vendor technology at relatively low cost	Highly vulnerable to continued success of provider Lowest degree of control over organizational data

TABLE 5.6 Relative Features of ERP Implementation Methods

Method	Time and Budget	Risk	Access to Technology	Security
Single vendor source	Very good	Lowest risk	Subject to vendor upgrades	High
Single vendor with modifications	Good	Modifications inherently risky	Very good	High
Best-of-breed	Poor	Development of interfaces problematic	Ideal	High
Multiple vendor modules with modifications	Very poor	Very high risk	Theoretically very good	High
In-house	Worst	The worst kind of IS project	Very risky	High
In-house with modules	Better than all in-house	Very difficult IS project	Less risky than all in-house	High
Application service providers	Can be best	Low project risk; Highly vulnerable to continued success of ASP	Can be ideal, if ASP can afford to buy the best	Very low

increases with the complexity of the ERP implementation. For instance, mixing modules calls for a great deal of difficult coordination, and consultants can be very helpful.

Table 5.5 compares the relative advantages and disadvantages of seven implementation methods.

Table 5.6 Compares implemantation methods on the specific aspects of time and budget, risk, access to technology, and security for organizational data.

Real Application: Xerox Focuses Its Information Technology Efforts

Early in 1994 Xerox Corp. outsourced its information systems operations to Electronic Data Systems Corp.[32] This 10-year outsourcing contract would cover Xerox data center operations, telecommunications, desktop systems support, and maintenance of existing business applications for $3.2 billion.[33] EDS also obtained responsibility for new client/server projects. Xerox retained control of its architecture, strategy, and new program development. Of Xerox's 2,700 IS/IT jobs, 1,700 were moved to EDS, 750 were retained, and 250 were eliminated.

While outsourcing often is used by companies needing quick cash, in the case of Xerox the firm was quite sound. Xerox had an operating profit of $620 million on sales of $14.6 billion at that time. The aim was to shed noncore business to focus on the strategically more important document business as well as to save roughly $1.2 billion. The stated motivation was to speed the rate at which Xerox could move into new technologies and to free management to focus on strategic information management issues. The remaining Xerox information technology staff worked on moving Xerox into flexible network computing (architecture, strategy, and application development) to support Xerox's long-term needs.

This Xerox initiative was part of a massive reengineering effort.[34] Rao cited Xerox as only one example of a large company choosing to outsource core business systems. While Xerox's system was a legacy system rather than an ERP system, it was the collection of core business computing support. Outsourcing allows tapping the expertise of others in taking care of cost center activities, while allowing the firm to focus on its core competencies. The Xerox technology transition has been reported to be painful, but represents an effort to deal with complex issues involved in delivering computer support.[35]

[32] M. Halper, "Xerox Signs up EDS," *Computerworld*, March 28, 1994, www.computerworld.com.

[33] M. Kerr, "Xerox, EDS Sign $3.2 B Deal," *Computing Canada* 20, no. 14 (July 6, 1994), pp. 1–2.

[34] S. S. Rao, "When in Doubt, Outsource," *FW* 164, no. 25 (December 5, 1995), pp. 77–78.

[35] "Working out the Kinks in a Megadeal," *Datamation* 43, no. 6 (June 1997), p. 45.

Tables 5.5 and 5.6 indicate why most ERP adopters utilize vendor systems with modifications. This method provides access to well-tested software while allowing some ability to maintain organizational competitive advantages through modifications. Many adopters use a single vendor source, which is the fastest and cheapest way to develop an ERP system within an organization. However, this approach means the information system is available to all customers of that vendor. The best-of-breed approach in theory adopts the best features of a variety of ERP vendors, but is rarely used, as are in-house methods. They involve high levels of risk and are appropriate only in special circumstances. Use of ASPs is relatively new. ASPs offer great reductions in time and budget risk in the short run, but entail future risks.

The preceding real IS/IT approach demonstrates how a very large firm can utilize outsourcing to reorganize its information system service. Xerox signed a $3.2 billion, 10-year contract with EDS in 1994 50 Xerox's reduced IT staff could focus on flexible network computing, a key strategic core competency.[36]

Summary

ERP is fundamentally based on obtaining quality software support. Implementation of an ERP is an IS/IT project. There are a number of ways to accomplish this, ranging from in-house development of the entire system (considered by most to be the most painful way), through direct adoption of an unmodified vendor product (the least painful, but also most inflexible way), to outsourcing through application service providers (a more recent phenomenon whose success is still questionable).

All IS/IT projects are difficult to bring in on time, in budget, with full designed functionality. Risk is an important element in any IS/IT project. It is present in ERP projects too, but in different ways from other types of IS/IT projects. ERP has less risk in the technology-enabled BPR form, in that a clear path of what needs to be done is available for many project activities. However, the risk dimension of scope is very high, in that if the ERP project goes wrong, it has a dramatic impact on the organization due to the scope of investment involved, as well as the impact on how organization members accomplish their work. The systems failure method offers a systematic way to apply the principles of the systems approach to the analysis of new project proposals. It is based on a simple idea—learn from the experience of others. While other projects clearly face different environments, the key is to see the pertinent factors that apply to the project being designed.

Consideration of system architecture can make ERP implementation projects more rational, in that they can support the addition of many attractive supplemental systems. Application of analysis and design control frameworks provides better means of controlling IS/IT projects, including ERP implementation. The traditional approach to an IS/IT project design is the waterfall model. If a direct implementation of a software vendor's system is adopted, this is probably sufficient, as there are relatively low levels of risk involved (the vendor has worked out the bugs of implementation). For ERP systems involving modification (or at the extreme of in-house implementation), high levels of risk would be involved, and Boehm's spiral model may be more appropriate. This model considers risk directly and uses prototypes as a means to assess the success of the system in dealing with project risks.

Application service providers offer a new way to share risk by outsourcing. While this approach seeks to shift the burden of ERP implementation and operation to others, it is not a foolproof approach. New risks are introduced relative to security, control, and what to do if the ASP provider fails.

[36] J. W. Verity, "Megadeals March On," *Computerworld*, July 28, 1997, www.computerworld.com.

Key Terms

Application service provider (ASP) Organization that offers computing services for an organization at a fee. (Use ASP computing facilities.)
ERP implementation strategy Strategic approach adopted to implement an ERP system.
Negative disaster Substantial modification, reversal, or abandonment of a computer system project after commitment of substantial resources.
Object-oriented enterprise frameworks (OOEFs) Formal set of criteria designed to systematically assist development or selection of an ERP using object-oriented technology.
Outsourcing Contracting with others external to the organization to operate an organization's computing on the organization's computer system.
Positive disaster Computer system implementation that is technically successful, but receives high levels of criticism by key users.
Prototyping Development procedure involving iterative development of small-scale versions of a system with the intent of identifying needed modifications.
Software life cycle Stages typically involved in developing a software or installing software such as ERP.
Spiral Model Software development procedure designed to reduce risk through careful analysis of prototypes.
System architecture Layout of computer systems used to provide an organization with an information system.
Systems failure method Application of soft-systems thinking to analyze a new computer implementation with the intent of learning from the mistakes of prior attempts to do similar things.
Waterfall model Standard software development sequence of interrelated activities.

Questions

1. Identify a relative advantage for each of the seven ERP implementation methods given in this chapter.
2. Why would you expect such a heavy proportion of ERP systems reported by Mabert et al. to involve vendor packages?
3. What is the general track record of information system organizations with respect to completing projects on time and within budget?
4. How can the systems failure method lead to reduction of information system project risk?
5. Discuss the applicability of waterfall model stages to implementation of an ERP vendor product.
6. For what type of ERP implementation might the spiral model be most appropriate?
7. Research the library and/or Internet for links between ERP and rapid application development, or joint application development.
8. Discuss some limitations of application service providers as a means to implement ERP.
9. Search the library and/or Internet for use of systems failure analysis or other systems approaches in information system project management, especially ERP.

Chapter 6

ERP Project Management

ERP projects can involve widely varying levels of complexity. The simplest way to implement ERP is to either go with full-scale vendor implementation (leaving the complexities of project management to the vendor) or to outsource ERP through an application service provider. Even in these simple cases, however, a great deal of coordination is needed for training and switching to the new way of doing things. Whether ERP is accomplished by modifying a vendor product or developing the ERP in-house, a great deal of project management support is needed.

Project management is critically important in information systems projects. The critical path method (CPM) provides a basic framework for planning and control of coordinated projects of all types, including ERP. This chapter presents fundamental project management concepts, based on the critical path method. Project management issues specific to ERP are also presented.

This chapter:

- Discusses ERP project features.
- Examines the critical path method.
- Explains the use of buffers in critical path scheduling.
- Outlines resource leveling adjustment of schedules.
- Studies the impact of critical path model assumptions.

Normal IS/IT projects have an implicit trade-off among time, cost, and function. In ERP systems, the importance of the project does not allow for sacrifices in time or in functionality. Therefore, cost becomes the primary variable to deal with project contingencies. As discussed in Chapter 1, the cost of this training component is typically greatly underestimated. To allocate an adequate budget to training, the many interrelated activities involved in training as well as in implementing the ERP system need to be carefully coordinated.

Characteristics of ERP Installation Projects

ERP systems involve a large collection of complex hardware and software. Many organizational, employee, and political issues further add to implementation project complexity.[1] ERP project management has been found to benefit most from clear definition of objectives, development of a work plan and a resource plan, and careful tracking of progress.[2] These are features that critical path tools are designed to support.

Project plans need to be aggressive because ERP systems are very critical to organizational efficiency. It is difficult to reliably estimate durations of any information systems projects. Due to the need to balance realism with urgency, schedules should be aggressive but achievable. Clear definition of project aims can reduce the risk of scope creep, the tendency for information systems projects to be changed during implementation. Scope creep arises because the need for change (modification) is identified after the project is under way. Careful planning would reduce such changes.

The type of ERP system adopted will affect the need for changes. Adoption of a single vendor package without modifications will reduce the need for customization, and thus will reduce project complexity, which fosters better schedule performance. However, the primary objective is to develop the right system for the organization. Implementing the ERP system on time and on budget is important, but it is more important to implement the right ERP system.

A project management steering committee is very important to ERP implementation project success.[3] This committee should include senior management representing affected corporate functions, as well as representative end users. This committee usually is involved in system selection, as well as monitoring project progress and management of external consultants. Consultants provide experience missing from the organization and can be invaluable. However, consultants should be screened to avoid those with financial ties to software vendors and inexperience in the specific system being implemented.

The Critical Path Method

The critical path method provides a way to easily identify how fast a project can be completed, given that the estimated durations of activities are accurate. Even though estimated durations are usually at variance with actual outcomes, the critical path method provides a useful analysis of which activities are time bottlenecks. The input to the critical path method is a list of each **activity,** its expected duration, and those activities that immediately precede this activity. "Immediately precede" means that predecessor activities must be completed before the subject activity can begin, and there are no other activities between the predecessor and the activity in question.

[1] T. M. Somers and K. G. Nelson, "The Impact of Strategy and Integration Mechanisms on Enterprise System Value: Empirical Evidence from Manufacturing Firms," *European Journal of Operational Research* 146 (2003), pp. 315–38.

[2] E. L. Umble, R. R. Haft, and M. M. Umble, "Enterprise Resource Planning: Implementation Procedures and Critical Success Factors," *European Journal of Operational Research* 146 (2003), pp. 241–57.

[3] Somers and Nelson, "Impact of Strategy and Integration Mechanisms."

TABLE 6.1 Activity List for ERP Project Selection Scenario

Activity	Duration	Predecessors
A: Select consultant for choosing system	2 weeks	None
B: Meet with consultant to discuss ERP	4 weeks	A
C: Meet with board of directors to explain ERP concept	2 weeks	A
D: Develop rough outline to solicit proposals	1 week	B, C
E: Obtain vendor proposals	4 weeks	D
F: Design alternatives for consideration	3 weeks	E
G: Develop cost accounting analysis of alternative designs	8 weeks	F
H: Present proposals with estimated costs to board	1 week	G
I: Redo estimates in light of board requests for changes	3 weeks	H
J: Obtain board approval	1 week	I

FIGURE 6.1 Network for ERP System Selection Scenario

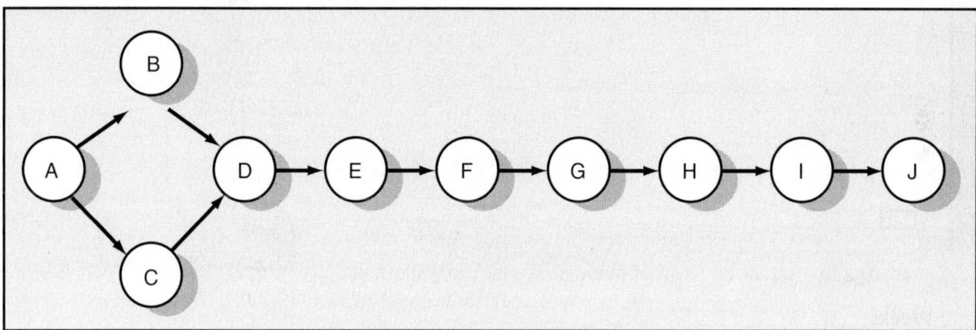

To demonstrate, consider the following project to select an ERP system, as shown in Table 6.1. This is a fairly straightforward sequence of activities, which can be graphically displayed in a **network,** as shown in Figure 6.1. Networks also provide a valuable visual aid for managers to identify relationships among activities. The sequence of events here is clear — activities B and C can work in parallel once activity A is accomplished. All other activities are sequential; they can't begin until their predecessors are finished. A predecessor relationship is captured by the critical path method. In reality, these relationships are often not as rigid as the critical path method assumes. For instance, analysts could anticipate and begin work on activity D before the board approved the concept. Such an early start would run the risk of wasting time if the board were to disapprove the proposal. But if management considered this to be of low likelihood, and if the benefit of getting a jump on estimation seemed worth the risk, modifications to the implied set of precedence relationships could be made. It is necessary to understand specifically what the critical path method assumes in order to use its output.

Another graphical outcome of the critical path method is a **Gantt chart,** which displays the early start schedule versus time (Figure 6.2). An **early start schedule** can be generated over a period of weeks based on the early start implied for all activities.

Figure 6.2 gives the Microsoft Project Gantt chart for this project, followed by a more detailed spreadsheet layout. A Gantt chart shows the time periods when each activity is

FIGURE 6.2 Schedule for ERP System Selection Scenario

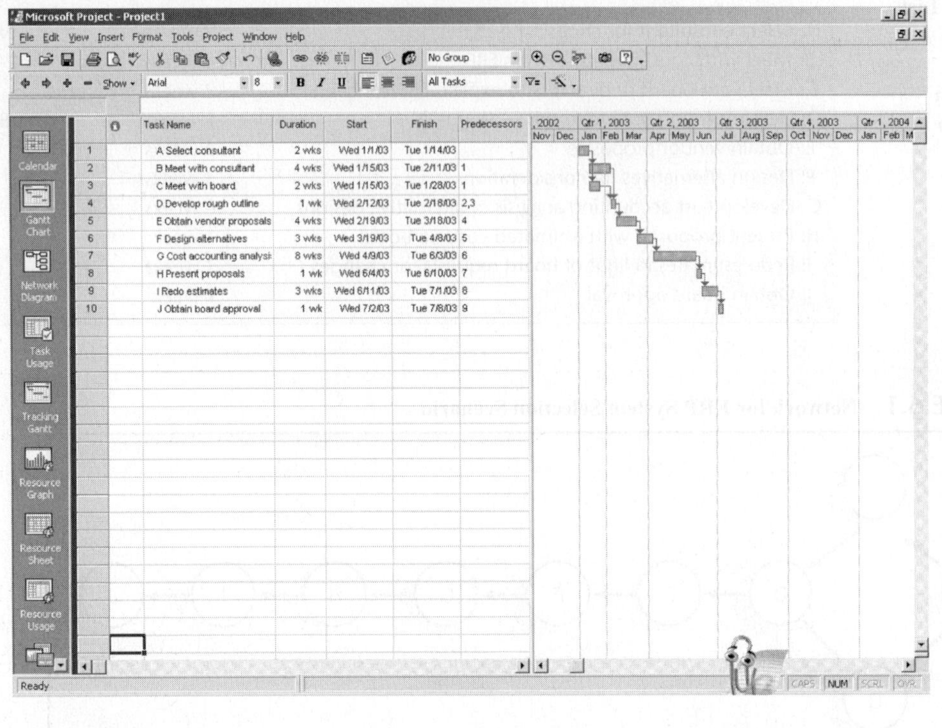

	Task Name	Duration	Start	Finish	Predecessors
1	A Select consultant	2 wks	Wed 1/1/03	Tue 1/14/03	
2	B Meet with consultant	4 wks	Wed 1/15/03	Tue 2/11/03	1
3	C Meet with board	2 wks	Wed 1/15/03	Tue 1/28/03	1
4	D Develop rough outline	1 wk	Wed 2/12/03	Tue 2/18/03	2,3
5	E Obtain vendor proposals	4 wks	Wed 2/19/03	Tue 3/18/03	4
6	F Design alternatives	3 wks	Wed 3/19/03	Tue 4/8/03	5
7	G Cost accounting analysi	8 wks	Wed 4/9/03	Tue 6/3/03	6
8	H Present proposals	1 wk	Wed 6/4/03	Tue 6/10/03	7
9	I Redo estimates	3 wks	Wed 6/11/03	Tue 7/1/03	8
10	J Obtain board approval	1 wk	Wed 7/2/03	Tue 7/8/03	9

Weeks

Activity	Duration	1	2	3	4	5	6	7	8	9	10										20										30
A	2 weeks	X	X																												
B	4 weeks			X	X	X	X																								
C	2 weeks			X	X																										
D	1 week							X																							
E	4 weeks								X	X	X	X																			
F	3 weeks												X	X	X																
G	8 weeks															X	X	X	X	X	X	X	X								
H	1 week																							X							
I	3 weeks																								X	X	X				
J	1 week																											X			

scheduled to occur. If everything went according to plan, this project would be completed in 27 weeks.

The activity list, estimated durations, and predecessor relationships are all the information items required to develop a critical path model. That also means that all other information, such as uncertain durations and limited resources, is assumed away in the critical path method. The initial step of the critical path method is to generate the early start schedule.

Early Start Schedule

For every activity that has no unscheduled predecessors, schedule the activity to start as soon as possible (either the project start time—usually time 0 for reference—or the maxi-

TABLE 6.2 Early Start Schedule for ERP System Selection Scenario

Activity	Duration	Predecessors	Early Start	Early Finish	Consequence
A	2 weeks	None	week 0	week 2	Releases B, C
B	4 weeks	A	2	6	Releases D
C	2 weeks	A	2	4	Must be done to start D
D	1 week	B, C	6	7	Releases E
E	4 weeks	D	7	11	Releases F
F	3 weeks	E	11	14	Releases G
G	8 weeks	F	14	22	Releases H
H	1 week	G	22	23	Releases I
I	3 weeks	H	23	26	Releases J
J	1 week	I	26	27	Finishes project

mum early finish of all predecessors). The critical path schedules are optimal with respect to time. This process continues until all activities are scheduled. The early finish is the sum of the early start time plus the duration as shown in Table 6.2.

Late Start Schedule

The next phase of the critical path analysis is the late start schedule. The **late start schedule** is the latest an activity can be scheduled without delaying project completion time. The final ending time for the project can be some contract deadline, which may be different from the early finish schedule, or the early finish project completion time can be used. If the deadline is earlier than the project early finish time, the project is infeasible (can't be completed on time with given durations). If the deadline is later than the project early finish time, all activities in the project will have slack, or spare time. If the deadline coincides with the project early finish time, there will be at least one **critical path** connecting activities in a chain with zero slack.

The late start schedule is calculated in reverse. Networks are not really needed for development of early start schedules, but are very useful in sorting out the relationships for late start schedules. Begin with the end time (deadline or early finish time). All activities that do not appear on the list of predecessors for unscheduled activities can be scheduled. The late finish time will be either the project end time, or the minimum of the late start times for all following activities. While networks usually aren't required to do an early start schedule, they can be handy in sorting out the abstraction involved in working backward during development of the late start schedule. The late start schedule for our scenario is shown in Table 6.3. Here the only case where there were multiple early starts to compare was for activity A. Activity A's early finish was the minimum of the early start for all activities that were followers of activity A (in this case activities B and C). The minimum early start for those two activities was 2, so the earliest A could finish without delaying the overall project would be the end of week 2.

Slack

Slack is the difference between the late start and early start schedules (it doesn't matter which you use, because in both cases the difference between start and finish is the duration). Those activities with zero slack are critical. If they are delayed, the project completion time would be delayed. There can be more than one critical path for a project, and

TABLE 6.3 Late Start Schedule for ERP System Selection Scenario

Activity	Duration	Followers	Early Finish	Early Start	Consequence
J	1 week	None	week 27	week 26	Releases I
I	3 weeks	J	26	23	Releases H
H	1 week	I	23	22	Releases G
G	8 weeks	H	22	14	Releases F
F	3 weeks	G	14	11	Releases E
E	4 weeks	D	11	7	Releases D
D	1 week	E	7	6	Releases B, C
B	4 weeks	D	6	2	Releases A
C	2 weeks	D	6	4	Must be started before A can finish
A	2 weeks	B, C	2	0	Late start schedule done

TABLE 6.4 Calculation of Slack for ERP Project Selection Scenario

Activity	Early Start	Early Finish	Late Start	Late Finish	Slack	Critical?
A	0	2	0	2	0	**Yes**
B	2	6	2	6	0	**Yes**
C	2	4	4	6	2	No
D	6	7	6	7	0	**Yes**
E	7	11	7	11	0	**Yes**
F	11	14	11	14	0	**Yes**
G	14	22	14	22	0	**Yes**
H	22	23	22	23	0	**Yes**
I	23	26	23	26	0	**Yes**
J	26	27	26	27	0	**Yes**

the project network presented in Figure 6.1 can be useful in ensuring identification of each critical path. Table 6.4 shows identification of slack.

Slack in the case above exists for only one activity, C. There is a critical path of activities with zero slack, consisting of the chain of activities A-B-D-E-F-G-H-I-J. More complex projects will include slack for multiple activities, as in the following project in Table 6.5.

Activity A is an example of a **milestone,** an activity with zero duration. This is an event, in this case triggering the development of an employee training program for an organization adopting ERP. The network for this project is given in Figure 6.3.

The Gantt chart from Microsoft Project is given in Figure 6.4, with the critical path displayed in bold. This project has the slacks shown in Table 6.6.

In this case, there is one critical path consisting of activities A-B-D-F-G-I. It is possible to have parallel sets of critical activities in more than one path. Looking at the list of critical activities will not automatically identify the critical path. This list needs to be considered in light of the network. There are two kinds of slack. **Shared slack** is slack that is shared across more than one activity. For instance, both activities C and E have 28 weeks of slack. This implies that there is some spare time available in the accomplishment of these activities. However, if a week of delay were encountered in activity C, this

TABLE 6.5 Activity List for Employee Training Program

Activity	Duration	Predecessors
A: Obtain mission statement	0	None
B: Reengineers business process	24 weeks	A
C: Obtain vendor specifications	2 weeks	A
D: Obtain list of job skills affected	1 week	B
E: Develop training module explaining overall concept	4 weeks	C
F: Develop training module for affected job skills	12 weeks	D
G: Obtain CD-ROMs for programs	2 weeks	E, F
H: Train help desk staff	5 weeks	D, E
I: Open help desk	1 week	G, H
J: Obtain training facility	1 week	A

FIGURE 6.3 Network for Employee Training Program Scenario

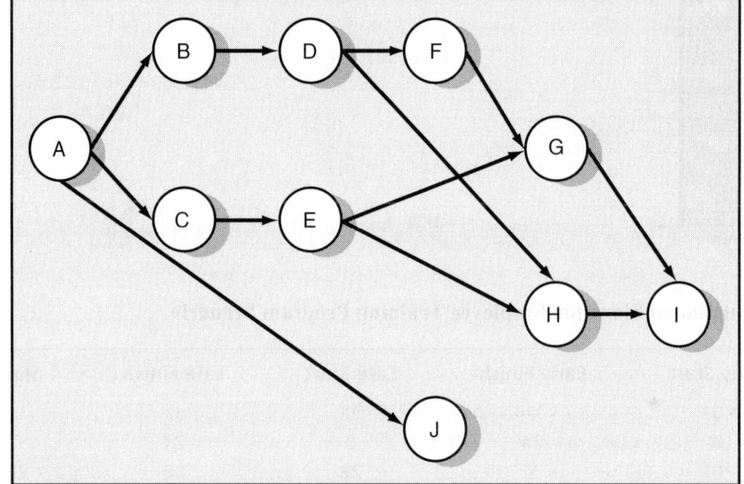

would reduce the time available for activity E as well. That is because it is the same 28 weeks of spare time in this case. Activity H also shares 9 of these 28 weeks of slack. The reason activity H's slack is lower than that for its predecessor activity E is that it must also wait for activity D to be finished, and that is 19 weeks later than activity E could be completed. Activity J has 39 weeks of independent slack.

Schonberger recommended focusing on scheduling the critical chain of activities closely, to make sure that they have the resources needed to proceed as scheduled.[4] Goldratt adopted the same view.[5] The critical chain of activities includes those activities that are critical (as long as managerial control can influence their duration), but is not limited to these activities. Activities with very little slack can become problems if they are delayed

[4] R. J. Schonberger, "Why Projects Are 'Always' Late: A Rationale Based on Manual Simulation of a PERT/CPM Network," *Interfaces* 11, no. 5 (1981), pp. 66–70.

[5] E. M. Goldratt, *Critical Chain* (Great Barrington, MA: The North River Press, 1997).

FIGURE 6.4
Employee Training Program Gantt Chart

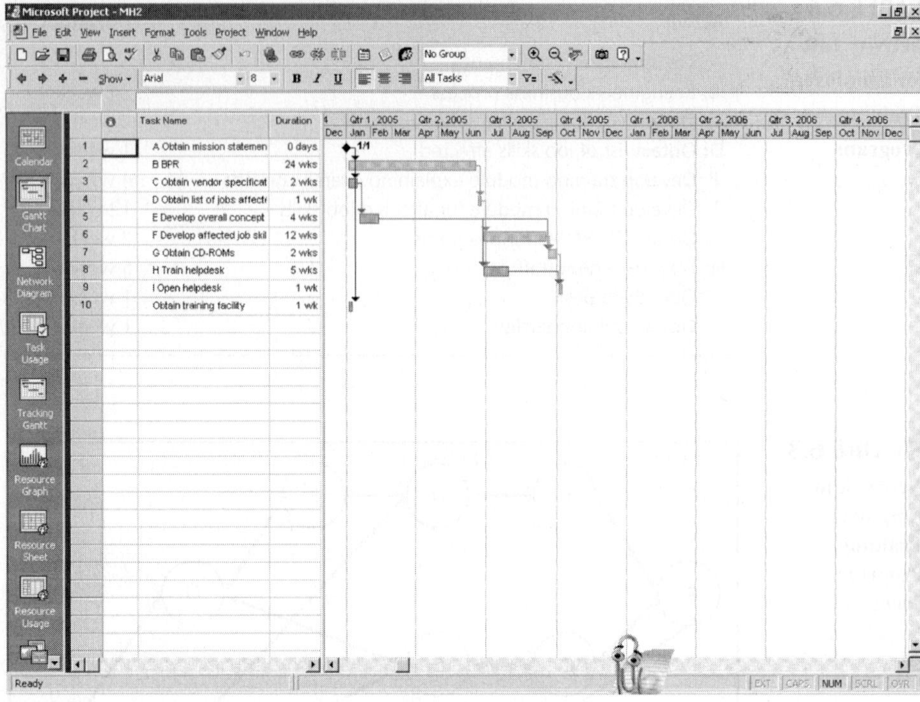

TABLE 6.6 **Calculation of Slack for Employee Training Program Scenario**

Activity	Early Start	Early Finish	Late Start	Late Finish	Slack	Critical?
A	0	0	0	0	0	**Yes**
B	0	24	0	24	0	**Yes**
C	0	2	28	30	28	No
D	24	25	24	25	0	**Yes**
E	2	6	30	34	28	No
F	25	37	25	37	0	**Yes**
G	37	39	37	39	0	**Yes**
H	25	30	34	39	9	No
I	39	40	39	40	0	**Yes**
J	0	1	39	40	39	No

up to or beyond their slack. Therefore, the slack of noncritical activities should also be monitored, to make sure that new critical activities are identified.

There is a bias in projects, in that activity delays accumulate while gains from finishing early do not.[6] This is because when an activity is late, those that must wait for it to be completed start later than scheduled. But if an activity is finished ahead of schedule, the advantage rarely can be used, because in complicated projects different crews and

[6] Ibid.

TABLE 6.7 Activity List for Single Module ERP System Installation Scenario

Activity	Duration	Predecessors
A: Work with consultant to develop initial specifications	2 months	None
B: Gather vendor proposals	1 month	A
C: Gather in-house team	1 month	none
D: Select vendor	0 (1 day)	B
E: Work with installation consultant and design system installation	3 months	C, D
F: Install system	1 month	E
G: Test system	1 month	F
H: Hire implementation consultant	0 (1 day)	None
I: Develop training program	1 month	H
J: Train users	2 months	I
K: Go on-line	0	G, J

materials have to be gathered, and many different people need to be coordinated. The early finish time is not usually known much before the activity's completion. Therefore, it is very difficult to gather all of the following activities' resources together in time to start early.

Buffers

Buffers are a means to ensure that critical activities are completed on time.[7] A buffer is time that is included in the schedule to protect against unanticipated delays and to allow early starts. Buffers are viewed by Goldratt and Newbold as different from slack. Slack is spare time. Buffers are time blocks that are not expected to be used for work time (the same as slack), but are dedicated to cover most likely contingencies and are closely watched so that if they are not needed, subsequent activities can proceed at the earliest time possible. **Project buffers** are used after the final task of a project to protect project completion time from delays. **Feeding buffers** are placed at each point where a noncritical activity is related to a critical path activity. Feeding buffers protect the critical activities from tasks that precede them and allow for early starts of critical activities. **Resource buffers** are placed before resources that are scheduled to work on critical activities to ensure that resources will be available and that their shortage will not delay critical activities. Either resource buffers can be implemented by warning notices to those managing the resource ahead of the required time, or a time can be scheduled to mobilize the resource as a predecessor to the critical activity using it. In multiple-project environments, **strategic resource buffers** can be used to ensure that key resources are available for critical activities.

To demonstrate the use of buffers, consider a third small project, in this case installation of a single module ERP, due to be completed in 10 months. The activity list is given in Table 6.7. The network for this scenario is given in Figure 6.5. As with the two prior examples, our plan involves a small number of activities. As further detail is added, an

[7] Goldratt, *Critical Chain,* and R. C. Newbold, *Project Management in the Fast Lane: Applying the Theory of Constraints* (Boca Raton, FL: The St. Lucie Press, 1998).

FIGURE 6.5 Network for Single Module ERP System Installation Scenario

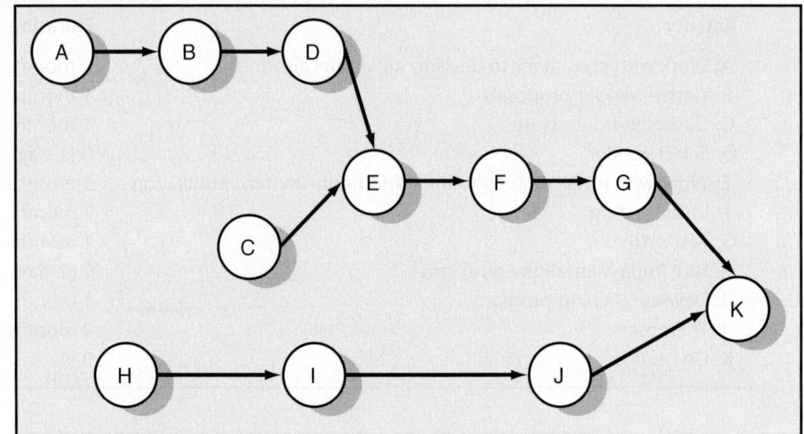

TABLE 6.8 Calculation of Slack for Single Module ERP System Installation Scenario

Activity	Early Start	Early Finish	Late Start	Late Finish	Slack	Critical?
A	0	2	0	2	0	**Yes**
B	2	3	2	3	0	**Yes**
C	0	1	2	3	2	No
D	3	3	3	3	0	**Yes**
E	3	6	3	6	0	**Yes**
F	6	7	6	7	0	**Yes**
G	7	8	7	8	0	**Yes**
H	0	0	5	5	5	No
I	0	1	5	6	5	No
J	1	3	6	8	5	No
K	8	8	8	8	0	**Yes**

ERP project can expand to tens of thousands of activities. The procedure presented here would still apply, only on a much larger scale.

Calculation of slack is shown in Table 6.8. The critical list of activities consists of developing specifications (activity A), gathering vendor proposals (activity B), designing (activity E), installing (activity F), and testing (activity G) the system, and the milestone activities of selecting the vendor (activity D) and going on-line (activity K, which it is hoped does not involve unexpected delays). There are two spare months of time to accomplish activity C, gathering the in-house team. Because the total time devoted is probably the same, there is no benefit to the firm in delaying the team's selection, and it would seem wisest to get the team started as soon as possible. There are five months of shared slack in the chain of training activities. Since a hired consultant is involved, it would be prudent to do this activity as late as possible. This plan would result in the Gantt chart given in Figure 6.6. There now are two months

FIGURE 6.6 Single Module ERP System Installation Scenario

Activity	Duration	Months 1	2	3	4	5	6	7	8
A: Work with consultant to develop initial specifications	2 months	X	X						
B: Gather vendor proposals	1 month			X					
C: Gather in-house team	1 month	X	S	S					
D: Select vendor	0 (1 day)				∅				
E: Select installation consultant and design system installation	3 months				X	X	X		
F: Install system	1 month							X	
G: Test system	1 month								X
H: Hire implementation consultant	0 (1 day)						∅		
I: Develop training program	1 month						X		
J: Train users	2 months							X	X
K: Go on-line	0								∅

∅ — milestone scheduled; X — activity scheduled; S — slack

FIGURE 6.7 Single Module ERP System Installation Scenario with Project Buffer

Activity	Duration	Months 1	2	3	4	5	6	7	8	9
A: Work with consultant to develop initial specifications	2 months	X	X							
B: Gather vendor proposals	1 month			X						
C: Gather in-house team	1 month	X	S	S						
D: Select vendor	0 (1 day)				∅					
E: Select installation consultant and design system installation	3 months				X	X	X			
F: Install system	1 month							X		
G: Test system	1 month								X	**P**
H: Hire implementation consultant	0 (1 day)						∅			
I: Develop training program	1 month						X			
J: Train users	2 months							X	X	**P**
K: Go on-line	0								∅	**P**

∅ — milestone scheduled; X — activity scheduled; S — slack; P — project buffer

available before the project needs to be completed. One of these months can be used as a project buffer, insulating the work that needs to be done from the project deadline. (This leaves one additional month of slack for each activity, making no activities critical at this point.) Project buffer is not planned to be used, but is available should something go wrong with critical activities or with noncritical activities beyond their available slack. Figure 6.7 displays this revised schedule, promising management completion in nine months.

Feeding buffers can be used as pseudo-activities to marshal required resources, making sure that they are available in time and that critical activities are not delayed. For instance, activity E, design of the installation, is crucial (and critical). Those activities immediately preceding activity E can be provided a buffer (say one month) to ensure that activity E gets done on time. There are two ways of implementing that. If the predecessors of the target activity are already critical, inserting a feeding buffer will delay expected completion time of the project. For instance, if activity B is given one month of feeding buffer, that will delay activity E and all subsequent critical activities. This would be counterproductive (and would delay the expected project completion time to month 10, in essence doing the same thing that the project buffer already does). However, applying feeding buffers to slack predecessors accomplishes the intended purpose without delaying the expected project completion time. Here, activity C can be given one month of feeding buffer with no problem. Instead of a deadline of the end of month 3, activity C can be given a deadline of the end of month 2, providing a cushion of one month in case things go wrong, during which remedial action can be taken without delaying the project completion time. Figure 6.8 displays this feeding buffer. Feeding buffers should not be used unless necessary. They should not be used as an excuse to delay activity C until the end of month 2 unless there is some beneficial reason to do so. Care must be taken to ensure that buffers do not make organizations lax.

Two other types of buffers are described by Goldratt. Resource buffers are applied around critical resources to ensure that they are available when needed. This concept is not usually important in ERP projects. A conceivable application in ERP might be the case of a critical consultant, without whom progress on a particular project may not be possible. In such a case, one view of a resource buffer would be to make sure this critical consultant is there a little earlier than really required. But such treatment would only make the critical consultant irritated and would certainly be counterproductive. The case of strategic resource buffers is sort of the reverse. It would make sense to have all required organizational personnel available when the critical consultant was present. In this case, the focus would be on not starving the important resource of productive work to do. But other than conceptually, the strategic resource buffer concept is not as germane to ERP as the ideas of project buffer and feeding buffer.

FIGURE 6.8 **Single Module ERP System Installation Scenario with Feeding Buffer**

		Months								
Activity	**Duration**	**1**	**2**	**3**	**4**	**5**	**6**	**7**	**8**	**9**
A: Work with consultant to develop initial specifications	2 months	X	X							
B: Gather vendor proposals	1 month			X						
C: Gather in-house team	1 month	X	**F**	S						
D: Select vendor	0 (1 day)				Ø					
E: Select installation consultant and design system installation	3 months				X	X	X			
F: Install system	1 month							X		
G: Test system	1 month								X	P
H: Hire implementation consultant	0 (1 day)						Ø			
I: Develop training program	1 month						X			
J: Train users	2 months							X	X	P
K: Go on-line	0								Ø	P

Ø — milestone scheduled; X — activity scheduled; S — slack; P — project buffer; F — feeding buffer

Resource Leveling

Resource leveling involves extending schedules so that particular resources are not over-scheduled. For instance, if a particular specialist is needed to accomplish more than one activity, and these activities happen to be scheduled during common periods, something would have to give. One or the other of the activities sharing the common resource would have to be delayed (or additional resource acquired).

Resource leveling becomes important in ERP installation projects when crucial human resources are overtaxed. The critical path method assumes unlimited resources are available. This assumption needs to be checked to ensure that bottlenecks are not unexpectedly encountered.

Projects will inevitably experience gaps in work, along with some periods of critical resource shortage. The quality of project management can be measured by the proportion of waste time encountered. However, priority should be given to ensuring that critical activities have the resources they need, even if this involves some waste. It is more important to get the job done right, on time, and within budget, than to obtain a perfectly smooth schedule.

Many ERP projects involve the coordination of resources in phased implementation of modules. We demonstrate such a case involving the phased implementation of two ERP modules (financial and accounting, to be followed by materials management). Note that ERP implementations involve the coordination of many people and many activities. The number of specific activities at the lowest level could easily be in the tens of thousands. However, that would be far too unwieldy to be of value to any one individual. The level of detail can vary across individual managers. The overall project manager would have quite an aggregated level of activities. Each subordinate would focus on his or her area of responsibility, with a higher level of detail. In this case, we view the project from a high level, beginning with the charge from the board to examine alternative systems. The network for this scenario is given in Figure 6.9. The Gantt chart from Microsoft Project is

TABLE 6.9 Activity List for Multiple Module ERP System

Activity	Duration	Predecessors
A: Select vendor	1 week	None
B: Hire FI (Finance module) consultant	2 weeks	A
C: Hire MM (Materials Management module) consultant	2 weeks	A
D: Develop internal team	6 weeks	None
E: Select client/server system	3 weeks	B, C
F: Implement client/server system	6 weeks	E
G: Develop FI interfaces	8 weeks	F
H: Install FI module	3 weeks	F
I: Test FI module	1 week	G, H
J: Bring FI module into production	0	I
K: Develop MM interfaces	12 weeks	F
L: Install MM module	5 weeks	J, K
M: Test MM module	3 weeks	L
N: Bring MM module into production	0	M
O: Develop FI training	5 weeks	D, G
P: Develop MM training	7 weeks	D, K

FIGURE 6.9 Network for Multiple Module ERP System

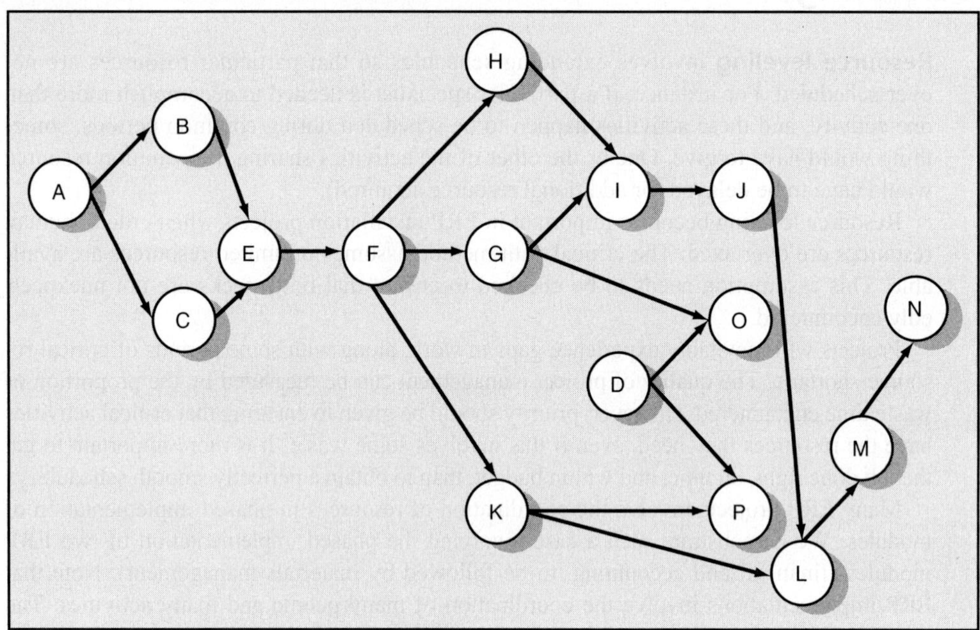

shown in Figure 6.10. In this case, if all goes according to schedule, the project will be complete by August 6. There is slack for the FI module, because of the time that development of MM interfaces is expected to take. If the same people were required to work on both FI and MM interfaces (activities G and K), this schedule would not work, as the schedule obtained from Microsoft Project (the CPM early start project) has both interface development activities occurring at the same time. Either additional interface development people are required, or leveling could be applied. Figure 6.11 shows the leveled project. The leveled project is not completed until October 7, in order to stay within available resources to develop module interfaces. The solutions provided are not necessarily the best possible, but are usually very good. The activity of smoothing is not as critical in project management, because efficiency is not as important as dealing with the high levels of uncertainty present in projects. Smoothing in uncertain environments is usually not effective.

Critical path models are very useful to sort out the complexity of projects with many interrelated activities (such as ERP installations). As long as the assumptions made by the method are understood, the approach is quite useful. Microsoft Project (and other vendor products) provide excellent tools to do computations and present graphical displays. To better understand the limitations of the method, we examine some criticisms of it.

Critical Path Criticisms

Like any model, the critical path approach makes a number of assumptions. Usually, the more convenient the assumptions are for mathematical solution, the less realistic the assumptions are relative to the real decision. The critical path model as demonstrated

FIGURE 6.10
Gantt Chart for Multiple Module ERP System

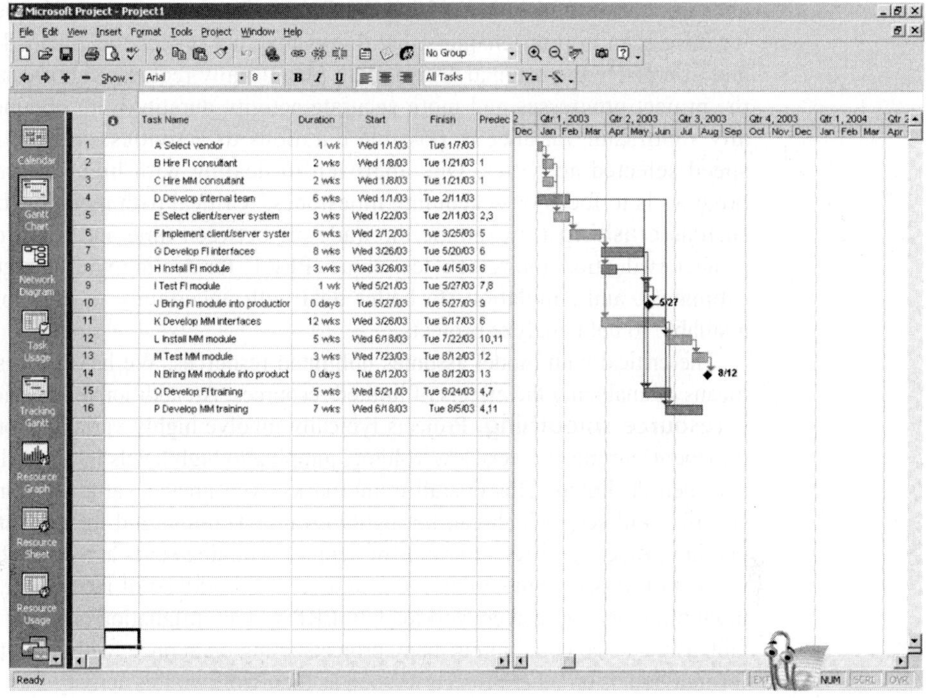

	Task Name	Duration	Start	Finish	Predec
1	A Select vendor	1 wk	Wed 1/1/03	Tue 1/7/03	
2	B Hire FI consultant	2 wks	Wed 1/8/03	Tue 1/21/03	1
3	C Hire MM consultant	2 wks	Wed 1/8/03	Tue 1/21/03	1
4	D Develop internal team	6 wks	Wed 1/1/03	Tue 2/11/03	
5	E Select client/server system	3 wks	Wed 1/22/03	Tue 2/11/03	2,3
6	F Implement client/server syster	6 wks	Wed 2/12/03	Tue 3/25/03	5
7	G Develop FI interfaces	8 wks	Wed 3/26/03	Tue 5/20/03	6
8	H Install FI module	3 wks	Wed 3/26/03	Tue 4/15/03	6
9	I Test FI module	1 wk	Wed 5/21/03	Tue 5/27/03	7,8
10	J Bring FI module into productior	0 days	Tue 5/27/03	Tue 5/27/03	9
11	K Develop MM interfaces	12 wks	Wed 3/26/03	Tue 6/17/03	6
12	L Install MM module	5 wks	Wed 6/18/03	Tue 7/22/03	10,11
13	M Test MM module	3 wks	Wed 7/23/03	Tue 8/12/03	12
14	N Bring MM module into product	0 days	Tue 8/12/03	Tue 8/12/03	13
15	O Develop FI training	5 wks	Wed 5/21/03	Tue 6/24/03	4,7
16	P Develop MM training	7 wks	Wed 6/18/03	Tue 8/5/03	4,11

FIGURE 6.11
Gantt Chart for Multiple Module ERP System—Leveled

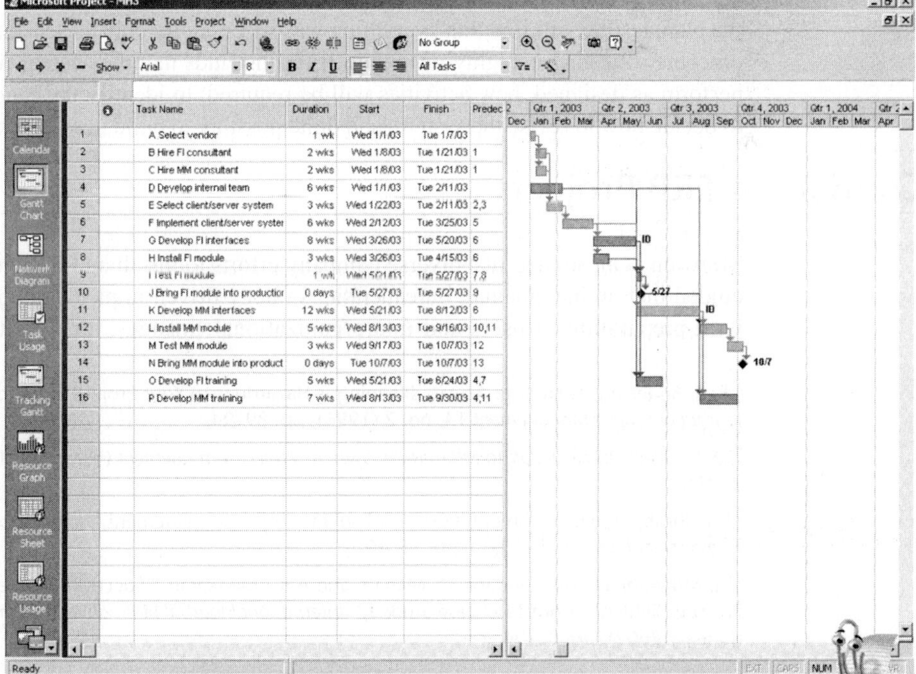

	Task Name	Duration	Start	Finish	Predec
1	A Select vendor	1 wk	Wed 1/1/03	Tue 1/7/03	
2	B Hire FI consultant	2 wks	Wed 1/8/03	Tue 1/21/03	1
3	C Hire MM consultant	2 wks	Wed 1/8/03	Tue 1/21/03	1
4	D Develop internal team	6 wks	Wed 1/1/03	Tue 2/11/03	
5	E Select client/server system	3 wks	Wed 1/22/03	Tue 2/11/03	2,3
6	F Implement client/server syster	6 wks	Wed 2/12/03	Tue 3/25/03	5
7	G Develop FI interfaces	8 wks	Wed 3/26/03	Tue 5/20/03	6
8	H Install FI module	3 wks	Wed 3/26/03	Tue 4/15/03	6
9	I Test FI module	1 wk	Wed 5/21/03	Tue 5/27/03	7,8
10	J Bring FI module into productior	0 days	Tue 5/27/03	Tue 5/27/03	9
11	K Develop MM interfaces	12 wks	Wed 5/21/03	Tue 8/12/03	6
12	L Install MM module	5 wks	Wed 8/13/03	Tue 9/16/03	10,11
13	M Test MM module	3 wks	Wed 9/17/03	Tue 10/7/03	12
14	N Bring MM module into product	0 days	Tue 10/7/03	Tue 10/7/03	13
15	O Develop FI training	5 wks	Wed 5/21/03	Tue 6/24/03	4,7
16	P Develop MM training	7 wks	Wed 8/13/03	Tue 9/30/03	4,11

above is very useful in identifying the fastest one can expect to complete a project. But we have seen in prior chapters that things may not proceed as planned in ERP projects, and in practice the original critical path plan usually requires significant modification as the project progresses and more accurate activity durations are obtained. There is usually significant variance in possible durations of activities, with options available to speed selected activities. One approach to dealing with high uncertainty in activity progress is to focus on scheduling milestones.[8] Critical path methods, including variants such as **crashing** (to examine the trade-off between time and resource requirements), project evaluation and review technique (PERT, for dealing with uncertainty in duration estimates), and simulation (to better deal with uncertainty in duration estimates), are available to help analyze projects.[9]

The critical path model assumes unlimited resources. We have discussed leveling as a means of analyzing the effects of limited resources. An additional extension of this concept is **resource smoothing.** Projects typically involve highly variable workloads, with employment starting at a very low volume, jumping to high levels in the middle of the project, and then declining. This overall trend masks even greater variations for the workload of specific skill sets, which can be highly erratic. Training and implementation progress in parallel (affecting different groups of people). Training starts at a low effort level, increasing as time passes. Smoothing seeks to level the workload of the project, sacrificing minimum time for a more even workload. In ERP system installation projects, this is less important, as the usual condition is many projects going on at once, with more than enough work for individuals on other projects as soon as their work on this activity is completed.

The critical path model assumes that activities can be addressed as entities, with clear beginning and ending points.[10] In reality, the content of complex projects changes over time. As new events unfold, project progress may require a change in direction. An obvious impact relative to information systems projects is the outcome of testing. According to the plan, testing will find that everything was successfully built as scheduled. In reality, the outcome of testing is highly uncertain. If testing finds that the system components do not perform as designed, new activities will be required: to identify the cause of the problem, to decide how to revise the system, and quite possibly to build new system components.

Conduct of ERP Projects

Motwani et al. studied two diverse company efforts to install an ERP system.[11] They concluded that an incremental, bureaucratic, strategy-driven implementation process backed with preparation of users and interorganizational linkages, along with careful change

[8] E. S. Andersen, "Warning: Activity Planning Is Hazardous to Your Project's Health," *International Journal of Project Management* 14, no. 2 (1996), pp. 89–94.

[9] D. L. Olson, *Introduction to Information Systems Project Management* (New York: Irwin/McGraw-Hill, 2001).

[10] A. Shtub, "Project Segmentation — A Tool for Project Management," *International Journal of Project Management* 15, no. 1 (1997), pp. 15–19.

[11] J. Motwani, D. Mirchandani, M. Madan, and A. Gunasekaran, "Successful Implementation of ERP Projects: Evidence from Two Case Studies," *International Journal of Production Economics* 75, nos. 1–2 (January 2002), pp. 83–94.

Real Application: Siemens ERP Implementation Project

Siemens Power Corp. (SPC) manufactured nuclear fuel assemblies. The firm adopted an SAP R/3 system and brought the first set of R/3 modules on line in 1996. Hirt and Swanson's longitudinal study began in January 1997.[12] The 1,100-employee operation was engineering-oriented, the third largest competitor in its industry. This industry was suffering from stagnation in the mid-1990s, with facility utilization at about 50 percent. SPC began a major reengineering effort in 1994, with changes planned for implementation from 1995 through September 1997. This reengineering was to reduce the number of employees by 30 percent. Replacement of the information system was budgeted at $4 million.

During fall 1995, SAP's R/3 suite was selected, utilizing the following modules:

- Finance (FI)
- Controlling (CO)
- Accounts receivable (AR)
- Accounts payable (AP)
- Materials management (MM)
- Production planning (PP)
- Quality control (QC)

Several legacy systems were retained, making it a single vendor system with modifications. The implementation of the ERP system was to be led by users. The project manager and most of the implementation team came from the user community rather than from the IS group. A consulting firm was hired to provide most of the IT support, and the SPC IS group had only marginal involvement with the implementation.

Financial modules were installed in October 1996. The remaining modules were installed by September 1997, at which time the project was completed on time and within budget. The project manager and key users responsible for quality control and production planning modules left the company by that time. However, the original project structure was still intact.

SPC decided to make the project team permanent. The project manager in place at the end of the project was retained, and an SAP steering committee and SAP project team formed. The steering committee of seven representatives of major user stakeholders provided guidance in operating policy, major expenditure approval, and major design changes. The project team of about 15 members from key user groups devoted part of their time to help implement modification projects. This team acted as trainer and help assistance for users and as adviser to middle management. Training of end users dropped over time as users became more proficient with the system. It took an average of three months for users to learn what they needed about the system. Involvement with managers continued. Management did not understand the system well and continued to make unrealistic requests.

During the first year of operation, major errors appeared in the ERP configuration. It was evident that users needed additional training. New opportunities to expand system scope were suggested. A number of small improvement projects were adopted. Two years after project completion, an R/3 system upgrade was undertaken.

[12] S. G. Hirt and E. B. Swanson, "Emergent Maintenance of ERP: New Roles and Relationships," *Journal of Software Maintenance and Evolution: Research and Practice* 13 (2001), pp. 373–97.

management, was a more effective method to implement an ERP than the reverse. Specific factors in the project management area were:

- Redefinition of the project was experienced in the more successful project. This was credited to that organization's monitoring of project progress and taking action to ensure success. Project redefinition involves adjustment of project scope, usually downward, and focus on important system features and deliverables.
- Efforts to improve project management (such as use of the critical path method) also were taken in the more successful project, but not in the less successful implementation. This also can be correlated with efforts to monitor project progress. More meetings and tighter control are means of improving project management.
- Change in project leadership was not a factor in either case studied. However, it clearly can have a disruptive effect on project progress. Project leadership should be changed only if the situation is viewed as unacceptable.
- The more successful organization subdivided the project, while the less successful one didn't. Dividing the project activities into more manageable parts creates a need for careful coordination, but also brings more resources to bear on getting things done.
- Both organizations acted to resolve specific problems. It is important to carefully monitor project progress to identify when problems arise. Problems encountered are usually related to external relationships (vendors, consultants) or technical issues (hardware, software problems). It is possible to overreact, but usually it is less costly and easier to make corrections early.

Critical factors involving resource management were evaluated as well.

- Adding and removing resources as needed is an important factor in making the ERP implementation work. The level of resources obviously needs to be sufficient to get this key project completed, but should not waste personnel resources.
- Layoff and hiring of personnel is also important. Especially important is the management of external consultants.
- Training is critically important in making ERP systems work. There is a need to adequately train organizational users of ERP systems if organizations are to hope for any gains from adopting them.

The Siemens case not only demonstrates many of the project management aspects of implementing an ERP system, but it also shows some of the uncertainty involved in ERP projects (in this case, for instance, key personnel left the organization in the midst of the project). Careful project management led to successful completion of the project. The importance of user training was demonstrated as well.

Summary

ERP implementation can be very beneficial to firms by improving business processes. Such implementation projects share many of the characteristics of other information systems projects. However, they tend to be much larger than the norm and to involve more work with external people (vendors and consultants). Careful design of functionality needs to be supported by adequate budget to keep on schedule. The vast impact of ERP systems on organizational operations makes user training a critical project activity. Project management methods can assist in obtaining timely ERP implementation.

The critical path method provides project managers with valuable information. The criticality of project activities can be identified, and those activities that are critical can be managed more closely. The critical path method provides an estimate of how long the project will take if everything takes no longer than estimated. The critical path method displays what can happen due to predecessor relationships. However, the critical path method assumes unlimited resources, which may not be realistic.

There are some things managers can do when facing resource limits. Buffers provide a way to better manage the chain of critical activities. Most project management software systems allow managers to level resources, generally following a priority system as outlined. While not guaranteed to give the best solution, this ability of software packages to level resources is extremely useful. Projects can also be leveled to stay within available resources.

Key Terms

Activity Event scheduled in critical path method.

Buffers Time built into a schedule to allow for anticipated contingencies.

Crashing Compressing an activity duration at a cost.

Critical path Chain of activities with zero slack that must be completed on time for project to meet its scheduled completion time.

Early start schedule Schedule designed to accomplish each task as early as possible.

Feeding buffers Buffers preceding the juncture of noncritical activities leading into critical activities, to ensure that the noncritical activities will not delay critical activities.

Gantt chart Bar chart of project tasks plotted against time units.

Late start schedule Schedule designed to accomplish each task as late as possible while maintaining expected project completion time.

Milestone Event marking end of project phase.

Network Sketch showing the predecessor relationships among project tasks.

Project buffer Buffer added to the end of a project to ensure against general delays.

Resource buffer Buffer placed before resources scheduled to work on critical activities to ensure that resource shortage will not delay critical activities.

Resource leveling Adjusting a critical path schedule to avoid overuse of limited resources.

Resource smoothing Adjusting a schedule to make the use of resources more uniform, minimizing resource usage peaks and valleys.

Shared slack Slack that is common to two tasks (if one of these tasks were to be late, it would exhaust its own slack, as well as the slack of the sharing task).

Slack Extra time available to accomplish a task beyond the time scheduled, while still allowing the project to be completed as scheduled.

Strategic resource buffers Buffers used to ensure that key resources are available for critical activities.

Questions

1. If no project completion time is given or stated, what is conventionally used as the project completion time for calculation of slack activities?
2. A network is not needed to calculate the critical path start times and finish times. What value does a network have?
3. What is slack?
4. What is a critical path?
5. Identify the early start, early finish, late start, late finish, and slack for each activity, and the critical path for the following project.

Activity	Duration	Predecessor	ES	EF	LS	LF	Slack
A: Get ASP quote	3 weeks	none					
B: Design interfaces	3 weeks	A					
C: Program interfaces	8 weeks	A					
D: Test	4 weeks	B, C					
E: Install	2 weeks	D					

6. Identify the critical path(s) of the following project:

Activity	Duration	Predecessors
A	5 weeks	None
B	4 weeks	None
C	4 weeks	A
D	5 weeks	A, B
E	6 weeks	B

7. Goldratt pointed out that the critical chain of activities (which should be managed closely to do all that can be done to keep on schedule) will not necessarily coincide with the critical path. Why might other activities also be important to manage?
8. Describe the difference between slack and buffers.
9. Four kinds of buffers were discussed. Compare project buffers, feeding buffers, resource buffers, and strategic resource buffers.
10. The following ERP development project is scheduled in weeks. Identify early start times, slack, and critical paths.

ID	Activity	Duration	Predecessors
A	Obtain plan from selection consultant	3 weeks	None
B	Collect vendor proposals	2 weeks	A
C	Perform Economic analysis	3 weeks	B
D	Select ERP vendor	1 week	C
E	Obtain plan from design consultant	3 weeks	D
F	Get hardware	4 weeks	D
G	Set up network	3 weeks	F
H	Develop training plan	5 weeks	E
I	Install vendor software	2 weeks	E, G
J	Train users	16 weeks	G, H
K	Test system	1 week	I
L	Implement system	1 week	K

11. Level the following project.

Activity	Duration	Predecessors	Resource
A	5	None	Henry
B	4	None	Mark
C	4	A	Louise
D	5	A, B	Daniel
E	6	B	Daniel

12. You have been asked to organize a business process reengineering study for your group, consisting of sections A, B, and C. As an initial step, you have identified the following work packages, durations, and precedence relationships. Identify the early start schedule, slack by activity, and critical paths.

ID	Activity	Duration	Predecessors
A	Meet with personnel	1 week	None
B	Identify business functions	2 weeks	None
C	Interview section A	3 weeks	A, B
D	Interview section B	2 weeks	A, B
E	Interview section C	2 weeks	A, B
F	Meet with consultant to identify best practices	1 week	C, D, E
G	Obtain corporate approval	4 weeks	F

Identify:

Early starts and finishes for each activity.

Late starts and finishes for each activity.

Slack by activity.

Critical path activities.

Chapter 7

ERP Implementation and Maintenance

ERP systems are adopted in the hopes that they will improve the performance of an organization on a number of key performance indicators, such as profitability, efficiency, and accuracy in information system data and reports. ERP vendors typically promise gains of 10 to 15 percent in revenue, customer satisfaction, and other measures of value. The effort required to build these systems is significant. Meta Group found that the average ERP implementation takes 23 months with total ownership cost of $15 million.[1]

It is typical for firms adopting ERP to go through an initial period where they realize few improvements. Some firms even experience a decline in performance for a period. Major reasons for such declines are failure to thoroughly reengineer business processes, management errors in system configuration, failure to map changes to the system deriving from changing business needs, mistakes in estimating processing power and data storage requirements, and insufficient training of end users. In a perfect world, all of these factors would have been considered in planning and taken care of before going live. In practice, it is nearly impossible to anticipate every factor.

When new ERP systems are installed, the manner in which the organization does business is usually changed. Newly reengineered business processes have been designed to get more work done with fewer personnel. Caldwell reported three stages of change. In the first stage, there is a period of productivity decline while jobs are redefined, new procedures established, the ERP system is fine-tuned, and the organization learns to process new streams of information. This first stage typically takes three to nine months. A second stage includes development of new skills, organizational changes, process integration, and addition of bolt-on technologies to expand the functionality of ERP systems. The third stage is where ERP pays off, with transformation of organizational operations to an efficient level.[2]

[1] M. Wheatley, "ERP Training Stinks," *CIO Magazine,* June 1, 2000, www.cio.com/archive/060100_erp_content.html.

[2] B. Caldwell, "New IT Agenda," *Informationweek* 711 (November 30, 1998), pp. 30–38.

This chapter:

- Discusses factors found to be critical in IS/IT projects.
- Lists strategic options available for the implementation of ERP systems.
- Reports failure rates in general IS/IT projects.
- Discusses failure in ERP implementation.
- Defines the implications of training in making ERP systems pay off for organizations.
- Presents ERP maintenance activities.
- Reports on the migration of ERP systems to improved software products.

Critical Success Factors in ERP

A **critical success factor** is something that the organization must do well to succeed. In terms of information system projects, a critical success factor is what a system must do to accomplish what it was designed to do. Three factors consistently appear as critical success factors for information systems projects: top management support, client consultation (user involvement), and clear project objectives.[3]

Effective user involvement is often difficult to attain. A large manufacturing firm adopted a system that affected 12 departments at five sites and 280 users around the country. A project team was formed consisting of 15 consultants, 10 people from within the firm, and two project managers working for the firm. A committee of top managers was created to provide oversight, and met with the project team once a month. Weekly project meetings were held, chaired by the vice president for information systems. The project team encouraged user sign-offs at different phases of the project, such as software selection, and at the end of phases such as changes to system components and development of screens. Different levels of users were involved at different phases to get users to buy into the system. Training sessions were provided, as well as pilot sessions where user suggestions were encouraged. However, the project was not a success. Four months after the system was installed, over 1,000 requests for changes had been received. Even though many means of encouraging user involvement had been applied, poorly defined lines of responsibility and communication resulted in failure of communication between users and system designers. Users grew to feel that their input wasn't valued, and therefore they quit contributing.[4] The phenomenon of user failure to cooperate with ERP systems is common.

The percentage of ERP system failures was rated by one study as ranging from 40 to 60 percent,[5] and by another study as between 60 and 90 percent.[6] The latter study defined

[3] D. L. Olson, *Introduction to Information Systems Project Management* (New York: Irwin/McGraw-Hill, 2001).

[4] K. Amoako-Gyampah and K. B. White, "When Is User Involvement Not User Involvement?" *Information Strategy*, Summer 1997, pp. 40–45.

[5] G. Langenwalter, *Enterprise Resources Planning and Beyond: Integrating Your Entire Organization* (Boca Raton, FL: St. Lucie Press, 2000).

[6] C. Ptak and E. Schragenheim, *ERP: Tools, Techniques, and Applications for Integrating the Supply Chain* (Boca Raton, FL: St. Lucie Press, 2000).

failure as not attaining the return on investment claimed in the approval phase. Many examples of ERP failure have been reported. Some of these involve user factors (see the FoxMeyer case in Chapter 1). Others involve different complications. Motwani et al. reviewed four cases of ERP systems causing considerable problems for the organizations that adopted them:[7]

1. Hershey (see Chapter 9) had a 19 percent drop in quarterly profit after adoption of its ERP, and a 29 percent increase in inventory blamed on the ERP order-processing system.[8]
2. The city of Oakland adopted an ERP project but, when implementing that system, generated erroneous paychecks for city employees.[9]
3. Miller Industries suffered an operating loss due to inefficiencies in its ERP system in its first quarter of implementation.[10]
4. WW Grainger Inc. saw its operating earnings drop $11 million per year, blamed on improper ERP implementation.[11]

Many studies have examined critical success factors in ERP implementation. Umble et al. integrated these findings into 10 categories.[12]

1. Clear understanding of strategic goals.
2. Commitment by top management.
3. Excellent implementation project management.
4. Great implementation team.
5. Successful coping with technical issues.
6. Organizational commitment to change.
7. Extensive education and training.
8. Data accuracy.
9. Focused performance measures.
10. Multisite issues resolved.

Items 1 and 2 are classical information systems critical success factors for any IS project. (Clear statement of project objectives is inherently present in ERP implementations, and the scope of investment holds management attention.)

Item 3 relates to project management. Implementation project management should include accurate estimates of project scope, size, and complexity. As discussed in Chapter 3,

[7] J. Motwani, D. Mirchandani, M. Madan, and A. Gunasekaran, "Successful Implementation of ERP Projects: Evidence from Two Case Studies," *International Journal of Production Economics* 75 (2002), pp. 83–96.

[8] C. Stedman, "Failed ERP Gamble Haunts Hershey," *Computerworld* 33, no. 44 (1999), pp. 1–2.

[9] C. Stedman, "ERP Project Problems Plague City Payroll," *Computerworld* 33, no. 50 (1999), p. 38.

[10] A. Gilbert, "ERP Installations Derail," *Informationweek* 22 (November 22, 1999), p. 77.

[11] Ibid.

[12] E. J. Umble, R. R. Haft, and M. M. Umble, "Enterprise Resource Planning: Implementation Procedures and Critical Success Factors," *European Journal of Operational Research* 146, no. 2 (2003), pp. 241–57.

this is far from a trivial task. There should be a match between the business requirements set forth by management and the selected ERP system. Project management should also develop achievable schedules. Designed systems should not include non-value-adding or redundant processes. Tools to assist in this aspect of project management were discussed in Chapter 6. It is also important to convey realistic expectations to management and users.

Item 4 also relates directly to project management. The implementation team needs good people. Assignments of internal people are controllable. Vendor and consultant personnel are not, but care should be taken to keep the team productive. Item 5 is the technical side of project management. Vendor and consultant personnel can help a great deal in this area of ERP installation projects.

Item 6 is associated with item 2, top management commitment. ERP systems will usually involve significant changes in the way in which almost everyone in the organization works. This requires people to change, something that we all tend to resist. For as little productivity disruption as possible, the organization must be committed to carry through the project. Employees are also often quite concerned that the ERP system will eliminate their jobs (a reasonable fear). Middle managers may also be concerned with the greater visibility into business operations the ERP provides to top management. There will be a year or two of significant organizational change. Item 7 relates to the organization providing the needed training to employees, explaining to employees how they will fit in with the new system, and telling them what training and skill development is required of them to continue to be productive.

Item 8 relates to internal data. The ERP system must deliver useful information. The Hershey case is a counterexample. If the new system provides bad data, the company will suffer major losses. Hershey survived this period. Most organizations would have difficulty doing that. Item 9 concerns system design. The ERP system should provide reports of critical information to all levels of management. If it does not provide management with the information that it needs, the system obviously is not accomplishing its purpose. Item 10 relates to the organizational network design. If each site has its own location-specific (or functional-specific) needs, the information system needs to be responsive. The greater the diversity of needs, the less attractive big-bang implementation is and the more attractive a phased ERP implementation would be.

Implementation Strategy Options

ERP implementations encounter complications in business strategy, software configuration, technical platforms, and management execution. There are a number of **implementation strategies** available. Markus et al. reviewed observations of practice in all four of these areas in multisite ERP implementations.[13] At least five ways to arrange relationships among business units were identified, four ways to configure software, and two ways to accomplish execution of an ERP system in multisite implementations, as displayed in Table 7.1.

[13] M. L. Markus, C. Tanis, and P. C. van Fenema, "Multisite ERP Implementations," *Communications of the ACM* 43, no. 4 (2000), pp. 42–46.

TABLE 7.1 Multisite ERP Implementation Areas and Options

Control Strategy	Software Configuration	Technical Platform	Management Execution
Total local autonomy	Single financial/single operation	Centralized	Big bang
Headquarters control—financial only	Single financial/multiple operations	Distributed	Phased rollout
Headquarters coordination	Multiple financial/single operation		
Network coordination	Multiple financial/multiple operations		
Total centralization			

Source: M. L. Markus, C. Tanis, and P. C. van Fenema, "Multisite ERP Implementations," *Communications of the ACM* 43, no. 4 (2000).

An initial issue in multisite ERP is scope. The scope of the system defines expected benefits from the ERP. If only a few financial modules are adopted, benefits from the other modules are not obtained, and the full scope of ERP benefits is not gained. But projects of larger scope require higher levels of coordination and top management support, as the impact is much more pervasive.

Five business strategy alternatives were cited by Markus et al. One European multinational allowed its subunits nearly **total local autonomy** in ERP adoption. This firm had different product subsidiaries operating in different countries. While this strategy does not take advantage of ERP potential, it avoids conflict associated with centrally mandated changes and also allows companies the ability to pursue independent initiatives, and reduces the risk of implementation project failure. When *headquarters controls financial modules only,* business units were often observed to independently configure, implement, and maintain ERP software. If the activities of different business units are independent, this approach makes sense. It also allows application of the best-of-breed approach. Another pattern of implementation is for *headquarters coordination of operations,* with high degrees of local autonomy. This strategy seems to work best when benefits in some particular areas such as purchasing are available. The strategy of *network coordination of operations* allows local operations to access the information of other business units for lateral coordination without high levels of centralization. This approach works best when entities sell to each other as well as to external customers. *Total centralization* works best when companies are more tightly coordinated. With respect to the impact of ERP effectiveness, theoretically a centralized ERP system used throughout the organization makes the most sense in order to gain ERP's potential benefits of integration. However, in practice there are often overriding reasons decentralization makes greater sense.

Markus et al. also noted options for configuring software. Software configuration in ERP requires a logical structure of legal-financial entities with operational entities. *Single financial/single operation* configurations are often adopted in simple, geographically centralized organizations. Single site software configurations are also adopted by complex organizations if they operate as a single management entity (in one country with one set of financial reporting requirements) or if they have common business processes and centralized control of the flow of material. *Single financial/multiple operations* configurations are found when there is a single financial company with multiple operational entities. Kraft Foods, with 53 manufacturing sites in eight product divisions, was found to be too complex for a single operational ERP configuration. *Multiple financial/single operation* configurations are suitable for organizations with one manufacturing facility but sales outlets in multiple countries, each with different financial reporting requirements for tax purposes. Finally, a *multiple financial/multiple operations* ERP configuration is useful for the typical multinational firm.

For technology platforms, site refers to a combination of a central database and possibly multiple applications servers. Organizations with many units and locations may opt for a *centralized* architecture with remote access via telecommunications lines and PCs. Another extreme is to *distribute data and processing.* ERP configuration is easier and often cheaper if centralized. However, there may be advantages in distributed architectures relative to database size and performance, telecommunications costs, maintenance costs, and risk management.

Execution of ERP systems can be accomplished a number of ways. The extremes are the **big-bang deployment,** where on one magic day, the old system is unplugged and the new system turned on-line. Markus et al. cited use of this strategy by Quantum Corp., which shut down its operations worldwide for eight days to switch systems. This risky approach was motivated by that company's specific circumstances. The other extreme is **phased rollout,** with components of the system brought on-line serially and operated and observed before moving on to implementation of the next phase. Markus et al. cited BICC Cables, which adopted a lengthy process of consensus building in its global operation. The selected ERP system was implemented one step at a time, as BICC Cables wanted no more than three software versions in operation at any one time (old being replaced, new being installed, future version being tested at headquarters). This resulted in an environment with technology changes as often as every 12 months.

Mabert et al. surveyed manufacturing users of ERP, and found implementation results as shown in Table 7.2. The big-bang approach is a dangerous approach for general IS/IT projects, but often makes sense in the context of ERP. The alternatives are to roll out a system, or to do a pilot study (here labeled mini big-bang). Rolling out a system makes sense for larger firms where geographic dispersion is present or in conglomerates with diverse functional groups. The data indicates that phased rollouts are often used, sometimes by both module and site. The pilot approach is less reliable in ERP contexts than it is for general IS/IT projects because scalability is so often a problem in ERP implementations.

TABLE 7.2 Implementation Strategies Adopted

Strategy	Time in United States	Time in Sweden	% Adopting in United States	% Adopting in Sweden
Big-bang	15 months	14 months	41%	42%
Phased rollout by site	30 months	23 months	23	20
Phased rollout by module	22 months	20 months	17	17
Mini big-bang	17 months	16 months	17	20
Phased rollout by module and site	25 months	.	2	

Source: V. M. Mabert, A. Soni, and M. A. Venkataramanan, "Enterprise Resource Planning Survey of Manufacturing Firms," *Production and Inventory Management Journal* 41, no. 20 (2000), pp. 52–58 and J. Olhager and E. Selldin, "Enterprise Resource Planning Survey of Swedish Manufacturing Firms," *European Journal of Operational Research* 146 (2003), pp. 365–73.

The pilot test may work quite well, but the server system may be overwhelmed when the full computational load is applied.

The time required for installation varies a great deal depending upon installation strategy. A longer time frame is required for a rollout strategy. The duration averages identified by Mabert et al. are probably related to organization size, in that smaller organizations are likely to use the big-bang approach.

Levels of IS/IT Project Failure

Project failure can come in many forms (budget overrun, schedule overrun, technical inadequacy). Lyytinen and Hirschheim identified four major categories of project system failure.[14]

- Corresponding failure.
- Process failure.
- Interaction failure.
- Expectation failure.

A fifth category is strategic/competitive failure. Obviously some of these categories are more critical than others.

Corresponding failure alludes to the failure of the system to meet design objectives. This is a technical failure in that a computer program didn't do what it was intended to do. The Hershey ERP implementation to be covered in Chapter 9 was a failure of this type.

Process failure is a failure to bring in a project system on time and within budget. The system may technically work, but it is no longer economically justifiable, or at least not within current business plans. The FoxMeyer Drug ERP implementation discussed in Chapter 1 was an example of this category of failure.

Interaction failure occurs when a system is not used as much as it was planned to be. This can arise when a system is built to technical specifications within budget and on time, but the intended users do not use it. This can be because of some bias on the users' part to continue to operate the old way or because the planned system design doesn't effectively deal with the problem.

Expectation failure occurs when the system does not quite match up with the expectations of project stakeholders. The system may perform technically, and may be on time and within budget, and may be used, but it may not do the job as management was led to expect.

Strategic/competitive failure comes about when systems work, are used as designed, and even meet stakeholder expectations, but the organization is not able to compete successfully. No computer system is a guarantee of success. For businesses to succeed, they have to have a good fundamental business purpose, providing their customers with something that their competitors cannot.

[14] K. Lyytinen and R. Hirschheim, "Information Systems Failures — A Survey and Classification of the Empirical Literature," *Oxford Survey of Information Technology* 4 (1987), pp. 257–309.

Ewusi-Mensah and Przasnyski distinguished between total abandonment (complete termination of project activity before implementation), substantial abandonment (major simplification resulting in a project radically different from original specifications), and partial abandonment (reduction in original project scope without major changes in original specifications).[15] Dell Computer and Kellogg, discussed in Chapter 2, are examples of firms that abandoned ERP implementations, apparently applying successful alternatives. Sometimes managers became too committed to projects, extending the projects' life when they should be canceled.[16] Project failure causes can be grouped into inadequate economic payoff, psychological factors (managerial persistence in expecting positive project prospects when they feel personally responsible), escalation factors (throwing good money after bad), social factors (including competitive rivalry), and organizational factors related to a project's political support.

ERP Implementation Failure

ERP implementations tend to be large, require long times to put in place, have high levels of complexity, and involve new technology. These are all characteristics of difficult IS/IT projects. A number of problems have been observed in implementing ERP systems.

Mabert et al. analyzed survey data to identify those variables key to successful ERP implementation.[17] Seven issues were considered.

1. Use of a single ERP package versus use of multiple packages was discussed in Chapter 4. Both approaches have been successfully implemented, and neither was found significant in either ERP implementation time or budget performance.
2. ERP systems can be implemented at one time across the organization (the big-bang approach) or in phases (as well as other variations in between). Again, a variety of approaches have been used in successful ERP implementations, and the variants were not found significant for either time or budget performance.
3. The number of modules implemented was examined, with no significance found.
4. The order of module implementation also did not prove to be significant.
5. Application of major BPR initially, as opposed to limited reengineering, did not make a significant difference in time or budget.

The two variables that did prove significant were:

6. Modifications to the system, which were significant in both time performance and budget performance. If vendor systems are modified, it will cost more and take longer (but will likely provide a better system).

[15] K. Ewusi-Mensah and Z. H. Przasnyski, "On Information Systems Project Abandonment: An Exploratory Study of Organizational Practices," *MIS Quarterly* 15, no. 1 (1991), pp. 66–86.

[16] M. Keil, "Pulling the Plug: Software Project Management and the Problem of Project Escalation," *MIS Quarterly* 19, no. 4 (1995), pp. 422–47.

[17] V. A. Mabert, A. Soni, and M. A. Venkataramanan, "Enterprise Resource Planning: Managing the Implementation Process," *European Journal of Operational Research* 146 (2003), pp. 302–14.

TABLE 7.3
Factors in ERP Implementation Failure

Scenario	CIO/IT Focus	Typical Outcome
Technological determinism	Technical	Failure to gain business benefits
Supplier/consultant driven	Disregarded	Cost overruns
Outdated relationships & capabilities	Insufficient talent	Chaos

Source: L. P. Willcocks and R. Sykes, "The Role of the CIO and IT Function in ERP," *Communications of the ACM* 43, no. 4 (2000).

7. Use of accelerated implementation strategy, which was significant in implementing ERP systems on time (but not significant with respect to budget). Vendors have been successful in expediting implementation of their systems.

The relative roles of chief information officers and the information technology group are seriously neglected in many ERP implementations. Most ERPs studied by Willcocks and Sykes accomplished the integration of data into a common data structure, which vastly improved the development of new software applications.[18] However, the primary benefit of an ERP is through improving the way in which the organization does business (business process reengineering). Many organizations were observed to fail on this aspect of ERP implementation (a case of interaction failure). This failure was driven by the need for major changes in human, cultural, and organizational relationships. Table 7.3 displays three factors associated with ERP implementation failure.

Technological determinism arises from the view of an ERP system as a packaged solution to all of an organization's technical and business problems. This often is the view adopted when the CIO is too technically focused, and the IT group is developed around technical skills. In such organizations, the IT function is seen as the prime owner of IT issues. ERP implementation results typically include general resistance and high rates of failure. Willcocks and Sykes found technological determinism to be common in ERP implementations in the mid-1990s. Implementation in this model is typically handed over to the IT group, whose members focus on time and budget metrics, giving little attention to business benefits.

A **supplier/consultant-driven** ERP implementation commonly arises when senior business executives mandate ERP without significant consultation with the CIO and IT group. This can be because top management views ERP as a great strategic tool, or because it lacks trust in IT group abilities (and ERP is seen as a means of replacing the IT group). In this type of implementation, ERP is outsourced (either through vendors and consultants, or more recently through application service providers). This approach has been seen to suffer considerable cost overruns. Willcocks and Sykes reported one case where costs were 10 times what was estimated in the first feasibility study. Another feature is that the organization often does not buy into the system, which is viewed as imposed from above. While the focus is on business benefits, the means of attaining those benefits are not present.

[18] L. P. Willcocks and R. Sykes, "The Role of the CIO and IT Function in ERP," *Communications of the ACM* 43, no. 4 (2000), pp. 22–28.

TABLE 7.4 Core IT Capabilities Needed for ERP Implementation Success

Capability	Impact
IT leadership	Develop strategy, structures, processes, and staff
Business systems thinking	Adopt systems view
Relationship building	Cooperate with business users
Architecture planning	Create needed technical platform
Technology fixing	Troubleshoot
Informed buying	Compare vendor sources
Contract facilitation	Coordinate efforts
Contract monitoring	Hold suppliers accountable
Supplier development	Explore long-term mutual benefits

Source: L. P. Willcocks and R. Sykes, "The Role of the CIO and IT Function in ERP," *Communications of the ACM* 43, no. 4 (2000).

Outdated relationships and capabilities occur when the CIO and IT group are insufficiently prepared to cope with the challenges of new technologies. The focus tends to be on cost minimization rather than as a strategic resource. The IT function is largely responsible for the ERP system, but lacks the technical skills to make it work. External suppliers are often hired to fill skills gaps. Relationships with business users are not developed, and there is a failure to reorient business thinking to utilize ERP tools. Willcocks and Sykes found this third scenario to be the most common, even in some successful ERP implementations.

Features of Successful ERP Implementation:

The most successful approach was to develop key IT capabilities before adopting ERP. Feeny and Willcocks reported the nine core IT capabilities required for successful ERP implementation.[19] These factors were assessed as in Table 7.4. This approach involves development of a competent internal IT organization, along with a systems view of the organization. A systems view enables better understanding of what IT is needed for and how the organization's business processes can best be supported.

This list of core capabilities needs to be maintained in-house. If key skills are lacking, Willcocks and Sykes recommend hiring the skills required rather than relying on long-term consultant relationships, unless the need is very short-term.

Strategies to Attain Success

In addition to obtaining needed IT capabilities, Willcocks and Sykes suggested the following strategies to successfully implement an ERP system.

User versus Technology Focus

The focus can be given to better support methods currently in place (**user focus**) or on the ERP design (**technology focus**). An ERP is intended to enable users to do their jobs better. Business process reengineering inherently leads to changing views of busi-

[19] D. Feeny and L. Willcocks, "Core IS Capabilities for Exploiting IT," *Sloan Management Review* 39, no. 3 (1998), pp. 9–21.

ness requirements. Therefore, requirements lists tend to be unstable, and flexibility is required in ERP system implementation. This change can also outdate vendor software capabilities. Willcocks and Sykes recommend focusing on user needs over technology. Technology focus (whether internal IT or outsourcing) should be adopted only when the technological maturity required is high and detailed specifications can be developed.

Governance and Staffing

Willcocks and Sykes consistently found that effective business innovations require high-level support and a project champion. This top support usually comes from the business side rather than the IT side. Project managers for ERP implementation projects need to be credible to top stakeholders, have a record of success, and be able to keep the project on its critical path. A multifunctional team is essential, including end users, in-house IT specialists, people with the ability to get diverse groups to work together, and specialists in IT and business needs.

Time-Box Philosophy

A short time frame for ERP implementation may seem clearly preferable. From a systems perspective, this time frame is ideally six to nine months. Often this may be identified as impractical. If so, it might be possible to decompose implementation into smaller projects, each with tangible business benefits. This approach to time discipline helps reduce project risk of failure to satisfy business requirements. This approach was referred to as converting "whales" (large unmanageable projects) into "dolphins" (smaller and more manageable projects) by Willcocks and Sykes.

One reason short ERP implementation projects are undesirable is the time required for employees to adjust to the new system. If employees have been working with different systems for extensive periods, a longer transition will be required to refocus the thinking of these employees.

Supplier/Consultant Role in ERP

Consultants can provide a great deal of knowledge and ERP experience. In highly innovative ERP systems supporting activities that the organization has as core competencies, it is best to strictly control outside consultants. The alternative is to outsource management of business innovation. This is counterproductive because the consultant gains the business's expertise to sell to others.

User Training

The activities of selecting and installing an ERP system have received the greatest focus. However, there are many important issues remaining in making ERP systems work. Training of user personnel is critical. Usually for about one year the trauma of the new system is very difficult to bear by all concerned. Adopting a thorough training program makes this difficult period easier to cope with. There is a strong tendency to underestimate the magnitude required in such a training program.

Wheatley reported a vice president of research for a large consulting firm saying that ERP software is rarely the source of implementation problems.[20] Nor was there a detectable

[20] Wheatley, "ERP Training Stinks."

difference in problems across vendors or by location. Poor training of users was blamed for most of the problems. Organizations with higher proportions of new employees may find ERP implementation easier. Firms with many employees with many years of experience require greater levels of change. Managerial and professional employees are often easier to convince of the positive impact of ERP on organizational effectiveness.[21] Further, the degree of change required within the organization can have an impact on ERP installation timing. If the system is implemented too quickly, this may not provide sufficient time for the organizational climate to change.

Only 10 to 15 percent of ERP implementations run smoothly. Some of the pitfalls that Wheatley reported were:

- Placing employees in software-specific training, without attention to business processes.
- Focusing training on command sequences without explanation of why.
- Skimping on training time.
- Solving problems the old way rather than learning the new system.

Training in new ERP systems is difficult for several reasons, including user diversity, the complexity of the new system, and the variety of training methods available. By their nature, ERP systems are going to radically change how people do their jobs. The theory of ERP is to integrate computer support to all aspects of the business, naturally leading to user diversity. These people also are busy, especially in coping with the requirements of the new system. Training users in new ERP systems can be extremely expensive—more than 10 percent of total ERP system cost.

Experience has demonstrated the importance of training. The need for flexibility in timing and place as well as the need for training in specific functions rather than the comprehensive ERP system affect training delivery. This has led to creation of an entire industry providing ERP training. Available delivery formats include:

- Web-based virtual training.
- Computer-based training.
- Video courses.
- Self-study books.
- Pop-up help screens.

ERP Maintenance

Another activity that tends to receive insufficient attention is ERP system maintenance. All computer systems need to be maintained. Nah et al. classified ERP maintenance tasks, as outlined in Table 7.5.[22]

[21] S. Abdinnour-Helm, M. L. Lengnick-Hall, and C. A. Lengnick-Hall, "Pre-implementation Attitudes and Organizational Readiness for Implementing an Enterprise Resource Planning System," *European Journal of Operational Research* 146 (2003), pp. 258–73.

[22] F. F.-H. Nah, S. Faja, and T. Cata, "Characteristics of ERP Software Maintenance: A Multiple Case Study," *Jounal of Software Maintenance and Evolutions: Research and Practice* 13 (2001), pp. 399–414.

TABLE 7.5 Classification of ERP Maintenance Activities

Maintenance Class	Typical Tasks	Descriptions
Corrective	Application of vendor additions	Incorporate vendor patches and objects
	Troubleshooting	Fix problems submitted by users
Adaptive	Transfers	Implement new features
	Testing	Test after change
	Modifications/enhancements	Internal customization
	Authorizations	Password maintenance
	Interface tuning	Implement interfaces with other software
Perfective	Version upgrade	Justification, planning, and implementation of new versions
Preventive	Administration	Monitor response times, thresholds, file sizes, backups, error logs
	Work-flow monitoring	Track flow of maintenance activities

Source: F. F.-H. Nah, S. Faja, and T. Cata, "Characteristics of ERP Software Maintenance: A Multiple Case Study," *Journal of Software Maintenance and Evolution: Research and Practice* 13 (2001).

Maintenance activities can include corrective actions for problems that are detected, adaptive procedures as new feature requirements are generated, perfective maintenance as new software upgrades are developed, and preventive maintenance to deal with routine administrative functions. Additionally, training users and providing help are important, as well as coordinating with vendors, consultants, and other external organizations.

The degree of relative maintenance activity is expected to vary with system cycle, much as with other software. Initially, the focus is on adaptive, corrective, and preventive maintenance. These maintenance classes decline in volume with time, while perfective maintenance activities increase. The greatest volume of maintenance activity would be generated by version upgrades. This creates a natural opposition in interests, as ERP users will prefer system stability, while ERP vendors will emphasize the need for upgrades to improve system efficiency and capacity (while also improving vendor cash flow).

ERP System Migration

Implementing ERP conceptually implies the adoption of best practice processes. However, as ERP systems evolve, new versions are regularly developed. When organizations decide it is time to adopt changes, these changes will range from minor modifications to ERP system replacement.[23] Vendors find ERP **migration** important for a number of reasons. First, the older the installed system, the higher the switching cost for the organization. Second, it is easier for the vendor to support and service a smaller number of software versions. Thus, by upgrading older systems for customers, vendors simplify their maintenance headaches, as well as provide better value to customers. Third, migrations

[23] M. Kremers and H. van Dissel, "ERP System Migrations," *Communications of the ACM* 43, no. 4 (2000), pp. 53–56.

Real Application: The Importance of Scheduling Training in Dow Chemical Co.'s ERP

Dow Chemical was an early adopter of ERP in 1988, installing SAP's mainframe R/2 system in the early 1990s.[24] This was migrated to SAP R/3 after Dow merged with Union Carbide Corp., allowing access to SAP advances in supply chain, performance management, and e-commerce. Dow adopted PeopleSoft's HR and payroll modules in its European user special interest group.[25] Dow adopted a very large outsourcing contract with Andersen Consulting in 1996, teaming 550 Andersen and Dow IT personnel for application development and support projects.[26]

Part of adopting an ERP is BPR, which leads to retraining needs. After 10 years of experience with ERP, Dow Chemical undertook a training program for its 50,000 employees at about 900 worldwide sites. About 80 percent of this training was to be delivered on-line over three years. The new training system was expected to pay back investment in 17 months. Design of the training program involved transition teams that identified some 350 requirements. The transition elements included preliminary design, pilot projects, and full-scale implementation. This involved a set of interrelated activities.

Development of the training program started with identification of what needed to be done and then design of a program to accomplish it. At every stage, measures were applied against appropriate objectives. Measurement continued through operation of the training program elements. Rolling upgrades of computer technology were accomplished systematically, expanding the ability of the firm to deliver enterprisewide training.

[24] S. Collett, "Merger Marries 'Old' ERP to New," *Computerworld* 33, no. 32 (August 9, 1999), pp. 1, 95.

[25] D. Schaaf, "Where ERP Leads, Training Follows," *Training* 36, no. 5 (May 1999), pp. ET14–ET18.

[26] A. E. Hahki, "R/3 + Outsourcing Is Formula for Success," *Informationweek* 700 (September 14, 1998), pp. 105–10.

can lead to increased sales of new software applications, as well as of add-on products supported by new versions but not supported by older versions.

The most common reason for updating ERP systems was added functionality.[27] Technical reasons included compliance with new standards and dissatisfaction with technical performance, as well as a desire to keep ERP systems current. Sometimes vendors discontinued support for installed versions, providing another technical reason for switching. There also was some response for switching because of organizational issues. Customers encountered a number of problems. Fifty percent of the responses indicated time problems in implementing the new version, 31 percent technical problems with the new version, and 25 percent problems with costs. Other negative experiences reported were strain on the organization and quality of migration support tools. Still, many organizations found migration was necessary.

As noted in Chapter 1 as well as in this chapter, training is key to successful application of ERP. This can involve a complex set of interrelated activities calling for project management. Dow Chemical's experiences demonstrate an effective approach to ERP training in the Real Application.

[27] Ibid.

Real Application: Owens Corning ERP Implementation

Owens Corning installed an ERP system, beginning with a massive reengineering effort in 1992.[28] This ERP installation encountered difficulties in 1997.[29] In March 1997 a major installation of the SAP system was applied over a weekend, folding 16 customer service centers into 1. The remainder of 1997 was spent rebuilding the system and repairing damaged customer relations.

Full benefits of the ERP system required integrated processes. However, departmental and regional managers retained power from the pre-BPR system and were not cooperating with the new design. New software was either rejected or tailored to narrow needs. Top executives at Owens Corning responded by reorganizing the company into cross-functional teams, headed by process owners. Order fulfillment processes were standardized across all divisions, which shared many customers. Before the reengineered system, duplicate paperwork was needed for each division involved in an order. After reengineering, customers had to submit only one order, received only one invoice, and paid only one bill. The new organization motivated acceptance of the ERP, which resulted in benefits including a 50 percent increase in inventory turns, a 20 percent reduction in administrative costs, and large logistics savings. Ettlie reported Owens Corning estimated savings of $50 million per year through the ERP system.[30]

The Owens Corning experience involved a lot of learning. Ettlie reported that 7% of the original budget was allocated for training. This cost turned out to be about 13% of the final ERP cost, a common case of underestimation of the effort required for training personnel.

[28] C. Koch, "From Team Techie to Enterprise Leader," *CIO* 13, no. 21 (October 15, 1999), pp. 56–60.

[29] Hammer and Stanton, op cit.

[30] J. E. Ettlie, "The ERP Challenge," *Automotive Manufacturing & Production* 110, no. 6 (1998), p. 16.

The Owens Corning application demonstrates resistance to ERP. It also reveals that it is better to learn the new system than to fight it. This case also further reinforces the importance of training in ERP implementation.

Summary

The success of an ERP project is measured by the timeliness of project completion, whether it is within budget, and by the functionality attained by the system. Factors critical to success in general IT projects are top management support, client consultation, and clearly stated project objectives. The scope of ERP projects almost ensures that top management support and clear project objectives are present before funding can be gained. Other important success factors in ERP projects include sound project management, change management, and technical implementation. Project success is expedited by careful consideration of business strategy, software configuration, technical platform architecture, and management execution. Client consultation often is not considered and is probably a major factor in ERP implementation difficulties.

A number of different control strategies are available for ERP implementation. The degree of decentralization applied should match how the ERP system will be operated. It is possible to allow decentralized operation of ERP systems, including different modules. However, this decentralization should be reserved for cases where different organizational elements have diverse operational problems. Similar considerations need to be given to the centralization of technical platforms. Finally, ERP systems can be brought into production all at once or in phases. It is wiser to use a phased approach, except for very small and easy to control organizations.

There are many definitions of failure. If too much is promised, failure will be inevitable at some level, regardless of the degree of success attained in implementing the ERP. The probabilities of success can be enhanced by heavy communication among members of the installation team, as well as with top management to retain support. It also is critical to keep users involved and to impress upon them the benefits of the new ERP system.

Once an ERP system is installed, that is usually not the end of the story. Two factors of concern are maintenance and training. There is a need to maintain any type of software, and ERP systems also involve a number of maintenance activities. Additionally, vendors will likely improve their software products over time, and if the technology-enabled approach has been adopted, the organization will need to consider migration to new versions of software. The second factor relates to training of organizational users. To be considered successful, ERP projects need to be implemented throughout an organization in an effective way, changing how the organization does its work. An important element of implementation is training, making sure that all users are aware of the need to utilize the ERP system. This requires a great deal of information dissemination as well as a great deal of training.

Key Terms

Big-bang deployment Implementation of an ERP throughout the organization at one time.

Corresponding failure Failure of a system to meet design objectives.

Critical success factors Those activities that the organization must do well to succeed.

Expectation failure Failure of the system to perform as stakeholders expected.

Implementation strategy Alternative ways to implement an ERP.

Interaction failure Failure of the system to be used by those it was intended for.

Migration Upgrading to a new ERP system (mergers, acquisitions, growth, vendor upgrade).

Phased rollout Implementation of an ERP incrementally.

Process failure Failure to implement a project on time and within budget.

Strategic/competitive failure Working systems fail to match investor expectations.

Supplier/consultant driven ERP design driven by external agents.

Technological determinism ERP design focused on system capabilities.

Technology focus ERP design focused on minimizing problems for the organizational information system.

Total local autonomy Subsidiaries have authority to make ERP selection decision.

User focus ERP design focused on giving users the tools needed to perform their work.

Questions

1. What is a critical success factor?
2. Markus et al. considered five business strategies, ranging from total local autonomy to total centralization. What did Markus et al. conclude relative to ERP implementation and this range of business strategies?
3. When would it make the most sense to adopt a single financial ERP configuration in conjunction with multiple operations ERP modules?
4. Why might a distributed data and processing technology platform be used with an ERP system?
5. What advantages does a phased-rollout approach have over a big-bang ERP deployment?
6. In manufacturing practice (according to Mabert et al.), which is used more often: big-bang or phased-rollout?
7. Give an ERP example of corresponding failure, process failure, interaction failure, and expectation failure.
8. What did Willcocks and Sykes mean by technological determinism?
9. What did Willcocks and Sykes mean by a supplier/consultant driven ERP?
10. What problems can be expected from software-specific ERP training of employees?
11. What forms of training are used in ERP systems?
12. What is meant by ERP system migration?

Chapter 8

Business Intelligence Systems and ERP

Enterprise resource planning systems offer powerful tools to better measure and control organizational operations. Many organizations have found that this valuable tool can be enhanced to provide even greater value through the addition of powerful business intelligence systems. Business intelligence in this context is supported by storing data (data warehouse and related systems) and conducting studies using this data to solve business problems (one means to do this is through data mining). One of the most popular forms of data mining in ERP systems is support of customer relationship management (CRM). Data warehouses are one of the most popular extensions to ERP systems, with over two-thirds of U.S. manufacturers adopting or planning such systems (and slightly less than two-thirds of Swedish manufacturers doing the same).[1]

This chapter:

- Discusses forms of data storage available to support ERP systems.
- Introduces data mining concepts.
- Reviews typical data mining applications related to ERP systems.
- Presents real examples of successful use of a data warehouse system and data mining.

Data Storage Systems

There has been tremendous progress in computer storage of data. Many applications are being found for this new capacity. One major user of massive storage capacity is ERP systems, which have large storage requirements due to their comprehensive nature.

[1] V. M. Mabert, A. Soni, and M. A. Venkataramanan, "Enterprise Resource Planning Survey of U.S. Manufacturing Firms," *Production and Inventory Management Journal* 41, no. 20 (2000), pp. 52–58; and J. Olhager and E. Selldin, "Enterprise Resource Planning Survey of Swedish Manufacturing Firms," *European Journal of Operational Research* 146 (2003), pp. 365–73.

Data Warehousing

A **data warehouse** has been defined as an orderly and accessible repository of known facts and related data used as a basis for making better management decisions.[2] Another more complete definition is: "a subject-oriented, integrated, time-variant, and nonvolatile collection of data in support of management's decision-making process."[3] Data warehouses provide ready access to information about a company's business, products, and customers. This makes it possible to organize by subject rather than by process. These systems store massive quantities of data from a variety of sources in an integrated way. The data is identified by a time period. Nonvolatile means the data is stable after initial formatting and cleaning, and not removed. An additional feature is efficiency, allowing quick retrieval of specific types of data. ERPs generate massive amounts of data, and often data warehouses are used to support ERPs.

Data warehouse systems generally store data in fine granular form, which other related systems such as data marts, On-line Analytic Processing (OLAP), and other forms of decision support systems can summarize or aggregate. Data warehouses also include a metadata repository holding data about the data stored, which ensures data integrity and speeds retrieval. They have extraction/transformation/loading (ETL) tools enabling data extraction for specific applications.

It is important for data to be consolidated. First National Bank of North Dakota used to have a separate computer system for each bank division. This led to problems, such as one division bouncing a check for one account of a customer who had a trust fund worth several million dollars in another division. While technically the customer was overdrawn, the impact on bank profits was jeopardized unnecessarily.[4]

Within data warehouses, data is classified and organized around subjects meaningful to the company such as customers, employees, or products. The data is gathered from operational systems (in addition to ERP-generated data, data can be generated by bar-code readers at cash registers, information from e-commerce, daily reports, etc.) and external data sources (industry volumes, economic data, etc.). Data from different sources (shipping, marketing, billing) are integrated to a common format. Transformation also includes filtering data to eliminate unnecessary details, cleaning the data to eliminate incorrect data or duplications, and consolidating data from multiple sources. This transformation, part of the data warehouse management rather than the data mining process, makes accessing data more efficient.

To demonstrate these concepts, consider a dealer in toys sold over the Internet. Many toys are sold each day, with detailed information kept on each sale. The company is organized into regions, and it assigns an item number to each product. Lot numbers are assigned by the source.

The data warehouse would deal with **granular** data, information in its rawest form. Within the data warehouse, each transaction may be recorded. Figure 8.1 shows transactions for a small portion of specific date (Julian date 1131—the standard industry refer-

[2] M. Katz, ed., *Price Waterhouse Technology Forecast: 1997* (Menlo Park, CA: Price Waterhouse World Technology Centre).

[3] W. Inmon, "Data Mart Does Not Equal Data Warehouse," *DMReview.com,* July 18, 2000.

[4] R. Whiting and J. Sweat, "Profitable Customers," *Informationweek,* March 29, 1999, pp. 44–56.

FIGURE 8.1 Data Warehouse Example

Key	Date	Customer	Name	City	Region	Product	Item#	Quant	Lot #	Price	Source	Cost
7332	1131	C129	Kim	Seoul	Intl	Bat Mobile	B019	120	XY482	39.99	Hasbro	10.50
7333	1131	C320	Walters	Ledoux	SW	Ninja Turtle Doll	A001	1	BA2441	18.62	Lucas	2.50
7334	1131	C320	Walters	Ledoux	SW	Remote Control Car	A059	1	CAB12	59.95	Ford	13.25
7335	1131	C320	Walters	Ledoux	SW	Baby Rattle	B008	1	F431	8.62	Lucas	0.62
7336	1131	C289	Cheslow	Richmond	SE	Fuzzy Dice	C373	576	AZ26	3.59	King	0.25
7337	1131	C151	Silver	New York	NE	Ninja Turtle Doll	A001	20	BA436	18.62	Lucas	2.50
7338	1131	C151	Silver	New York	NE	Baby Rattle	B008	200	F431	8.62	Lucas	0.62
7339	1131	C238	Billman	Austin	SW	Remote Control Car	A059	3	CAB12	59.95	Ford	13.25
7340	1131	C241	West	Orlando	SE	Nuclear Tank	A007	1	RA69	231.12	Ford	36.67

ence to the dating system of year digit and sequential day of that year—the 131st day of year 2001).

The data warehouse's purpose is permanent storage of detailed information. This repository is a reliable source of detailed information. Data entered into a data warehouse needs to be processed to ensure that it is clean, complete, and in the proper format.

Data Marts

Data warehouses are intended as permanent storage facilities. **Data marts** can exist in a number of different forms. Three of these are:[5]

1. Data marts created with a subset of data warehouse information, usually focusing on information needed by a specific set of users.
2. Freestanding data marts, making them a quick and less expensive (although less powerful) means of implementing the data warehouse idea.
3. A prototype for a future full-scale data warehouse.

Data, once stored in a data warehouse, is usually not changed without a compelling reason. To apply **data mining,** an intermediate storage form is used. Data marts are sometimes used to extract specific items of information for data mining analysis. Data marts have a number of advantages. First, they are available for data miners to work with, transforming information to create new variables (such as ratios, or coded data suitable for a specific applications) without fear that these transformations will contaminate the data warehouse. Second, only that information expected to be pertinent to the specific data mining analysis is extracted. This vastly reduces the computer time required to process the data, as data marts are expected to contain small subsets of the data warehouse's contents and to have ample space available to generate additional data by transformation.

A data mart is interested in data relating to a question under study. For instance, a firm might be interested in examining the characteristics of customers who buy their products.

[5] D. Browning and J. Mundy, "Data Warehouse Design Considerations," Microsoft Corporation, December 2001, www.msn.com.

FIGURE 8.2 Example Data Mart

Customer #	Region	Item #	Quantity	Profit	Source	Media
C320	Southwest	A001	1	16.12	Lucas	Internet
C320	Southwest	B008	1	8.00	Lucas	Print
C289	Mideast	C373	576	3075.84	King	Internet
C151	Northeast	A001	20	322.40	Lucas	Internet
C151	Northeast	B008	200	1600.00	Lucas	Internet
X	Northeast	D412	24	1248.00	Vendor	Internet
X	Midwest	B429	1	8.77	Vendor	Mail
X	Northwest	B231	12	36.36	Vendor	Print
X	Northwest	A622	1	17.25	Vendor	Print

The firm might want to study the consumer response to advertising by mail, advertising by Internet, or advertising by print media. Or the firm might study who buys by region, as well as the profitability by product, and the effectiveness of advertising in increasing sales by product. The data warehouse would contain much useful information related to these questions.

As with all centralized data systems, technical expertise is required to operate a data mart. However, there is a slight difference in its application from that of a data warehouse. A data warehouse would have a permanent staff to operate that system, with an ongoing responsibility to clean and maintain data and to ensure data integrity and security. A data mart is typically applied to shorter-term projects, usually with the intent of collecting data for a specific study.

Analysts face choices about manipulating currently available information, generating additional information, or purchasing information from vendors. Information available from the data warehouse could include sales volume and profitability figures by time and region. Data marts could extract this data, aggregate it in a form useful for data mining, and keep only that information important for the study at hand (and possibly specify a time frame). But the data warehouse does not include the advertising media that triggered sales. This information would have to be generated by survey. Survey results could be added to the data mart. For observations where survey information is not obtained, the observation might be deleted, or it might be retained with a code for missing data. Additional observations or variable information might be available for purchase from information vendors. A subset of data mart entries for nonvehicular toy products is shown in Figure 8.2.

Using raw data from the data warehouse, profit rates are calculated based on multiplying volume by the difference between price and cost, and inserting this in the appropriate data mart column. Customers listed in Figure 8.2 were contacted by survey to identify media for product introduction. Survey results are appended within the data mart. The data warehouse provided the first five observations presented. External sources were used to supplement the data warehouse results. The last four observations presented are from this source, and they have no customer number. The items from these sources are keyed to this organization's catalog of products or to the nearest equivalent. Profit is estimated for these additional entries based on this organization's prices and costs. The purpose of the data mart here is to feed data mining.

FIGURE 8.3 Example OLAP

Product	Region	Q IV Last Year	Quarter I	Quarter II	Quarter III	Quarter IV	Revenue This Year	Profit This Year
Bat Mobile	Northeast	326	122	98	82	125	15,235	6,875
	Southeast	258	68	42	39	51	7,536	3,168
	Midwest	412	151	112	106	165	19,871	8,168
	Southwest	168	39	26	25	32	4,536	1,832
	Northwest	151	36	31	30	35	4,986	2,126
	International	56	65	73	86	92	11,965	3,965
	Total	1371	481	382	368	500	64,129	26,134

On-line Analytic Processing

On-line analytic processing (OLAP) systems are multidimensional databases. These systems allow analysts to display data in one or more of a number of different dimensions, such as time, geographic region, product, organizational department, customer, or other factors. While data warehouses focus on efficiently storing vast quantities of data, OLAP systems are designed to make it easy to analyze data.

OLAP systems allow firms to deliver access to data and report-generating tools throughout their organization in virtual time.[6] The ability to access OLAP packages has allowed Lockheed Martin Tactical Aircraft Systems to make data widely available for analysts. The OLAP system provided a single source to find program and business-management metrics, staffing information, risk and technical measurements, sales and cost forecasting, and overhead information.

The Case Corp. is another example of successful OLAP use. Case employees can view marketing, sales, and inventory data over their network and distribute reports to selected users. This system supports both queries and report generation.[7]

An OLAP application would focus more on analyzing trends or other aspects of organizational operations. It may obtain much of its information from the data warehouse. The OLAP application extracts granular information that is of interest to the users being supported, aggregates this information, and makes the information easily accessible on a number of dimensions. This information could be accessed to make a report by product, as shown in Figure 8.3.

The purpose of the OLAP here is summarizing data, with a report focus. OLAP products have spreadsheet computational capability, as well as organization expediting the layout of data by selected dimensions (here by region, by quarter).

Data Quality

Data warehouse projects can fail for a number of reasons. One of the most common reasons is users' refusal to accept the validity of data obtained from a data warehouse.[8]

[6] T. Barron, "OLAP Goes Online," *Informationweek,* September 20, 1999, pp. 90–93.

[7] Ibid.

[8] J. Wu, "Ensuring Data Integrity (Parts 1, 2, and 3)," *DM Review,* July 18, 2000, August 7, 2000, August 14, 2000, www.datawarehouse.com.

FIGURE 8.4 Extract from Database for Name Kim

Key	Date	Customer	Name	City	Region	Product	Item#	Quant	Lot #	Price	Source	Cost
7332	1131	C129	Kim	Seoul	Intl	Bat Mobile	B019	120	XY482	39.99	Hasbro	10.50
7671	1131	C129	Kimm	Inchon	Intl	Bat Mobile	B019	12	ZZ1243	41.16	Lucas	10.66
7822	1131	C729	JD Kim	Seoul	Intl	Bat Mobile	B019	144	TU642	37.65	Hasbro	10.12
7865	1131	C129	Kim	Seoul	Intl	Bat Mobile	B019	1	VV336	38.86	Hasbro	8.67

This is an issue of data integrity. Such problems can arise because of one or more of the following:

- Corruption of data or missing data from the original sources.
- Failure of the software transferring data into or out of the data warehouse.
- Failure of the data-cleansing process to resolve data inconsistencies.

In the initial stages of data warehouse use, data must prove to be reliable. Once a reputation is lost, it is very difficult to recover. The information system staff operating the data warehouse must verify the integrity of data, ensuring that when data is loaded into the data warehouse, it is stored as planned. Also, the systems used to extract data from the data warehouse must function properly. This is accomplished through cleaning up new data by removing redundancies, filling in blanks and missing fields, and organizing data into consistent formats.

Data integrity requires that meaningless, corrupt, or redundant data not be entered into the data warehouse. Controls can be implemented before loading data, in the data migration, cleansing, transforming, and loading processes. This is the most efficient stage to prevent meaningless, corrupt, or redundant data from entering the system.

An example of multiple variations for two of the variables in the example data warehouse is shown in Figure 8.4. In this case, the name variable includes three variations of the same customer. The second is a misspelling. The third is correctly spelled, but it includes a more complete definition. Since the name "Kim" is fairly common, it would probably be best to use the form "JD Kim," although this decision would be made dependent upon the use of the variable. The process of developing unique variable values is **data standardization.**

Matching involves associating variables. For instance, in this database, the variable "Customer" is clearly associated with a unique "Name." We can see that the Customer variable includes a misread value (C729 rather than C129) in the third row. It is often difficult to detect such errors, especially in conjunction with other problems such as variations in name spellings.

Efficient data warehouse operation requires that the database contain the minimal number of consistent entries for each variable. As discussed above, one name entry for "JD Kim" needs to be identified. The overall system needs to be adjusted to reflect these choices. Software used to introduce new data into the data warehouse needs to check that the appropriate spellings and entry values are used. This also includes matching companies with addresses, an obvious opportunity for variety. Care needs to be taken to keep up with changes, such as telephone area code changes, or new ZIP codes. Personnel turnover makes maintaining proper contact names a challenge.

TABLE 8.1
Comparison of Database Products Related to ERP

Product	Use	Duration	Granularity
Data warehouse	Repository	Permanent	Finest
Data mart	Specific study	Temporary	Aggregate
OLAP	Report and analysis	Repetitive	Summary

Means to guarantee **data quality** begin with ensuring that the data extraction process operates correctly. A framework for error identification and correction as well as reconciliation needs to be operating when the data warehouse is created. Data validation and testing tools are needed to monitor data quality and resolve problems as they arise.

Once data is stored in the data warehouse, controls can be applied to detect accuracy and completeness. Quick reviews should be performed soon after data is loaded to make sure the correct number of records was loaded. It is useful to check aggregate totals as a means of verifying a degree of accuracy. More detailed validation efforts are often performed during data warehouse implementation. Ownership and accountability for particular data are assigned to a specific person or organization. Detailed validation checks whether data is complete and correct, whether business rules are followed, and whether the transformation processes of consolidation, filtering, cleaning, and aggregating are done properly. Validation also checks to make sure data was loaded correctly. Data also is checked to make sure that entries are within tolerance levels. Any errors detected should be investigated to determine cause, so that appropriate changes can be made to the overall system.

Data marts are products designed to select particular data from data warehouses (as well as from external sources) to be used for analysis, especially data mining. OLAP products come in a variety of product forms, but all are intended to give users the ability to design reports that give them insight into their operational environment. Table 8.1 compares the three database products discussed in broad terms.

Data quality is very important in ensuring the accuracy needed for successful system use. Data needs to be checked for accuracy before entry into the data warehouse. In an ideal system, if accurate data is entered, few problems should occur during subsequent operations. Realistically, there are many required changes to data, which makes administration of a data warehouse challenging.

Data warehouses are capable of storing vast quantities of data. However, their implementation is not trivial. Missing and miscoded data has to be cleaned up, and variables often come in a variety of types, such as nominal data with no numeric content, dates, counts, averages, and many other forms. Relationships may be difficult to identify because of weak relations, often masked by other relationships. A number of publications are available to explain more about data warehouses.[9]

Now that we have established that the vast amounts of information generated by ERP systems can be efficiently stored and retrieved, we turn to ideas about how to utilize this information.

[9] W. Inmon and R. Hackathorn, *Using the Data Warehouse* (New York: John Wiley & Sons, 1994); R. Kimball, *The Data Warehouse Toolkit: Practical Techniques for Building Dimension Data Warehouses* (New York: John Wiley & Sons, 1996); M. Corey, M. Abbey, I. Abramson, L. Barnes, B. Taub, and R. Venkitachalam, *Data Warehousing* (New York: Osborne, 1999).

Data Mining Overview

Data mining refers to the analysis of the large quantities of data stored in computers.[10] For example, grocery stores have large amounts of data generated by purchases. Bar coding has made grocery checkout very convenient. Grocery stores and other retail stores are able to quickly process purchases, and use computers to accurately determine product prices. These same computers help the stores with inventory management by instantaneously determining the quantity of items of each product on hand. Stores can also apply computer technology to contact their vendors so that they do not run out of items. Computers allow the store's accounting system to more accurately measure costs and determine the profit that store stockholders are concerned about. All of this information is available based upon the bar coding information attached to each product. The benefits of bar coding encompass for more than faster checkout service. The entire business management process can use the information generated.

Data mining can use bar-code information to make better business decisions. Data mining is not limited to retail inventory control through bar coding. It is also widely used by banking firms in soliciting credit card customers, by insurance and telecommunication companies in detecting fraud, by manufacturing firms in quality control, and many other applications. One of the most prominent applications of data mining is support of **customer relationship management (CRM).** Great Atlantic & Pacific grocery stores use data mining to target customers and centralize buying. Fingerhut was very successful in **micromarketing,** targeting small groups of highly responsive customers. Media companies such as R. R. Donnelley & Sons provide consumer and lifestyle data, as well as customized individual publications to firms that use data mining for catalog marketing.

Data mining requires identification of a problem, along with collection of data that can lead to better understanding and computer models to provide statistical or other means of analysis. There are two general types of data mining studies. **Hypothesis testing** involves expressing a theory about the relationship between actions and outcomes. In a simple form, there is a hypothesis that advertising will yield greater profit. This relationship has long been studied by retailing firms in the context of their specific operations. Data mining can be applied to identify relationships based on large quantities of data, which could include testing the response rates to various types of advertising on the sales and profitability of specific product lines. The second form of data mining study is **knowledge discovery.** In this form of analysis, a preconceived notion may not be present, but rather be seen by looking at the data. This may be supported by visualization tools, which display data, or through fundamental statistical analysis, such as correlation analysis.

Data mining has been called exploratory data analysis. Masses of data (generated from cash registers, from scanning, from topic-specific databases throughout the company) are explored, analyzed, reduced, and reused. Searches are performed across different models proposed for predicting sales, marketing response, and profit. Classical statistical approaches are modified in data mining, due to the lack of time for systematic exploration through classical statistical methods. However, some of the tools developed by the field

[10] M. J. A. Berry and G. Linoff, *Data Mining Techniques* (New York: John Wiley & Sons, 1997).

of statistical analysis are harnessed through automatic control (with some key human guidance) in dealing with data.

Data mining can be conducted with a variety of statistical and data manipulation tools. For large projects, data mining tools need to be versatile, scalable, capable of accurately predicting responses between actions and results, and capable of automatic implementation. **Versatility** refers to the ability of the tool to apply a wide variety of models. **Scalability** implies the ability to efficiently analyze large and even very large data sets. Automation is sought, but its application is relative. Some analytic functions are often automated, but human setup before implementing procedures is required. Analyst judgment is critical to successful implementation of data mining. Proper selection of data to include in searches is critical. Too many variables produce too much output, while too few can overlook key relationships in the data.

Typical Benefits of Data Mining

Data mining is expanding rapidly, with many benefits to business. Most of these gains involve using minor relative advantages. Two of the most profitable application areas have been by direct marketing organizations (to identify those with marginally greater probabilities of responding to different forms of marketing media) and banks (to more accurately predict the likelihood of people to respond to offers of different services offered by the bank). Many companies are using this technology to identify their blue-chip customers so that they can provide them the service needed to retain them (customer relationship management).

First National Bank of North Dakota found that only 10 percent of its customers were providing almost all of the bank's profitability.[11] Bank of America in San Francisco also found that 20 percent of its customers determined bank profitability. Bank of America developed profiles of its top accounts to target services. It also was able to assess the likelihood that particular customers would take their business to a competitor (**churn,** in telephone business terminology, which we will see again later in this chapter).

The casino business has also adopted data warehousing and data mining. Historically, casinos have wanted to know everything about their customers.[12] Harrah's Entertainment Inc. is one of many casino organizations that use incentive programs.[13] About 8 million customers hold Total Gold cards, which are used whenever the customer gambles, eats, stays, or spends money in other way at the casino. Points accumulated can be used for complimentary meals and lodging. More points are awarded for activities that provide more profit to Harrah's. The information obtained is sent to the firm's corporate database, where it is retained for several years. Trump's Taj Card is used in a similar fashion. Recently, high competition has led to the use of data mining. Instead of advertising the loosest slots in town, Bellagio and Mandalay Bay are promoting luxury visits. Data mining is used to identify high rollers, so that they can be cultivated. Data warehouses enable casinos to estimate the lifetime value of players. Incentive travel programs, in-house promotions, corporate business, and customer follow-up are tools used to maintain the most

[11] Whiting and Sweat, "Profitable Customers."

[12] R. McKim, "Betting on Loyalty Marketing," *Zip/Target Marketing* 22, no. 3 (March 1999), pp. 42–43.

[13] Whiting and Sweat, "Profitable Customers."

profitable customers. Casino gaming is one of the richest data sets available. Very specific individual profiles can be developed. Some customers are identified as those who should be encouraged to play longer. Other customers are identified as those to be discouraged from playing.

Business Data Mining Applications

There are many uses for data mining in business. Table 8.2 shows a variety of techniques applied to a diverse set of problems.

Retailing

Data mining offers retailers in general, and grocery stores specifically, valuable predictive information from data. Grocery stores generate mountains of cash register data that require automated tools for analysis. Software is marketed to service a spectrum of users. In the past, it was assumed that cash register data was so massive that it couldn't be quickly analyzed. However, current technology enables grocers to study customers who have defected from a store, their purchase history, and characteristics of other potential defectors. Tom Rubel of Price Waterhouse Management Consulting viewed the greatest potential to come from retailers and manufacturers sharing data.[14] Targeted marketing programs are beginning to be successfully used by grocers. Single store operations may be able to operate with PC software for as little as $4,000. Free Internet software is emerging as well. Most larger chain operations will have to spend up to $750,000 for data mining operations.

Fingerhut has been a pioneer in the successful use of customer segmentation models to reach targeted customers with specialty product catalogs. This very effective utilization of data mining is reported in greater detail below.

Customer Relationship Management

The banking industry was one of the first users of data mining. Kiesnoski reported that banks were turning to technology to find out what motivated their customers and what would keep their business (customer relationship management).[15] Understanding the

TABLE 8.2 Data Mining Applications

Area	Applications
Retailing	Market basket analysis, affinity positioning, cross-selling
Banking	Customer relationship management
Credit card management	Lift, churn
Insurance	Fraud detection
Telecommunications	Churn (customer turnover)
Telemarketing	On-line caller information
Human resource management	Churn (employee turnover)

[14] S. Weinstein, "Tackling Technology," *Progressive Grocer* 78, no. 2 (February 1999), pp. 43–49.

[15] K. Kiesnoski, "Customer Relationship Management," *Bank Systems & Technology* 36, no. 4 (February 1999), pp. 30–34.

value a customer provides the firm makes it possible to rationally evaluate if extra expenditure is appropriate to keep the customer. A Tower Group analyst predicted that spending by U.S. banks on CRM would grow at 11 percent annually. Deloitte Consulting found that only 31 percent of senior bank executives were confident that their current distribution mix anticipated customer needs.

Support of customer relationship management is the form of data mining most commonly associated with ERP. CRM allows businesses to identify the profitability of specific customers and to increase chances of retaining them. This is accomplished by having all relevant information readily available that is needed for planning, product, and service throughout the customer life cycle. SAP has been a leader in enhancing its product's abilities to support CRM.[16] Retailers were expected to spend 15 percent of the IT application budgets on CRM (compared to 35 percent on ERP directly).[17] However, as with any innovative application of technology, there are growing pains. Ernst & Young studies noted CRM failure rates of 70 to 80 percent and large gaps between planned and actual benefits from CRM systems.[18] These numbers are typical in IS/IT projects, however. As with any technology, the risks must be realized along with the opportunities to much more effectively manage organizational resources.

Some customers are more profitable to banks than others. Only 3 percent of the customers at Norwest (which recently merged with Wells Fargo) provided 44 percent of the profits.[19] Bank of America utilized a program to cultivate ties to the top 10 percent of its customers. CRM products enable banks to define and identify customer and household relationships. This is the first step of the process, which must then be disseminated throughout the banking organization so that it can be taken advantage of through better product design and greater attention to key customers.

Fleet Financial Group has blended product and customer-based approaches. Information was being used to provide customer focus within a product-based organization rather than reorganizing around customer groups, as other financial institutions have done. Fleet invested about $30 million in a data warehouse to support the entire organization. It also hired about 60 database marketers and statistical/quantitative analysts as well as specialists in decision support and other areas.

First Union (now Wachovia) has concentrated on the contact-point end of CRM. The bank previously had very focused product groups with little coordination. First Union has created marketing customer information files, which integrate information across products through an enterprisewide data warehouse and marketing-based data mart. The CRM structure uses statistical tools to develop offers for customers.

Data mining provides a way for banks to identify patterns. This is valuable in assessing loan applications, as well as in target marketing. Credit unions use data mining to track member profitability, as well as to monitor the effectiveness of marketing programs and sales representatives. Data mining also is used in the effort of member care, seeking to identify what credit union customers want in the way of services.

[16] K. T. Higgins, "Tomorrow the Front Office," *Marketing Management* 8, no. 2 (Summer 1999), pp. 4–7.

[17] A. Bednarz, "Cents and Retail Sensibility," *Network World* 19, no. 1 (January 7, 2002), pp. 21–22.

[18] W. Holland and G. Skarke, "Is Your IT System VESTed?" *Strategic Finance* 83, no. 6 (December 2001), pp. 34–37.

[19] Kiesnoski, "Customer Relationship Management."

Credit Card Management

The credit card industry has proven very profitable, attracting many card issuers. A common practice for customers is balance surfing, where the card user pays off an old balance with a new card. These are not considered attractive customers, and one of the uses of data warehousing and data mining is to identify balance surfers. Michael Eichorst, vice president of analytics for Chase Manhattan Bank, says card issuers must maintain database marketing as a core competency.[20]

Bank credit card marketing promotions typically generate 1,000 responses to mailed solicitations, a response rate of about 1 percent. This rate is improved significantly through data mining analysis.[21] In a survey of 175 financial institutions, 24 percent were reported as using data warehouses in 1997, which rose to 36 percent in 1998.

Data mining tools used by banks include credit scoring.[22] A key is a consolidated data warehouse, covering all products, including demand deposits, savings, loans, credit cards, insurance, annuities, retirement programs, securities underwriting, and every other product banks provide. Credit scoring used to be conducted by bank loan officers, who considered a few tested variables, such as employment, income, age, assets, debt, and loan history. Automated credit scoring applies statistical and mathematical models including many more variables on a much larger scale. It provides a number for each applicant by multiplying a set of weighted numbers determined by the data mining analysis times ratings for that applicant. These credit scores can be used to make accept or reject recommendations, as well as to establish the size of a credit line.

Customers who usually use ATM machines can be presented with electronic sales pitches for products keyed to this particular customer. If a database indicates a new address for a customer with high credit scores, this customer may have traded up to a new, larger house, and may be a prime target for an increased credit line, a higher-end credit card, or a home improvement loan, which can be offered in a card statement mailing. Databases can also be used to support telephone representatives when customers call. The representative's computer screen can indicate the customer's characteristics as well as products the customer may be interested in.

The new wave of technology is broadening the application of database use and targeted marketing strategies. In the early 1990s, nearly all credit card issuers were using mass-marketing to expand their cardholder bases.[23] However, with so many cards available, broad-based marketing campaigns have not been as effective as they initially were. Card issuers are more carefully examining the expected net present value of each customer. Data warehouses provide information that allows issuers more accurately predict what the customer is interested in, as well as the customer's potential value to the issuer. Desktop campaign management software is used by the more advanced credit card issuers, utilizing

[20] P. Demery, "The Decade of Marketing," *Credit Card Management* 11, no. 11 (February 1999), pp. 74–84.

[21] Ibid.

[22] A. Levinsohn, "Modern miners Plumb for Gold," *ABA Banking Journal* 90, no. 12 (December 1998), pp. 52–55.

[23] Demery, "Decade of Marketing."

data mining tools such as neural networks to recognize customer behavior patterns to predict their future relationship with the bank.

Insurance

The insurance industry utilizes data mining for marketing, just as retailing and banking organizations do.[24] But insurers also have specialty applications. Farmers Insurance Group has developed an underwriting system that generates millions of dollars in higher revenues and lower claims. The system allows the firm to better understand narrow market niches and to predict losses for specific lines of insurance. One discovery was that it could lower its rates on sports cars, which increased its market share for this product line significantly. Farmers uses seven databases and 35 million records.

Our complex society leads to inappropriate business actions, including insurance fraud. Specialists in this underground industry often use multiple personas to bilk insurance companies, especially in the automobile insurance environment. InfoGlide specializes in products to identify insurance fraud.[25] InfoGlide's Fraud-Investigator system uses a similarity search engine, analyzing information in company claims for similarities. By linking names, telephone numbers, streets, birthdays, and other information with slight variations, patterns indicating fraud can be identified. The similarity search engine has identified up to seven times more fraud than exact-match systems.

Alta Analytics' NetMap for Claims searches for suspicious data using an industrywide database from the National Insurance Crime Board. Consolidating data internal and external to the insurance company creates a data mart that can be used for expanded search. This type of software can also identify unusual activity for specific chiropractors or attorneys. HNC Insurance Solutions focuses on workers' compensation fraud. Its VeriComp software is predictive, comparing claims to what is normally the pattern. VeriComp uses a neural network on historical claims data. This system was credited with saving the State of Utah more than $2 million and is used by the Province of British Columbia.[26]

Telecommunications

Deregulation of the telephone industry has led to widespread competition. Telephone service carriers fight hard for customers. But once a customer is obtained, it is attacked by competitors, and retention of customers is very difficult. The phenomenon of a customer switching carriers is referred to as churn, a fundamental concept in telephony as well as in other fields.

A director of product marketing for a communications company considered that one-third of churn is due to poor call quality and up to one-half is due to poor equipment. That firm has a wireless telephone performance monitor tracking telephones with poor performances.[27] This system reduced churn by an estimated 61 percent, amounting to retaining about 3 percent of the firm's overall subscribers over the course of a year. Given an average business volume of $150 per month, this churn reduction was estimated to be

[24] T. Hoffman, "Finding a Rich Niche," *Computerworld* 33, no. 6 (February 8, 1999), p. 44.

[25] T. Goveia, "Short Circuiting Crime," *Canadian Insurance* 104, no. 5 (May 1999), pp. 16–17.

[26] Ibid.

[27] B. Reeves, "All in the Family," *Wireless Review* 15, no. 7 (April 1, 1998), pp. 42–50.

worth $580,000 in revenue a year. The firm's cellular fraud prevention system monitors traffic to spot problems with faulty telephones. When a telephone begins to go bad, telemarketing personnel are alerted to contact the customer and suggest bringing the equipment in for service.

Metapath markets the Communications Enterprise Operating System to help identify telephone customer problems.[28] Dropped calls, mobility patterns, and demographic data are recorded. This allows the firm to target specific customers. Further, customers with faulty service can be contacted before they complain, allowing the firm to offer a solution before the customer switches service.

Another way to reduce churn is to protect customers from subscription and cloning fraud. Cloning (placing a call charged to someone else's number) has been estimated to have cost the wireless industry $650 million in 1996.[29] A number of fraud prevention systems are marketed. These systems provide verification that is transparent to legitimate subscribers. Subscription fraud has been estimated to have an economic impact of $1.1 billion. Deadbeat accounts and service shutoffs are used to screen potentially fraudulent applicants. Churn Prophet and Churn Alert are tools applying data mining to predict characteristics of subscribers who have canceled service in the past. Arbor/Mobile is a set of products including churn analysis. A number of other products also perform this service for telephone providers.

Churn is a concept that is used by many retail marketing operations. Banks widely use churn information to drive their promotions.[30] Once data mining identifies customers by characteristic, direct mailing and telemarketing are used to present the bank's promotional program. The mortgage market saw massive refinancing in the early 1990s. Banks were quick to recognize that they needed to keep their mortgage customers happy if they wanted to retain their business. This has led to banks contacting current customers if those customers hold a mortgage at a rate significantly above the market rate. While they may cut their own lucrative financial packages, banks realize that if they don't offer a better service to borrowers, a competitor will. By utilizing data mining and telemarketing, Crestar Mortgage reported increasing its retention rate from 8 percent to over 20 percent in one year.

Telemarketing

Telephone providers obviously are among the many marketing operations utilizing telemarketing. MCI Communications has utilized a strategy of data marts, extracting data on prospective customers from a data warehouse. This data is typically applied in a two-month program, after which the data mart is shut down. This approach has been credited with 20 percent improvement in the quality of sales leads.[31] The data system required a multimillion-dollar-investment in data marts and parallel hardware to support it and was staffed by 45 people.

[28] Ibid.

[29] Ibid.

[30] M. McGarity, "Keeping your Borrowers," *Mortgage Banking* 58, no. 9 (June 1998), pp. 12–23.

[31] T. Hoffman, "MCI Connects with Disposable Marts," *Computerworld* 31, no. 50 (December 15, 1997), pp. 67–70.

The ability to utilize comprehensive databases allows telemarketers to custom design their pitches. The Australian Tourist Commission has been a proactive user of telemarketing, utilizing detailed knowledge of prospective customers.[32] The commission has maintained a database since 1992, capturing all responses to travel inquiries about tour operators, hotels, airlines, travel agents, and consumers. Data mining is used to determine which travel agents and consumers are responding to promotional efforts by advertising media. The Australian Tourist Commission estimated its sales closure rate at 10 percent and up. Travel and tourism students from Australia have been hired by the data warehouse provider for 12 to 18 months, providing insider perspective enabling them to counsel consumers with detailed expertise. Lead lists are faxed weekly to productive travel agents.

Segmentation involves grouping data with common characteristics, such as the set of customers who respond to new promotions, the set of customers who respond to discounts, or the set of customers who respond to new product offers. This information is used to determine the group of customers offered a new service or to predict the set of customers most likely to commit fraud. Data mining can be used to determine segments. Once segments have been defined, on-line analytic processing tools can be used to explore in greater depth.

The MCI system has been used for trend spotting. If a prospect turns down one frequent-flier pitch enough times, the program can suggest a different approach, such as switching airlines. On the data mart, data can be updated by the user. Data marts for a specific application are designed to include only the information needed for the specific promotion. However, it is important that all required information be included, so initial design of the data mart is crucial. Too much data slows the system, while too little causes problems of inaccuracy.

Human Resource Management

Business intelligence is a way to truly understand markets, competitors, and processes. Software technology such as data warehouses, data marts, and data mining or on-line analytical processing (OLAP) makes it possible to sift through data to spot trends and patterns that can be used by the firm to improve profitability. In the human resources field, this analysis can lead to identification of individuals who are liable to leave the company unless additional compensation or benefits are provided.

Data mining can be used to expand upon things that are already known. A firm might know that 20 percent of its employees use 80 percent of services offered, but may not know which particular individuals are in that 20 percent. Business intelligence provides a means of identifying segments so that programs can be devised to cut costs and increase productivity. Data mining can also be used to examine the way in which an organization uses its people. It can help determine whether the most talented people are working for those business units with the highest priority or where they will have the greatest impact on profit.[33]

[32] R. Robinson, "1:1 Marketing: An Integrated Strategy to Reach Customers," *Telemarketing* 15, no. 11 (May 1997), pp. 66–74.

[33] B. Roberts, "HR's Link to the Corporate Big Picture," *HRMagazine* 44, no. 4 (April 1999), pp. 103–110.

Data Mining Tools

Many statistical and analytic software tools provide data mining. Connolly found the 77 companies he surveyed used more than 25 vendors, with no single vendor being used by more than 8 of the companies.[34] One of the most widely used products is SAS Institute's Enterprise Miner. But many other products also are being used.

These products use one or more of a number of analytic approaches. The major categories of methods applied are regression, decision trees, neural networks, cluster detection, and market basket analysis.

PNC Bank is using Model 1 data mining software to strengthen its target marketing.[35] The system is designed to better exploit customer contacts for more effective marketing and promotions. Modeling is expedited through wizards and a booster, software tools to aid marketers in better identifying potential customer needs. The firm also uses SAS Institute products to develop clean models, which are then automatically applied through Model 1. Model 1 modules include a response model, a customer segmentation module, a module to evaluate customer value, and a cross-selling support module.

Products used by banks include:

OLAP tools PowerPlay and Impromptu from Cognos.

DDS agent product from MicroStrategy for OLAP reporting.

Harland's householding algorithm.

Monica 1 data mining software from Unica Technologies.

Prime Vantage from Prime Response for CRM.

SAS Institute's analytical tool kit.

VALEX from Exchange Applications, a product for management of Customer Retention Model campaigns.

The market supplying software for both data warehousing and data mining is growing very rapidly. Vendors selling data access tools include IBM, SAS Institute Inc., Microsoft, Brio Technology Inc., Oracle, and others. IBM's Intelligent Mining Toolkit has a set of algorithms available for data mining to identify hidden relationships, trends, and patterns. SAS's System for Information Delivery integrates executive information systems, statistical tools for data analysis, and neural network tools.

The first example of real practice reviews Wal-Mart's highly successful data warehouse system, which has been a key element in Wal-Mart's retailing dominance. The second example demonstrates the highly successful use of large database systems through data mining to extract usable information leading to increased profitability.

34 J. M. Connolly, "Fast Facts," *Computerworld* 33, no. 20 (May 17, 1999), p. 98.

35 K. Kiesnoski, "PNC Add GUI-Based Modeling Solution," *Bank Systems & Technology* 36, no. 4 (April 1999), p. 18.

Real Application: Wal-Mart's Data Warehouse System

Wal-Mart was founded in 1962 and has grown to dominate the retail market. One primary reason for this dominance has been the use of information technology, used to support Wal-Mart's core competency of supply-chain distribution over its 2,900 outlets. Wal-Mart uses a data warehouse consisting of 101 terabytes, believed to be the world's largest commercial database.[36] The investment for this data warehouse operation was given as over $4 billion.

The initial Wal-Mart data warehouse was stocked with point-of-sale and shipment data. This has been supplemented with inventory, forecast, demographic, markdown, return, and market basket information. Data about competition is also included. The system processes 65 million transactions per week. The Wal-Mart data warehouse includes 65 weeks of data by item, by store, and by day.

This information supports decision making. Buyers, merchandisers, logistics personnel, and forecasters have direct access to the data warehouse, as do 3,500 vendor partners. The system can handle up to 35,000 queries per week. The benefits of this operation were estimated to be over $12,000 per query. A few power users were running about 1,000 queries per day.

[36] P. S. Foote and M. Krishnamurthi, "Forecasting Using Data Warehousing Model: Wal-Mart's Experience," *The Journal of Business Forecasting,* Fall 2001, pp. 13–17.

Caveats

Data mining involves the application of statistics and artificial intelligence. In business, one of the most popular forms of data mining is support to customer relationship management (CRM). While CRM is very promising, it has often been found to be less effective than hoped. Patton found that up to 70 percent of CRM projects did not produce measurable business benefits.[37] CRM systems can cost up to $70 million to develop, with additional expenses incurred during implementation. Patton cited problems with applications at Monster.com, Mshow, and CopperCom. One reason cited for problems in implementing CRM was that its users, marketing personnel for the most part, were not as computer familiar as were accounting and production personnel. At Mshow, the sales force refused to use a new CRM system. At CopperCom, a $500,000 CRM project was reduced in size due to lack of support from an applications service provider. Even Fingerhut, a pioneer at using data mining for business, saw their operations shut down after being absorbed by a large sales organization. On the other hand, Siebel Systems, the largest provider of CRM software, reported that the vast majority of its customers were happy with the product.

[37] S. Patton, "The Truth about CRM," *CIO Magazine,* May 1, 2001, www.cio.com/archive/050101/truth_content.html.

Real Application: Data Mining at Fingerhut

Fingerhut Companies, Inc., was a pioneer in the use of data mining for focused marketing in catalog retailing. Fingerhut was founded in 1948 and sent out about 130 different catalogs to more than 65 million customers.[38] The firm had a 6-terabyte data warehouse. Data mining analysis focused on 3,000 variables related to the company's 12 million most active customers. Over 300 predictive models were reported in use by Fingerhut.

Federated Department Stores purchased Fingerhut Companies for $1.7 billion in February 1999 to acquire its database.[39] In 2002, Fingerhut operations were curtailed. Fingerhut represents a highly successful use of data mining for market segmentation—it had a $1.6 billion to $2 billion business per year, targeting lower-income households.[40] The company had the ability to mail 400,000 packages per day, and it distributed 340 million specialty catalogs annually to 7 million active customers.[41] Each product line had its own catalog. Target customers were identified as the small subset of people with marginally higher probability of purchasing (the concept of lift in marketing terminology; see Appendex at end of chapter). Federated Department Stores planned to transfer Fingerhut's technology to its Macy's and Bloomingdale's stores.

Fingerhut used segmentation, decision tree, regression analysis, and neural modeling tools from SAS (for regression analysis tools) and SPSS Inc. (for neural network tools). When one of Fingerhut's 7 million active customers ordered a product (toys, games, household items, many others), transaction, demographic, and psychographic data were stored in the firm's relational database. There were up to 3,000 potential data items per customer. The firm had a staff dedicated to the data warehouse.[42] One of their roles was training other Fingerhut personnel in the use of the warehouse.

The segmentation model combined order and basic demographic data with Fingerhut's product offerings. This enabled Fingerhut to create new mailings targeted to customers with the greatest potential payoff. Fingerhut analysts determined that customers who recently had moved tripled their purchasing in the 12 weeks after the move.[43] Fingerhut therefore created a catalog containing products that those who were moving would likely be interested in, such as furniture, telephones, and decorations, while deleting products such as jewelry or home electronics.

A second application was mail-stream optimization. This model showed which customers were most likely to respond to existing catalog mailings. Massive growth in the late 1990s led to a dramatic increase in the number of catalogs mailed, leading to saturation of some customers. Campbell et al. reported a joint IBM-Fingerhut project to consider thousands of customer attributes in determining which customers would receive each catalog.[44] The purpose was to identify and eliminate unproductive mailings without harming

[38] J. Lach, "Data Mining Digs In," *American Demographics* 21, no. 7 (July 1999), pp. 38–45.

[39] G. Rosenberg, "The e-Tailing Phenomenon: Wall Street Helps Retailers' Mad Dash to the Internet," *Investment Dealers Digest,* May 31, 1999, pp. 18–22.

[40] Whiting and Sweat, "Profitable Customers."

[41] D. Campbell, R. Erdahl, D. Johnson, E. Bibelnieks, M. Haydock, M. Bullock, and H. Crowder, "Optimizing Customer Mail Streams at Fingerhut," *Interfaces* 31, no. 1 (2001), pp. 77–90.

[42] D. Pearson, "Marketing for Survival," *CIO* 11, no. 13, (April 15, 1998), pp. 44–48.

[43] S. Deck, "Mining Your Business," *Computerworld* 33, no. 20 (May 17, 1999), pp. 94–98.

[44] Campbell et al., "Optimizing Customer Mail Streams."

continued

TABLE 8.3 Fingerhut Mail-Stream Optimization System

Phase	Operation	Function
Data Extraction	Segment customers	Assign appropriate advertising levels by customer
	Allocate advertising	Assign budgets by micro class
	Profit score customers	Predict profit by customer
	Determine saturation	Identify interactions
	Reduce scores	Discount profit scores by interactions
Optimization	Cluster	Reduce problem size
	Generate mail-streams	Generate candidate mail-streams
	Select mail-streams	Identify best mail-stream by cluster
	Assign mail-streams	Assign customers to clusters
Mail	Send catalogs	Contact customers

Source: D. Campbell, R. Erdahl, D. Johnson, E. Bibelnieks, M. Haydock, M. Bullock, and H. Crowder, "Optimizing Customer Mail Streams at Fingerhut," *Interfaces* 31, no 1 (2001).

revenues. This led to the mail-stream optimization system, which considers saturation, advertising limits, and catalog preferences. The mail-stream optimization system had a planning horizon of about 12 weeks. Table 8.3 shows the system components.

This system was reported to be run weekly, considering six months of catalogs. The program was massive, running up to 12 hours on parallel computing systems. A second mail-stream optimization program, also run weekly, generated mail-streams for 1 million new customers. The goal of this second system was to control advertising and risk while boosting catalog response. Fingerhut estimated savings of nearly $3 million per year through mail-stream optimizing.[45] This system enabled Fingerhut to go against the trend of the catalog sales industry in 1998 and reduce mailings by 20 percent while increasing net earnings to over $37 million.[46]

Neural network models were used to identify overlaps in mailing patterns and order-filling telephone call orders. This enabled Fingerhut to more efficiently staff telephones and to handle heavy order loads.

[45] Deck, "Mining Your Business."

[46] S. Chiger, "Bragging Rights," *Catalog Age* 15, no. 9 (August 1998), pp. 1, 66.

Much of the problems in CRM expectations have been blamed on overzealous sales pitches. CRM offers a lot of opportunities to operate more efficiently. However, they are not silver bullets, and benefits are not unlimited. As with any system, prior evaluation of benefits is very difficult, and investment in CRM systems needs to be based on sound analysis and judgment.

Appendix

Lift in Data Mining

Retailers and manufacturers know they are wasting a lot of money on mass marketing. The concept of lift is critical to marketing promotion. Lift is the difference between the average probability of positive response and the response obtained. We can divide the data into groups as fine as we want (here we divide them into 20 equal portions of the population, or groups of 5 percent each). These groups have some identifiable feature, such as ZIP code, income level, and the like. We can then sample and identify the portion of sales for each group. The idea behind lift is to send promotional material (which has a unit cost) to those groups that have the greatest probability of positive response first. We can visualize lift by plotting responses against the proportion of the total population of potential customers.

Both the cumulative responses and the cumulative proportion of the population are graphed to identify lift. Lift is the difference between the two lines of the lift graph on the following page.

The purpose of lift analysis is to maximize profit by identifying the portion of the population to receive promotional materials. For instance, if an average profit of $6 is expected for each response, and a cost of $5 is expected for each set of promotional material sent out, it obviously would be more profitable to send to the first segment containing an expected 0.0987 of the total responses. But it still might be possible to improve overall profit by sending to other segments as well (always selecting the segment with the larger response rates in order). The plot of cumulative profit is shown in the next figure for this set of data.

The maximum profit is found by sending to the 15 most responsive segments of the 20 in the population. If there was a promotional budget, it would be applied to as many segments as the budget would support, in order of expected response rate, up to the 15th segment.

Response Proportions by Segment

Segment	Response	Segment	Response	Segment	Response
Largest Response	0.0987%	8th	0.0623%	15th	0.0273%
2nd	0.0923	9th	0.0573	16th	0.0223
3rd	0.0873	10th	0.0523	17th	0.0173
4th	0.0823	11th	0.0473	18th	0.0125
5th	0.0773	12th	0.0423	19th	0.0080
6th	0.0723	13th	0.0373	20th	0.0040
7th	0.0673	14th	0.0323		

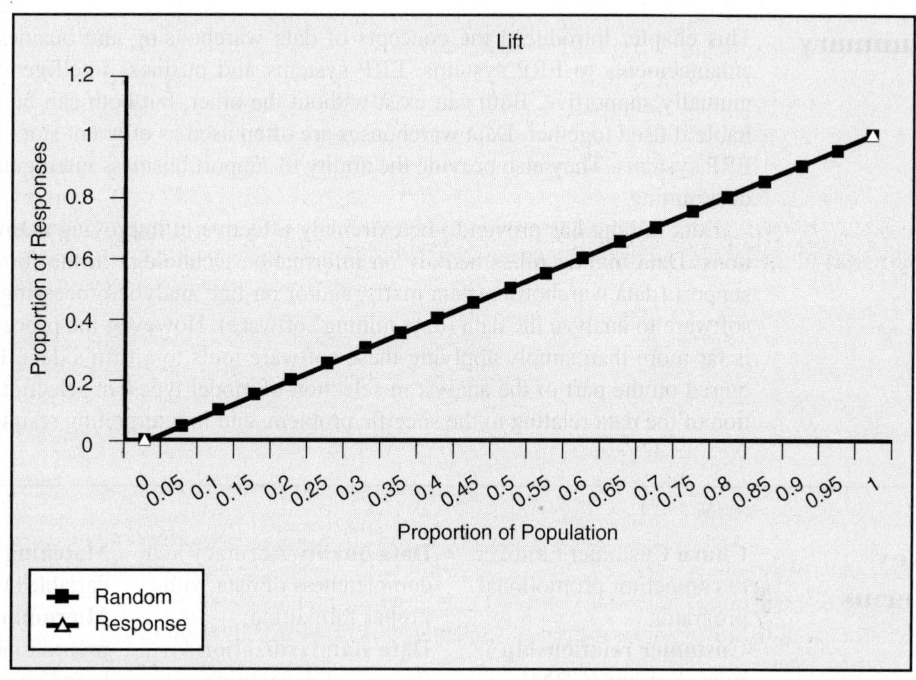
Lift
Proportion of Responses
1.2
1
0.8
0.6
0.4
0.2
0
0 0.05 0.1 0.15 0.2 0.25 0.3 0.35 0.4 0.45 0.5 0.55 0.6 0.65 0.7 0.75 0.8 0.85 0.9 0.95 1
Proportion of Population
Random
Response

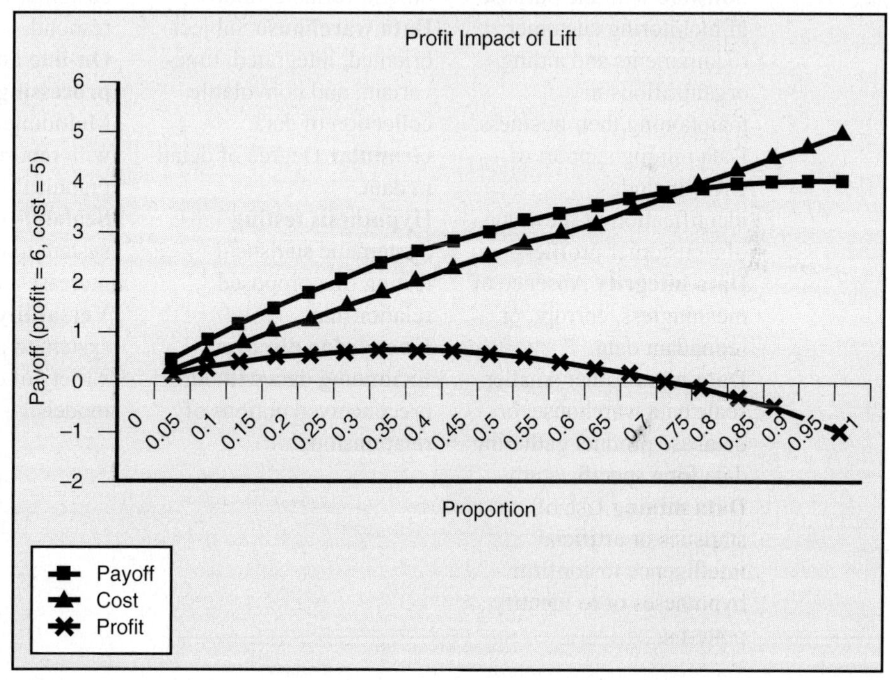
Profit Impact of Lift
Payoff (profit = 6, cost = 5)
6
5
4
3
2
1
0
−1
−2
0 0.05 0.1 0.15 0.2 0.25 0.3 0.35 0.4 0.45 0.5 0.55 0.6 0.65 0.7 0.75 0.8 0.85 0.9 0.95 1
Proportion
Payoff
Cost
Profit

Summary

This chapter introduced the concepts of data warehousing and business intelligence as enhancements to ERP systems. ERP systems and business intelligence operations are mutually supportive. Both can exist without the other, but both can be much more profitable if used together. Data warehouses are often used as efficient storage units for larger ERP systems. They also provide the ability to support business intelligence in the form of data mining.

Data mining has proven to be extremely effective in improving many business operations. Data mining relies heavily on information technology in the form of data storage support (data warehouses, data marts, and/or on-line analytic processing tools) as well as software to analyze the data (data mining software). However, the process of data mining is far more than simply applying these software tools to a firm's data. Intelligence is required on the part of the analyst in selection of model types, in selection and transformation of the data relating to the specific problem, and in interpreting results.

Key Terms

Churn Customer turnover to competitor promotional programs.

Customer relationship management (CRM) Software with the purpose of monitoring customer requirements and aiding organizations in maintaining their business. Data mining support of CRM includes identification of the value of a customer profile.

Data integrity Absence of meaningless, corrupt, or redundant data.

Data mart Either smaller scale data warehouse, or database product gathering data for a specific study.

Data mining Use of statistics or artificial intelligence to confirm hypotheses or to identify patterns.

Data quality Accuracy and completeness of data with proper formatting.

Data standardization Process of developing unique variable values.

Data warehouse Subject-oriented, integrated, time-variant, and nonvolatile collection of data.

Granular Degree of detail in data.

Hypothesis testing Systematic statistical testing of a proposed relationship.

Knowledge discovery Examining data without preconceived notions of relationships.

Matching Association of variables within a database.

Micromarketing Targeting promotional campaigns based on information about customer likelihood to respond.

On-line analytic processing (OLAP) Multidimensional database with report generation and graphical support.

Scalability Ability of system to cope with increases in volume.

Versatility Ability of system to apply a wide variety of data mining models.

Questions

1. Describe a data warehouse. What does that have to do with ERP?
2. What is data granularity?
3. What are data marts typically used for in CRM?
4. What is an on-line analytic processing system, and what relation does it have to data mining?
5. What is meant by data quality?
6. What is meant by data integrity?
7. What is meant by data standardization?
8. Describe micromarketing and its relationship to data mining.
9. What is the difference between hypothesis testing and knowledge discovery?
10. What does scalability mean in information systems?
11. What is meant by churn in data mining?
12. Search the library and/or the Internet for applications of CRM in ERP.
13. Search the library and/or the Internet for applications of data warehouses in ERP.

Chapter 9

ERP and Supply Chains

Supply chains are collections of organizations that work together to provide raw materials that are converted into products and delivered to retail outlets where customers can obtain them. In the past, monopolies would sometimes seek vertical integration so that they could control the entire supply chain (Standard Oil went a long way toward total vertical integration; steel companies also attained at least something approaching it). The Dutch East India companies are an early example of a global supply chain.[1] Military logistics systems are the epitome of a supply chain. The value of a supply chain is control and efficiency. Today's companies gain efficiency through a higher degree of specialization. This appears in various forms, including outsourcing. The idea behind outsourcing is that there are specialists throughout the supply chain who can do a better job of the specific function they perform.

In pure vertical integration, the idea was to closely coordinate the supply chain internally. Automobile firms in the 1970s and 1980s often tied vendors and retail outlets together into closely coordinated supply chains to gain production efficiency (appearing in the form of just-in-time manufacturing). Today, computer technology makes it possible to obtain many of the same benefits through coordination across organizations. With the advent of ERP systems, along with telecommunications technology, supply chains have provided increased efficiency.

While far from universal, almost 20 percent of U.S. manufacturers in one survey had implemented supply-chain extensions into their ERP systems. Less than one-third had no plans for such extensions (as opposed to 46 percent in a related Swedish study).[2]

This chapter:

- Describes what supply chains are and what advantages they provide.
- Describes advanced planning systems to support supply chains.
- Discusses the role of on-line marketplaces in supply chains.
- Reviews the concept of lean manufacturing in the context of ERP.

[1] K. Kumar, "Technology for Supporting Supply," *Communications of the ACM* 44, no. 6 (June 2001), pp. 58–61.

[2] V. M. Mabert, A. Soni, and M. A. Venkataramanan, "Enterprise Resource Planning Survey of U.S. Manufacturing Firms," *Production and Inventory Management Journal* 41, no. 20 (2000), pp. 52–58, and J. Olhager and E. Selldin, "Enterprise Resource Planning Survey of Swedish Manufacturing Firms," *European Journal of Operational Research* 146 (2003), pp. 365–73.

Advantages of Supply Chains

Supply chains can provide competitive advantage from a combination of cost and value.[3] On the cost side, production efficiencies can provide output less expensively. At the delivery end, added value may be gained through logistics efficiencies that lead to lower costs, better coordination of advertising campaigns, enhanced service from larger-scale operations, or other means.

One of the most important motivations for manufacturing firms to implement ERP has been to improve interactions and communication with suppliers and customers[4]. Thus, ERP has a role in supporting supply-chain activities. A study of more than 400 Midwestern manufacturers reported that 20 percent of the firms surveyed had already implemented supply-chain extensions to their ERP systems and another 25 percent were planning to.[5]

Typical ERP installations can also impose some restrictions on this communication. Internally focused ERP systems can constrain supply-chain coordination.[6] ERP systems should be able to provide useful integration over supply-chains in the long run, but in the short run could hinder logistical operations.[7] ERP systems make integrated information available within the organizations that adopt the systems. However, unless all business units in the supply chain use the same system, ERP systems can be barriers to communication. Units across supply chains would benefit by adopting a single vendor.[8] (This could work well in the long run, but imposes very high costs if a supplier is required to spend millions of dollars on a system to do business with one client, as some automobile manufacturers have done in the past.) Many of the problems of communicating across ERP systems relate to data incompatibility, as well as different software tools.

Part of the problem relates to system openness. Supply chains require open systems. ERP systems were developed on the assumption that a relatively small proportion of the workforce would need access to information.[9] This led to a pricing mechanism where license fees for each user were set at a high level. Edwards et al. gave a framework of three enterprise categories, shown in Table 9.1.

While theoretically open supply chains linked across organizations would have major advantages, currently this degree of openness is rare. Edwards et al. found that 6 of the 11 companies they interviewed felt that transaction processing systems hindered linkage development. There are benefits to be gained, however. Those organizations moving toward

[3] E. Christaanse and K. Kumar, "ICT-Enabled Coordination of Dynamic Supply Webs," *International Journal of Physical Distribution and Logistics Management* 30, nos. 3–4 (2000), pp. 268–75.

[4] V. A. Mabert, A. Soni, and M. A. Venkataramanan, "Enterprise Resource Planning Survey of U.S. Manufacturing Firms," *Production and Inventory Management Journal* 41, no. 2 (2000), pp. 52–58.

[5] Ibid.

[6] T. Davenport, "Putting the Enterprise into the Enterprise System," *Harvard Business Review* 76, no. 4 (July–August 1998), pp. 121–31.

[7] D. J. Bowersox, D. J. Closs, and T. P. Stank, "21st Century Logistics: Making Supply Chain Integration a Reality," *Supply Chain Management Review* 3, no. 3 (1999).

[8] T. Baron, "One Vendor, One Solution," *InformationWeek* 760 (November 8, 1999), pp. 108–12.

[9] P. Edwards, M. Peters, and G. Sharman, "The Effectiveness of Information Systems in Supporting the Extended Supply Chain," *Journal of Business Logistics* 22, no. 1 (2001), pp. 1–28.

TABLE 9.1 Characteristics of Different Categories of Organizational Openness

Source: P. Edwards, M. Peters, and G. Sharman, "The Effectiveness of Information Systems in Supporting the Extended Supply Chain," *Journal of Business Logistics* 22, no. 1 (2001).

	Extended Enterprise	Cooperative Enterprise	Traditional Company
Profile	Agile	Lean	Profit focus
Strategy	Adaptive	Value maximizing	Cost minimizing
Goal emphasis	Flexibility	Effectiveness	Efficiency
Operations	Collaborative, open	Selective sharing	Limited sharing
Planning	Joint performance measures	Moving from push to pull	Push orientation
Relationships	Extended alliances	Qualified relationships	Limited sharing
Technology	Linked systems, Internet ERP	ERP and selected SCM software	No linkage of ERP

more open systems have been reported to gain advantages in ordering and logistics operations[10]. The Internet offers a rich information infrastructure making negotiation, knowledge sharing, and transaction processing much easier and faster. Traditional firms can be pushed aside by more effective and competitive Internet-based supply-chain groups.[11]

Advanced Planning Systems

Computer technology makes it possible for improvements at both the cost and value ends of the supply chain. Demand uncertainties can be better managed through improved inventory demand forecasting, reduction of inventories, and improved transportation costs through optimization of coordinated activities across the supply chain. **Advanced planning systems (APS)** provide decision support by using operational data to analyze material flows throughout the supply chain. Increased computing power enables more sophisticated analysis. APS products are available from:

BAAN
CAPS Logistics
i2 Technologies
J.D. Edwards
Manugistics
Numetrix
Oracle
PeopleSoft
SAP.[12]

[10] J. Curry and M. Kenney, "Beating the Clock: Corporate Responses to Rapid Change in the PC Industry," *California Management Review* 42, no. 1 (1999).

[11] D. Tapscott, *Creating Value in the Network Economy* (Boston: Harvard Business Press, 1999).

[12] T. Baron, "One Vendor, One Solution," and K. Kumar, "Technology for Supporting Supply".

Advanced planning systems use historical demand data as the basis of forecasts that are used to manage future demand. However, to optimize systems, a certain stability level is required. John D. Rockefeller was able to manipulate demand for petroleum products more than 100 years ago. Demand manipulation is still possible in some markets today, but it is much more difficult. The idea of supply-chain optimization is more difficult to implement in conditions of constant product innovation, highly volatile global demand, and increased product customization (such as applied by Dell and other computer vendors allowing customers to custom design their computer systems on-line). This turbulent market environment makes it difficult to obtain extensive pertinent demand history. It is easy to collect data, but demand changes too rapidly to take advantage of it for extended periods.

ERP vendors are expanding their functionality to provide services formerly supplied by supply-chain vendors such as Manugistics and i2 Technologies.[13] SAP has introduced mySAP.com, which is an open collaborative system integrating SAP and non-SAP software. SAP APO supports supply-chain activities such as forecasting, scheduling, and other logistics-related activities. PeopleSoft has Enterprise Performance Management to support decisions at many levels. J.D. Edwards products have support for planning and execution. Oracle's 11i Advanced Planning and Scheduling system was designed to automate customer, supplier, and firm interactions. Vendors are moving toward greater integration of supply-chain products.

In dynamic market environments, supply-chain software may not be able to attain optimization, but there still is a great deal of benefit to be obtained from coordination of supply-chain partners. IT also provides rapid coordination that can be even more beneficial than optimization in a stable supply-chain environment. Technology makes it possible to find new partners at short notice in response to new market developments.[14]

On-line Marketplaces

Open Internet marketplaces are becoming more widespread. These exchange mechanisms benefit suppliers and purchasers by providing a more competitive environment with broader access. E-marketplaces aggregate buyers, sellers, content providers, and business services. They also provide a single point of integration for interaction of buyers and sellers. A buyer can log on to an e-marketplace, issue a request for proposal, and be flooded with bids. This creates a problem of bid comparison and interpretation. **On-line marketplaces** also provide services to help sift through large numbers of bids. Table 9.2 lists types of on-line marketplaces.

Vertical on-line marketplaces have narrow but deep product lines. Multivertical marketplaces access multiple sources of product lines in the same way. These site types are particularly useful for those seeking products that are difficult to find. Horizontal on-line marketplaces deal with a broader set of products and more extensive linkage to buyer purchasing systems. A number of ERP vendors have horizontal on-line marketplaces, such as mySAP and Oracle exchange.

[13] T. Baron, "One Vendor, One Solution,"

[14] A. Moshowitz, "Virtual Organization," *Communications of the ACM* 40, no. 9 (1997), pp. 30–37.

TABLE 9.2
Types of On-line Marketplaces

Source: J. Manetti, "How Technology Is Transforming Manufacturing," *Communications of the ACM* 42, no. 1 (2001), pp. 54–64.

Target Market	Charateristics
Vertical	Deep and narrow product access
Multivertical	Multiple vertical sites
Horizontal	Broader, more extensive linkage to sites
Transaction Method	**Characteristics**
Auction-based	Seeks simultaneous bids
Future contract variants	Reduces risk
Pure auction systems	Establishes prices for buyers
Reverse auctions	Establishes prices for sellers
Metacatalogs	Reduces search costs
Mall-based	Accesses multiple suppliers at single site

These marketplaces also can be grouped by transaction methods. Auction-based services are common. One use of auction-based methods is as an exchange, seeking simultaneous bids and offers to determine efficient prices. Future contract variants allow buyers to lock in supplies or hedge prices. Pure auctions seek only bids to establish prices for unique products. Reverse auctions do the same, only from the perspective of offers rather than bids. Metacatalogs focus on reducing search costs rather than on pricing. Mall-based on-line marketplaces allow buyers to surf a single site, with visits to individual areas representing different suppliers.

Advanced planning systems and on-line marketplaces represent two applications of technologies making supply chains more efficient. Lean manufacturing was originally proposed as a way to make supply chains efficient as a strategy not supported by information technology. ERP vendors are seeking to show how their systems can support lean manufacturing ideas.

Lean Manufacturing

Lean manufacturing is a bundle of techniques pioneered by Toyota in the 1950s. It has become a common philosophical approach to supply-chain organizational design in the automobile industry. The key principles of lean manufacturing are to cut out waste by eliminating activities that don't add value, by making sure that this principle is applied throughout the supply chain, by creating continuous flows of product without bottlenecks, by producing to order (demand-pull rather than supply-push), and by emphasizing quality. This approach will typically lead to elimination of backlogs and more synchronized production to forecast. Lean manufacturing approaches have been credited with improved customer service as well as reduced procurement and plant-floor costs.[15]

Initial ERP applications often did little to obtain efficiency on plant floors. Problems with early ERP systems were complex bills of materials, inefficient work flows, and unnecessary

[15] M. Bradford, T. Mayfield, and C. Toney, "Does ERP Fit in a Lean World?" *Strategic Finance* 82, no. 11 (May 2001), pp. 28–34.

TABLE 9.3
Lean Business Strategies

Source: M. Bradford, T. Mayfield, and C. Toney, "Does ERP Fit in a Lean World?" *Strategic Finance* 82, no. 11 (May 2001).

Discrete Manufacturing Processes	Characteristics
Build-to-stock	Customer orders filled from existing finished-goods inventory
Configure-to-order	Products assembled to order from prebuilt components
Assemble-to-order	Batch formulated to fill a specific order from prebuilt components
Engineer-to-order	Each order designed to customer specifications
Continuous Manufacturing Processes	**Characteristics**
Make-to-stock	Customer orders filled from existing inventory
Configure-to-order	Batches mixed in common, but packaged and processed to fill specific orders
Make-to-order	Batch is formulated to specific order

data collection. Switching plant-floor management in ERP systems to demand-pull (lean manufacturing) was cited as a way to overcome these limitations.[16]

There are differences in emphasis between ERP and lean manufacturing. ERP emphasizes planning based on sales forecasts. Lean manufacturing ties production to actual customer orders. Lean manufacturing emphasizes continuous improvement.[17] ERP tracks every activity and material price, which often generates many non-value-added transactions, contrary to the lean philosophy's emphasis on speedy and smooth production. Some ERP users have dealt with this difference in philosophy by turning off ERP logs and reports that involve push motivation rather than pull.[18] Other companies prefer a change in ERP software.

Many ERP vendors have expressed lean features of their systems, but not all customers have been convinced of ERP's comprehensive support of lean ideas. Bradford et al. surveyed 14 ERP vendors, all of whom indicated their product supported at least one lean manufacturing feature. Specific lean manufacturing features that vendors have included are demand smoothing, mathematical models to synchronize daily production to demand, *Kanban* replenishment calculation, and exception reporting. Bradford's overall assessment of ERP vendor products' ability to support the lean business strategies in discrete and continuous manufacturing environments is summarized in Table 9.3.

The J.D. Edwards' basic ERP system supports mixed-model scheduling, demand-pull production, flexible material and capacity planning, distribution scheduling, and supply-chain information sharing and analysis. The J.D. Edwards' One World ERP system supports quality management, shop-floor management, product data management, forecasting, and material planning, all of which relate to lean manufacturing.

Many modern ERP systems allow users to configure more than one of these business strategies. Most ERP vendors support all but the engineer-to-order strategy, which was

[16] Ibid.

[17] D. Bartholomew, "Lean vs. ERP," *Industry Week* 248, no. 14 (July 19, 1999), pp. 24–30.

[18] Bradford et al., "Does ERP Fit?"

found in less than half of the ERP vendors surveyed by Bradford et al.[19] While it appears that ERP vendors are providing greater support to lean manufacturing, the current state of systems has not yet achieved that ideal. The limitations of current ERP software led Bartholomew to view ERP and lean manufacturing to be competing approaches to plant operations. Bartholomew's view is supported by the actions of Dell Computer, which has used customer demand as the basis of its system, the pull approach. As discussed in Chapter 3, Dell discarded a proposed ERP system after two years of study, concluding that the ERP approach was too inflexible for its demand-pull system.

Key Trends in Supply-Chain Management

Akkermans et al. conducted a Delphi workshop of 23 Dutch supply-chain executives of European multinational firms.[20] That study reached consensus of over 50 percent on only two issues:

1. Further integration of activities between suppliers and customers across the entire chain (87 percent support). Thus current ERP systems require greater openness.
2. Maintaining flexibility in ERP systems to deal with changing supply chain needs (57 percent support). Vendors have moved to increase their ability to support Internet operations.
3. Mass customization (39 percent support).

There is an inherent trade-off in centralized, controlled, internally focused ERP systems and the openness of systems required to adequately support supply-chain connectivity. This relates to both of the two most important issues identified. ERP systems do support mass customization by providing standard interfaces (given that the same system is used by all supply-chain participants).

Implementing ERP in a supply-chain environment takes great care, as demonstrated in the Hershey case. While Hershey continues to be a strong producer in its market, its installation experience emphasizes the need for allowing sufficient time to adequately plan and implement ERP systems. The idea of applying ERP and related hardware to supply-chain environments clearly has a great deal of potential benefit.

Summary

In the past, vertical integration was a way to gain efficiency in supply chains. Today, vertical integration doesn't work as well, because specialty organizations have developed to perform specific tasks very efficiently. Efficiency is gained today through supply chains linking specialists throughout the vertical business hierarchy.

ERP systems were initially focused on integrating internal operations. Their high investment cost and often rigid procedures made them barriers to effective supply-chain linkage. However, recent trends toward more open systems allow closer coordination across supply chains. One way to accomplish this efficiency would be through all elements in a supply chain adopting the same ERP vendor products, as well as software

[19] Ibid.

[20] H. A. Akkermans, P. Bogerd, E. Yücesan, and L. N. van Wassenhove, "The Impact of ERP on Supply Chain Management: Exploratory Findings from a European Delphi Study," *European Journal of Operational Research* 146 (2003), pp. 284–301.

Real Application: ERP Impact on Supply Chain at Hershey

Hershey Foods Corp. adopted an ERP system budgeted at over $110 million in 1997 to replace scores of legacy systems dealing with inventory, order processing, and other applications.[21] The system was originally scheduled as a four-year project.[22] This schedule was compressed into 30 months to go live before the peak sales period preceding Y2K. By July 1999, the project was three months behind schedule, but the system was implemented using the big-bang approach anyway.

By mid-September, a busy season for Hershey, the company was experiencing serious order processing and shipping problems with the system. Large customers load up on Halloween candies in the third quarter of every year. After implementing its new systems, Hershey faced shipment delays and deliveries of incomplete orders. Typical delivery times increased from 5 days to 12. In third quarter 1999, Hershey sales dropped by more than 12 percent relative to 1998, while inventory piled up in warehouses. This strained many customer relationships and threatened market share.

Diagnosis of the problems of implementing this large-scale ERP in a supply-chain environment focused on implementation timing.[23] Hershey sought to implement its system during the peak season. A second problem was trying to do too much at once.[24] In addition to the SAP R/3 software, Hershey added a CRM system from Siebel Systems and a logistics package from Manugistics that would balance inventories across warehouses. This made the project quite complex, and while such installations have been accomplished, it proved to be too daunting in Hershey's case. Hershey also faced perceived time problems with respect to Y2K concerns, which probably induced it to attempt to accomplish ERP implementation in too short a time frame. Specific problems were identified in the area of correct identification of business processes.

Case Questions

1. Supply-chain networks are adopted to expedite communication among supply-chain members. Logistics is a forte of Hershey. What pitfalls did Hershey encounter relative to its logistics supply chain?
2. In this case, it appears that performance deteriorated when an ERP system was adopted. How could that happen? What specific circumstances can be blamed for this deterioration?
3. Hershey added a sound CRM package to its system, as well as a very reputable logistics package. Both packages have proven successful in similar applications. What went wrong here?

[21] A. Osterland, "Blaming ERP," *CFO*, January 2000, pp. 59–62.

[22] C. Stedman, "Failed ERP Gamble Haunts Hershey," *Computerworld* 33, no. 44 (November 1, 1999), pp. 1–2.

[23] M. L. Songini, "Halloween Less Haunting for Hershey This Year," *Computerworld* 34, no. 45 (November 6, 2000), p. 12.

[24] A. Osterland, "Blaming ERP."

enhancements. However, this is not economically viable for most supply-chain components. Many suppliers may not have the millions of dollars necessary to invest in technology adopted by the core company in the supply chain.

Other approaches are toward open ERP software. Advanced planning systems were originally developed to enhance the ability of firms to deal with other organizations in their supply chain. More recently, ERP vendors are providing this functionality within their products, especially through Internet technology.

Lean manufacturing is another philosophy related to gaining efficiency in production operations. While the concepts of lean manufacturing initially seem in conflict with the idea of ERP, imaginative developments allow ERP systems to support lean manufacturing.

Key Terms

Advanced planning systems (APS) Software to analyze material flows throughout a supply chain.

Lean manufacturing Philosophical approach for efficient supply-chain organization without bottlenecks.

On-line marketplaces Systems connecting parties potentially interested in a supply chain.

Supply chain Network of organizations working together to produce a product, from raw materials to delivered goods.

Questions

1. What advantages do supply-chain relationships provide participating businesses?
2. According to Edwards, what feature of traditional ERP systems was incompatible with supply-chain relationships?
3. Describe an advanced planning system.
4. Search the library and/or the Internet for advanced planning systems. Report on their use in support of ERP systems.
5. What are on-line marketplaces?
6. Search the library and/or the Internet for applications of on-line marketplaces related to ERP. Report on their use in support of ERP systems.
7. Describe lean manufacturing.
8. Search the library and/or the Internet for applications of lean manufacturing. Try to find ERP relationships.
9. Search the library and/or the Internet for linkages between supply chains and ERP. Report on ERP value to supply chain operations.
10. Search the library and/or the Internet for the Hershey ERP case.

Chapter 10

Advanced Technology and ERP Security

Information technology has developed many useful tools, including PDAs (personal digital assistants) and pocket PCs as well as other means of mobile computer access, wireless systems for connecting PDAs to the Internet, and other forms of technology that expand our ability to do many things. These technology tools have had and will continue to affect ERP systems.

The fundamental idea behind ERP systems was to integrate all business reporting systems within an organization. SAP pioneered products that were inherently secure because they were focused internally. However, the advance of technology has made it apparent that there are many reasons to prefer open systems. This not only improves communication with suppliers and customers (discussed in Chapter 9), but also allows the use of more advanced technological tools.

This chapter:

- Considers different views of future ERP development.
- Presents the idea of middleware to allow enhancement of ERP.
- Discusses trends toward open ERP systems.
- Discusses security aspects of ERP.

Manetti argued that ERP is on the verge of another major evolutionary advance, with the following major changes occurring soon:[1]

- Broader use of Web-enabled systems to support closer coordination, especially in supply chains.
- Greater artificial intelligence (AI) driven systems supporting more powerful advanced planning.
- Greater ERP presence in midrange manufacturing, with more stable technology enabling less time and money for installation.

[1] J. Manetti, "How Technology Is Transforming Manufacturing," *Production and Inventory Management Journal* 42, no. 1 (2001), pp. 54–64.

- More flexible, modular systems (the best-of-breed concept).
- More third-party applications (bolt-ons) to perform specialty applications accessed by middleware.

We have seen some of these ideas earlier in the book. Supply-chain systems were discussed in Chapter 9. Chapter 8 discussed the link between business intelligence software and ERP. In Chapter 7, we discussed ERP implementation, and the trend toward easing implementation problems by vendor attention to more standardized and easier-to-implement systems. The best-of-breed concept was presented in Chapter 1. This chapter discusses enhancements to ERP in the form of bolt-on software and AI, as well as trends in more open data input.

Open Architecture and ERP Bolt-ons

Bolt-on is ERP jargon for third-party applications. More specifically, a **bolt-on** is an artificially intelligent, comprehensive execution system providing very specific functionality or technology to complement ERP software.[2] Bolt-ons employ client-specific business rules to meet unique needs. There are many useful applications of this type. The usual means of connection to other organizations with ERP systems is through software components. Most software had historically been delivered as monolithic code focusing on its originally intended application.[3] A much easier approach is the idea of components, where separate, encapsulated software code is written that is easier to manage, upgrade, and connect to host systems. Open systems can easily accept modifications, additions, or linkages to external software. Components make open systems possible.

Since the underlying philosophy in early ERP systems was internal integration, there was initially little apparent value in developing open systems. However, the ERP user market soon identified the benefits of best-of-breed selection of modules, sometimes across vendors. Vendors then realized the need to offer applications components. The focus shifted from internal design coherence to the ability to communicate with external software. Service-based architectures were created enabling business transactions and data transfer from outside the core application.

Table 10.1 lists types of bolt-on software and vendors, and shows that both ERP vendors (BAAN and J.D. Edwards) and other software providers are involved in developing bolt-on products to enhance ERP systems. Some of these products reflect the focus on materials planning, originally found in MRP (demand planning, inventory management products, order tracking). Others extend support to that originally provided by MRP II software (factory planning and scheduling). Others focus on intranet and Internet communication (e-procurement, business-to-business products, on-line collaboration). The last two types of system (warehouse management and data mining) are a bit different, in that they support business intelligence.

[2] J. Glazer, "Make the Choice Between Bolt-on and Middleware Solutions," *Automatic I.D. News* 14, no. 8 (July 1998), pp. 46–48.

[3] D. Sprott, "Componentizing the Enterprise: Application Packages," *Communications of the ACM* 43, no. 4 (2000), pp. 63–69.

TABLE 10.1 Bolt-on Products and Providers

Source: V. M. Mabert, A. Soni, and M. A. Venkataramanan, "Enterprise Resource Planning: Common Myths versus Evolving Reality," *Business Horizons* 44, no. 3 (2001), pp. 69–76.

Bolt-on Feature	Example	Vendor
Demand planning	Demand Planner	BAAN
Inventory management	Warehouse Management System	Catalyst
E-procurement	Ariba Network	Ariba, Inc.
Business to business	MANAGE:Mfg	Cincom
Integrated suite systems	Manugistics 6	Manugistics, Inc.
Order tracking	Intelliprise	American Software, Inc.
Factory planning and scheduling	Capacity Planning	J.D. Edwards
On-line collaboration	Aspen OnLine	Aspen Technology, Inc.
Warehouse management	CSW Warehouse Management System	Cambar
Data mining systems	Enterprise Miner	SAS Institute

Example of an Optimization Bolt-on

Optimization is a powerful tool that planning systems sometimes include as a feature. The following real application on page 160 demonstrates how a custom-built ERP system was augmented by optimization software in a complex production scheduling/inventory management environment.

Other types of software bolt-ons can be added to ERP systems. Examples include auction management software, shopping cart management software, and credit authorization software. There is no end to the variety of products that the marketplace develops to utilize computers to do business better. Growth in the acquisition of components from multiple sources seems inevitable. Some firms may avoid the addition of such software, but competitive pressures will probably require adoption of some.

Middleware

External applications to ERP systems were initially accessed through **application programming interfaces (APIs),** which can access ERP data. APIs are pieces of computer code at low level, which is time consuming, costly, and difficult to maintain.

A more recent trend has been the development of software with the specific purpose of accessing application packages to ERP. **Middleware** is an enabling engine to tie applications together. Middleware removes the need for APIs. Kara divided ERP middleware vendors into data-oriented products (supporting ERP integration through sharing data sources) and messaging-oriented vendors (supporting direct data sharing between programs without the need for data files or databases).[5] Data-oriented vendor products ex-

[5] D. Kara, "ERP Integration," *InformationWeek,* March 8, 1999, pp. 3A–6A.

Real Application: Optimization Add-On at Kellogg

The Kellogg Company developed its own internal enterprise resource planning (ERP) system to forecast demand, take orders from customers, coordinate purchases of raw material, produce over 100 food products, and distribute these products.[4] To complement this ERP, Kellogg utilized a large-scale linear program that it named the Kellogg Planning System (KPS) to help develop weekly production, inventory, and distribution decisions for the various food products it produced. This system also assisted in other decisions, such as budgeting and capacity expansion.

Kellogg had long been a user of software such as material resources planning (MRP) and distribution resource planning (DRP) to aid in planning operations. In 1987, the company realized that the growth in product line and international expansion required more complete planning and control, to include optimization. That led to development of the KPS, originally focused on operational planning. The KPS prototype was installed in 1989, and its use inspired expansion of capabilities to other applications, such as analysis of capacity expansion. The complete KPS was installed in 1990 and was modified over several years. By 1994 a sophisticated and accurate cost system was in place, which produced savings of $4.5 million in 1995.

The basic core of the KPS is a linear programming model minimizing total cost of purchasing, manufacturing, inventorying, and distributing each item (product, package size, and case size) by week over a 30-week planning horizon. Constraints reflect processing line capacities, packaging line capacities, flow-balance constraints between processing and packaging, inventory balances, and safety stock requirements. Some of these constraints are modeled as elastic, meaning that they can be violated at a price (overtime, for instance). Other constraints impose restrictions reflecting Kellogg policies.

Raw materials are not modeled, but some intermediate products are. Input data that is relatively constant over time includes product codes, relationships of intermediate and final products, and product-facility possibilities. Costs include inventory cost, shipping cost, and penalties for unmet demands, safety stock, and overuse of production facilities. More variable inputs include production capacities by shift, costs by time of year, estimated demands, and target safety stocks.

The model has about 700,000 variables and 100,000 constraints, with 4 million nonzero coefficients. This is a very large linear programming model. Technically, the model would be more precise were mixed-integer restrictions imposed, but the continuous linear programming model taxes solution capabilities too much to add this refinement. The continuous model takes several hours to run. Solutions are viewed as beginning production plans that managers modify to reflect integer restrictions.

A great deal of uncertainty also is associated with the long-term inventory aspects of the model. Again, technically this could be modeled as a stochastic (and nonlinear) model, but such a model would require an unwieldy amount of data and would be very difficult to solve. Therefore, probabilistic features of the real problem are dealt with through imposition of safety stocks. The output of the model is used in a rolling-horizon environment, where production and packaging decisions are fixed in the first week from prior decisions, and model output is used to establish plans for the second week out.

[4] G. Brown, J. Keegan, B. Vigus, and K. Wood, "The Kellogg Company Optimizes Production, Inventory, and Distribution," *Interfaces* 31, no. 6 (2001), pp. 1–15.

tract and transform data and then exchange data files between ERP packages and other applications. Middleware can transform data into standard formats readable by source and host systems. Most middleware products also avoid hub-and-spoke bottlenecks in single-server computer architectures by providing load balancing in their execution environments if multiple servers are present.

A major change in ERP systems has been the emergence of Web-delivered ERP. J.D. Edwards has designed an ERP product for that mode of delivery. SAP's mySAP.com also is oriented to Web delivery, and all vendors have moved that way. Kumar and van Hillegersberg expect expansion to multimedia documents, including engineering drawings, scanned documents, and audiovisual products.[6] Mullin noted a similar trend in the chemical industry (a big user of ERP), as well as increased emphasis on customer service and marketing rather than on internal transaction processing.[7] Every vendor has developed a **portal,** which provides linkage to sites of interest to specific users.

Middleware can support many forms of data acquisition. This includes bar-code data collection and radio-frequency data collection. When Web systems are used, the term *Web portal* applies to software providing user-friendly access to data. Portals can act as middleware, giving organization members the ability to find technical information about engineering specifications, status information about promised shipments, and data about product prices and availability. Portals provide user-friendly access to data. Osram Sylvania developed a company-built portal for human resources information using Lotus Domino.[8] Table 10.2 shows all ERP vendors also provide portals, although each tends to emphasize something different.

Portals enable ERP vendors to maintain a presence in a dynamic market. ERP vendor portals can focus attention on products. Portals are also offered by third-party vendors, as shown in Table 10.3. Companies that are not ERP vendors provide portals to provide access to information in files, data warehouses, e-mail systems, the Internet, and many other applications.

Portals provide value to supply-chain environments, feeding data across the entire supply chain and tapping into the power of an ERP system. For instance, Gillette had a private exchange allowing suppliers and customers to view forecasts and actual orders to monitor production target performance. A portal provides a unified interface to various data sources.[9]

While opening ERP systems provides a competitive advantage, it also introduces concerns about security. Initial ERP systems were very closed, with limited numbers of organizational employees having access to the system. However, the strong trend toward

[6] K. Kumar and J. van Hillegersberg, "ERP Experiences and Evolution," *Communications of the ACM* 43, no. 4 (2000), pp. 23–26.

[7] R. Mullin, "Priorities Shift Away from ERP," *Chemical Week,* September 29, 1999, pp. 44–45.

[8] R. Michel, "ERP Gets Redefined," *MSI* 19, no. 2 (2001), pp. 36–44.

[9] S. Greengard, "New Connections: Manufacturers Are Opening up ERP Systems to Enhance Communication with Business Partners," *Industryweek,* August 13, 2001, pp. 21–24, www.industryweek.com.

TABLE 10.2 Portals Developed by Major ERP Vendors

Source: T. Stein and B. Davis, "Portal Push: ERP Vendors Join the Rush of Software Companies with Plans to Deliver Gateways That Integrate Applications with Other Data Sources," *Information Week,* May 10, 1999, pp. 190–91, www.informationweek.com, and T. Stein, "ERP Points to Portals," *Information Week,* May 31, 1999, p. 26.

Vendor	Portal	Function
BAAN	IBAAN	Application integration
J.D. Edwards	ActivEra Portal	Single interface access to ERP, e-mail, spreadsheets, Internet data
	With CPqD Technologies and Systems	Telecommunications support to operations
Oracle	11i	Connect to business intelligence tools
	Oracle Portal Partner Initiative	Partnership of enterprise information providers (closed system)
PeopleSoft	PeopleSoft Business Network	Customers can tie applications to build on-line communities
	PeopleSoft Enterprise Portals	Data integration and aggregation targeted by employee
SAP	mySAP-Employee Workplace	Travel reservation, on-line procurement, etc.
SAP	Business-to-Consumer Selling	Tools to build Internet storefront
SAP	Business-to-Business Selling	Share production data
SAP	mySAP.com	Center for SAP users
Lawson	Insight II Seaport	File, data warehouse, e-mail, Internet

TABLE 10.3 Portals Developed by Other Vendors

Type	Third-Party Vendor	Function
Business intelligence	Cognos	Access to data warehouses, data mining, and other business intelligence tools
	Information Advantage	
	SAS Institute	
Documentation management	Documentatum	Manage text
Other	Glyphica	Integrate ERP data into various applications
	Plumtree Software	
	Viador	

Source: T. Stein and B. Davis, "Portal Push: ERP Vendors Join the Rush of Software Companies with Plans to Deliver Gateways That Integrate Applications with Other Data Sources," *Information Week,* May 10, 1999, pp. 190–91.

more open ERP systems to gain advantages from supply-chain connectivity and other features changes this circumstance dramatically.

Security and ERP

Security is considered foremost in matters of national welfare. In the military, elaborate systems to safeguard information have always been important. Knowledge of enemy plans has been critical in influencing the course of human history. In classical business operations, just as in governmental and military operations, there have long been security issues concerned with physical protection. This physical protection could be of human

TABLE 10.4 Security Threats by Type

Type of Security	Threat
Physical	Theft, damage, copying
	Unauthorized access to information
	Natural disasters or accident
Social	Tricks to gain information
Network	Telephone taps
	Dial-up entry
	Internet hacking
	Viruses

access to buildings and information stored in critical rooms, much the same as banks are secured. With the advent of computer systems, this security expanded to data.

There also has always been a concern about the security of individuals. In a military context, patrols are sent out to capture enemy personnel with critical information. Business firms have been known to hire away from competitors individuals with key information.

Computer systems involve a new level of detailed complexity, providing many opportunities to obtain key competitive information. Information is stored on computers and, with the advent of networks, is in most cases accessible by networks. There are many threats to the security of information found on ERP systems. Threats across all three forms of access are addressed in Table 10.4.

The traditional forms of physical spying can still be applied. This can include any form of unauthorized access to information. The most common forms of security threats to ERP are those made possible because of computer technology, including invasive electronic entry through some form of tapping or hacking.

In addition to these security risks faced by all computer systems, two aspects of security are critical to ERP. One aspect concerns the quality of data generated and housed on the ERP. Data warehouses, discussed in Chapter 8, provide tools to ensure data quality. The other aspect is control over who can access data.

One major benefit of a Web-delivered system is the flexibility afforded to users through the ability to log on to the ERP system from any terminal (not only throughout the company, but also at airport terminals, hotels, or client offices). However, Liebmann reports that this creates a serious security problem.[10] One difficulty is that providers use forms of caching to improve performance. There is a serious risk arising from the user walking away from the terminal before deleting the cache. This can be cured by software designed to turn off caches once the need for them has gone. Another form of control is a log-in page showing only those applications that the user is authorized to view. Some systems also provide access to HTML code that can reveal link information. The Web page access system can preclude user access of this HTML code.

While moving to the Web may make tight control more difficult, this is not insurmountable. A digital certificate sign-on can act as one security measure, with log-on to a directory protocol permitting access to authorized ERP applications.[11] The ability to

[10] L. Liebmann, "ERP's Housekeeping Headaches," *InternetWeek* 866 (June 18, 2001), pp. 37–38.

[11] S. Tiazkun and C. Dunlap, "Security Strategies Refined as ERP Apps Move to Web," *Computer Reseller News,* January 18, 1999, pp. 5–6, www.crn.com.

Real Application: Dow Corning and Middleware

Dow Corning began to integrate its global business practices in 1995 when it adopted the R/3 ERP system from SAP. This system replaced many legacy systems. But that was only the initial purpose of an overall strategy to incorporate business intelligence. This second overall objective was furthered by adoption of a data warehouse, also provided by SAP.[12] The data warehouse was intended to consolidate information generated both internally and externally, and to allow deeper analysis of data. The types of data added to that generated by the R/3 system included plant-floor data, patent information, and benchmarking from outside the firm.

The system was designed to allow over 4,000 users to access the R/3 ERP. By using SAP data warehouse products, some integration and data compatibility problems were avoided. However, Dow Corning also added an automated data collection system that needed integration through middleware.[13] The middleware was reported to streamline work flow information and would allow expansion into supply-chain management.

[12] J. Teresko, "Leveraging the ERP Backbone," *IndustryWeek*, February 1, 1999, www.industryweek.com.

[13] "Dow Corning Finds Middleware to Marry ERP and ADC," *Automatic I.D. News Europe* 15, no. 2 (February 1999), p. 10.

maintain ERP security in a Web environment is mandatory, given that all ERP vendors are responding to demand to provide Web products.

The real application above demonstrates how middleware can enable communication of data across software applications. It is an example of an **optimization system.**

Summary

The evolution of ERP has been meteoric. Before the early 1990s, ERP was mostly a vision on the part of SAP. During the 1990s, ERP evolved into a critically important backbone of software systems in large organizations. Late in the 1990s, the benefits of opening ERP systems became apparent, leading to a new generation (in a very compressed timetable) of ERP products.

Open architecture is necessary for the addition of valuable bolt-ons to ERP systems. Bolt-ons provide organizations the means to do many specialized tasks. Another source of value comes from accessing data-oriented products, especially for data entry using modern technology. Middleware supports ERP access of external applications. Portals are specific forms of middleware, focusing on Internet connections to data and applications. Portals allow access to vendor enhancements, as well as individualized access to important information, no matter where that information is located.

This openness makes security an important issue. However, tools to obtain security are available. This makes it possible for all ERP vendors to deliver Web-based ERP systems.

Key Terms

Application programming interface (API) Software providing access to external applications to ERP systems.

Bolt-on Artificially intelligent execution system to add specific functionality to an ERP system.

Middleware Software tying applications together.

Open architecture Computer system environment where there are not excessive barriers to linking to other systems.

Optimization system Algorithmic software, such as mathematical programming, capable of identifying the best solution to a given model.

Portal Software providing linkages from an ERP.

Questions

1. Describe the term *bolt-on*.
2. What does an open architecture have to do with bolt-ons?
3. Search the library and/or the Internet for ERP bolt-ons. Report on their use in support of ERP systems.
4. What is middleware and what does it have to do with ERP?
5. Search the library and/or the Internet for applications of middleware. Report on their use in support of ERP operations.
6. Search the library and/or the Internet for applications of portals. Report on their use in support of ERP operations.
7. Portals have been defined by vendors in different ways. Describe some of these different definitions.
8. Discuss the relative trade-off between security and open access in ERP.
9. Compare physical, social, and network security.

Chapter 11

Trends in ERP

The intent of the book was to describe enterprise resource planning systems, considering what they are, their purpose, and some of the issues involved in their application. ERP has had a major impact on organizational computing. In the boom period of the 1990s, large companies were willing to spend tens and hundreds of millions, and even billions of dollars to advance a level in computing sophistication.

Either through legitimate concerns over nonexistent dangers (a common human response to uncertainty) or through insidious marketing efforts, there was a great deal of concern about Y2K problems. This led to the boom period in ERP sales. Just before Y2K, this boom ceased. ERP vendors responded by making products that were faster and easier to install, and they broadened their target market to include nonprofit organizations and smaller businesses. They also have developed Internet products, which fly in the face of the inherent conflict between the closed nature of 1990s ERP systems and the openness needed in supply-chain environments. Further openness is needed to accommodate the many auxiliary products that have been developed to enhance ERP.

Benefits perceived from adopting an ERP system were studied by Mabert et al. in Midwestern U.S. manufacturing, and replicated in Sweden by Olhager and Selldin.[1] Both studies used a 1 to 5 scale, with 1 representing "not at all" and 5 representing "to a great extent." Average ratings are given in Table 11.1.

The results in the two studies were very similar. ERP systems had support above 3 for providing information faster, for increasing interaction within organizations, and for providing better performance with respect to taking care of business within required cycles. However, ERP systems received support less than 3 for interaction with customers, or in getting work done more efficiently. Most notable were the low ratings for ERP systems in reducing direct operating costs. (This rating was slightly higher among Swedish manufacturers than among U.S. respondents.)

Similar questions were asked about those operational areas of organizations benefiting from ERP, as shown in Table 11.2.

[1] V.M. Mabert, A. Soni, and M. A. Venkataramanan, "Enterprise Resource Planning Survey of U.S. Manufacturing Firms," *Production and Inventory Management Journal* 41, no. 20 (2000), pp. 52–58, and J. Olhager and E. Selldin, "Enterprise Resource Planning Survey of Swedish Manufacturing Firms," *European Journal of Operational Research* 146 (2003), pp. 365–73.

TABLE 11.1 Expected Benefits of ERP Systems

ERP Performance Outcomes	United States	Sweden
Quicker information response time	3.51	3.81
Increased interaction across the enterprise	3.49	3.55
Improved order management/order cycle	3.25	3.37
Decreased financial close cycle	3.17	3.36
Improved interaction with customers	2.92	2.87
Improved on-time delivery	2.83	2.82
Improved interaction with suppliers	2.81	2.78
Lowered inventory levels	2.70	2.60
Improved cash management	2.64	2.57
Reduced direct operating costs	2.32	2.74

Source: V.M. Mabert, A. Soni, and M.A. Venkataramanan, "Enterprise Resource Planning Survey of U.S. Manufacturing Firms" *Production and Inventory Management Journal* 41, no. 20 (2000); and J. Olhager and E. Selldin, "Enterprise Resource Planning Survey of Swedish Manufacturing Firms," *European Journal of Operational Research* 146 (2003).

TABLE 11.2 Areas Benefiting from ERP Systems

Area	United States	Sweden
Availability of information	3.77	3.74
Integration of business operations/processes	3.61	3.42
Quality of information	3.37	3.31
Inventory management	3.18	2.99
Financial management	3.11	2.98
Supplier management/procurement	2.99	2.94
Customer responsiveness/flexibility	2.67	2.95
Decreased information technology costs	2.06	2.05
Personnel management	1.94	2.06

Source: V.M. Mabert, A. Soni, and M.A. Venkataramanan, "Enterprise Resource Planning Survey of U.S. Manufacturing Firms" *Production and Inventory Management Journal* 41, no. 20 (2000), and J. Olhager and E. Selldin, "Enterprise Resource Planning Survey of Swedish Manufacturing Firms," *European Journal of Operational Research* 146 (2003).

Again, the results are very similar. ERP systems were credited with making information more available, at higher quality, and with integrating operations. There was relatively neutral support for crediting ERP with providing benefits in specific materials management and financial functions. The ratings of support for customer response and personnel management were quite low (although the Swedish rating for customer response was very close to neutral). Interestingly, both surveys found low support for crediting ERP systems with decreasing information technology costs. Given the high level of investment, and the disruption to the organization, that seems appropriate.

ERP Expectations

Management of organizations that adopt ERP expect many benefits from their systems. These expectations are often difficult to meet. ERP can be seen to provide more responsive information to management. There also is more interaction across the organization and more efficient financial operation. There is weaker perceived benefit from operational performance, such as improved operating efficiency, inventory management, and cash management. While more information is available, at higher quality, this does not directly translate to cost efficiencies across the board.

Part of this failure to meet expectations is due to the time element. During ERP installation, organizations are disrupted. People are trying to get on with their jobs, and management attention is diverted to designing this new mammoth system. The first year of operation, most in the organization feel the full impact of the ERP system changing the ways they do their jobs (sometimes for the better). There are consistent reports of a difficult transition period. Three broad ways to deal with this massive change in working environment are:

1. Enthusiastically cooperate.
2. Go on with life.
3. Fight the problem.

Those who enthusiastically cooperate with the system usually gain. They develop key skills in the new environment that enable them to contribute more to the organization. Those who passively go on with work as they had before ERP will be the targets of intensive training programs that try to instill in them an appreciation for the better way of doing things. With time, these people will learn to adapt, working for those in group 1. The last group will leave the organization. An ERP system is too much of an investment for most companies to retreat from (barring bankruptcy, as in the FoxMeyer case). Dell Computer was a rarity in that it canceled its ERP project after significant investment. Most organizations don't have the courage to do that.

Review of Real Applications Covered

The book has presented a number of real application examples. These were selected to demonstrate various points and do not provide a representative sample. However, they do provide a frame of reference for review of issues involved in ERP systems. Table 11.3 lists these studies.

ERP implementation takes a great deal of effort. The FoxMeyer Drug implementation was not a bad idea, but it was poorly executed. It is a premier example of how not to undertake a large-scale information technology project. McKesson bought out FoxMeyer assets and systematically implemented the ERP.

There are a number of ways to implement ERP systems. Chapter 2 presented the modules offered by vendors. Despite the underlying logic of ERP being applied throughout an organization, vendors quickly adapted their products to modularity. This was undoubtedly a response to the reticence of potential customers to jump to full-scale implementation of ERP systems all at once. ERP vendors also argue that their products include the best way of accomplishing business functions and processes. Yet customization is almost inevitable, as demonstrated by a cable firm and a home products firm from Great Britain.

Chapter 3 presented a variety of formal and less structured techniques for organizations to evaluate the relative benefits and costs of ERP systems. The Dell Computer example demonstrates that not all organizations find ERP appropriate. Even here, it is a

TABLE 11.3 Real Applications Presented

Chapter	Firm	Project Elements	ERP Issues
1	FoxMeyer Drug	Anti-example	ERP installation as a project
	McKesson	Systematic counter	
2	Two British firms		Customization
3	Dell Computers	Selection	System adoption
4	McDonnell Douglas		BPR
5	Xerox		Outsourcing
6	Siemens		Phasing, uncertainty
7	Dow Chemical		User training
	Owens Corning		
8	Wal-Mart		Data warehousing
	Fingerhut		Data mining
9	Hershey		Supply-chain aspects
	Kellogg		
10	Dow Corning		Middleware

matter of the degree of customization, because the system adopted by Dell does many of the functions of ERP. It just does it by combining a number of software products.

The remainder of the book focused on other issues in ERP. Chapter 4 focused on business process reengineering. The McDonnell Douglas example demonstrated how BPR can benefit an organization (in this case through an internally developed ERP). The Xerox example reported a firm that outsourced its computing. That is an extreme way to implement information systems. Other ways to install ERP systems were reviewed in Chapter 5. Another major ERP issue is training end users. Facets of this issue were touched upon in the Dow and Owens Corning examples given in Chapter 7.

In addition to customizing ERP systems, there is a noted trend to adding external software products to enhance ERP. Chapter 8 presented examples of data warehousing and data mining. Wal-Mart implemented a very large data warehouse. Data warehouses are important storage facilities that don't have to be part of an ERP, but that would make ERP systems much more effective. Given that all of this data is available, it is natural to take advantage of its availability for analysis, through data mining. Fingerhut was presented as one of the more technically successful data mining applications. Chapter 9 discussed supply-chain issues with respect to ERP. Hershey sought to apply ERP to its supply chain, but did a poor job of managing that implementation project. Kellogg was more successful (and Hershey has subsequently successfully implemented a system as well). All of the openness required to support external software products has led to the development of middleware. In Chapter 10, the Dow Corning example shows how middleware can streamline work flow information and connect systems to supply chains.

Conclusions

ERP has had a major impact on information systems. Most of that impact has been positive. During the boom period of the late 1990s, investors seemed to throw money at ERP without much analysis of its appropriateness for their operations. Economic realities since

2000 have proven the need for sound analysis. ERP is not automatically best for everyone. There are ways to implement it poorly, and not all organizations need what it provides. However, the market has evolved to provide very flexible products so that firms can choose systems appropriate to them. ERP needs to be considered by most organizations in order to utilize information technology to efficiently manage businesses (including cash flow, materials flow, and personnel flow). The precise form of ERP appropriate to an organization requires careful evaluation.

There is a trend toward more open ERP systems. Vendor products have a tendency to be inner-directed, a major driver for which is the need for security. However, the growth in the desire for supply chain support has led to more open systems, as has the growth in auxiliary software to provide organizational computing with more sophisticated features.

Probably the most important factor that is overlooked in practice is user training. ERP systems can involve massive change in how many within the organization do their work. Even though ERP vendors have been very successful in reducing installation time, most organizations that adopt an ERP underbudget for training. It is important to get quality systems in place, but it is also necessary to allow time for employees to learn the new system and to adapt their work methods.

Index